Clare Abbott

SAFARI PRESS ©

DEER HUNTING COAST TO COAST

DEER HUNTING COAST TO COAST
Craig Boddington & Bob Robb

SAFARI PRESS
(A Division Of The Woodbine Publishing Co.)
P.O. Box 3095, Long Beach, CA 90803, USA.

Boddington, Craig and Robb, Bob

Second edition

ISBN 0-940143-46-1

1990, Long Beach, California.

10 9 8 7 6 5 4 3 2 1

Readers wishing to receive the Safari Press catalog featuring many fine books on hunting big game all over the world should write to: Safari Press, P.O. Box 3095, Long Beach, CA 90803.

21st book published by Safari Press
Printed in the U.S.A.

TABLE OF CONTENTS

FOREWORD

It is sometimes said that deer are the poor man's big-game animal. Whoever first said this must not have hunted deer very much and had only the vaguest notion of what hunting is all about. For an appreciation of deer hunting is synonymous with an appreciation of the art of hunting itself.

While it is true that deer are hunted throughout the whole world more than any other big-game animal, it is nevertheless far from easy to obtain a fine trophy. It is also true that deer are the big-game animal most accessible to the greatest number of hunters. It is, perhaps, the very accessibility of the deer that makes many people eschew this fine hunting animal for more exotic trophies. But the challenge in obtaining a legal deer, let alone a trophy buck, has so many rewards that I could not begin to describe them in the limited space of a foreword.

I have been fortunate enough to have hunted not only North American deer, but also the deer of Europe, the South Pacific, and Asia. In addition I've had the privilege of treading the soil of Africa in pursuit of the many varieties of big-game found on that great game continent. However, in all my travels I have never found any animal quite as challenging as the deer of North America, particularly when it comes to trophy specimens.

Craig Boddington and Bob Robb have done a fine job of making the North American hunter realize how lucky he or she is. North American hunters are surrounded by unprecedented plenty. Deer live in all states and provinces of this continent. Currently most deer populations are at a peak, and bag limits are generous. In fact it could be argued that overall deer hunting has never been better than it is right now. Hunting in far-flung places has its rewards, of course, but we must not belittle the fortune we have in our abundant deer. If I had to chose but one game animal to hunt for the rest of my life, there is no doubt I would be hunting the "poor man's" game: deer. Pity the "rich" hunter!

Ludo Wurfbain, Publisher
June 1989

CHAPTER I

NORTH AMERICAN WHITETAIL DEER

It doesn't matter whether you talk about sheer numbers of animals, hunter participation, or extent of range. By any of those criteria, America's whitetail deer must rank as the greatest game animal in the world. If you choose, instead, to use hunters' criteria such as elusiveness, craftiness, and ability to use terrain to best advantage, then the whitetail deer must again come out at the top of the heap. In the ranking of game animals, if you choose to indulge in such a pastime, you could instead consider more subjective factors such as local rarity, beauty, or the sheer imposing aura of an animal. If these are your yardsticks, then a bighorn sheep, or a six-by-six elk, or perhaps a foreign prize such as a greater kudu rank higher on your scale.

And then again they may not, for regardless of how common the whitetail is in a given area, a truly fine, mature buck will never come easy. Such a buck, too, with his heavy, multi-tined antlers and ghostlike grace, will indeed be an animal of matchless beauty. If you succeed in taking such an animal, you'll probably enjoy his venison. Undoubtedly you'll bring his antlers home, and quite possibly you'll mount his head. Regardless of how many beautiful trophies you bring home in the course of your career, you'll be a rare hunter if that whitetail rack doesn't occupy a place of honor—both in your den and in your hunting memories.

If you have been fortunate to have taken a really fine, mature whitetail buck, you have indeed taken one of the world's great game animals—regardless of how you judge such things. You will have taken an animal whose senses have been honed through centuries of contact with man. By inheritance, in his genetic makeup, a whitetail buck possesses the cunning and defense mechanisms to provide protection against most hunters. By the time he reaches maturity, he has combined experience with inheritance to become virtually unapproachable.

There are, of course, chinks in the whitetail's armor of sharp eyes, radar hearing, near-perfect sense of smell, and the species' exceptional ability to adapt to habitat. One of these chinks is the whitetail's tendency to stay within a relatively small area. A buck may come to know it perfectly, but so can a man . . . Another chink is the buck's tendency to let down his guard during the rut, if ever so slightly. One must also never forget the vagaries of sheer chance. This element of luck seems usually to ride with the deer, but once in a great while chance dictates that we, with all of our natural disadvantages on the whitetail's home turf, will be in the right place at the right time and do the right things.

When you go in search of a great whitetail buck, you accept that the odds are against you—or you should, because they are indeed. But in spite of the odds, the chinks in the whitetail's armor are wide enough—and Lady Luck fickle enough—to allow an amazing number of great whitetails to be taken every fall. Enough to give all of us hope that someday such a buck will belong to us.

There are many different criteria for determining what is a great whitetail and what is not. Certainly the criteria may not be, and need not be, the same from one hunter to another or from one part of the country to another. One common yardstick is the Boone & Crockett Club's system of measuring, which is used not only for their book of records, *North American Big Game*, but also for the Pope & Young Club's book of archery records.

The B&C system measures, in essence, inside spread, beam length, point length, and four circumferences at different points on each beam. In the case of a typically antlered buck, where the points rise from the main beam, only the typical points are counted while abnormal points—plus any differences from one side to the other—are deducted from the final score. A buck with a significant number of abnormal or nontypical points may be scored as nontypical, a separate record book category. In general, such a head is measured as a typical buck first, then the lengths of all the abnormal points are added in rather than subtracted.

The total score is in points rather than inches. It requires 170 points to enter the all-time record book for a typical head; 195 for a nontypical. Such a buck is huge beyond belief, and also, if typical, very symmetrical. And very uncommon. Yet, in a recent three-year period the Boone & Crockett Club accepted 110 new typical entries and 70 new nontypical entries. They're out there!

The much newer Safari Club International record book, kept for its members, uses a simpler system that has no deductions for lack of symmetry and no spread credit. The SCI system measures circumference of burr, length of beams, length of points, and adds in the number of points. Only typical points are counted for a buck to be entered as typical, while all points are scored if a buck is to be entered as nontypical.

There are other local clubs, and record books may use these or other measurement systems. And you may have your own yardsticks of excellence. It's clearly ridiculous to say that a buck isn't worth taking, or keeping, unless he reaches 170 Boone & Crockett points. Few of us have ever laid eyes on such a buck, or will ever—and they may not exist in the area you hunt. In fact, in hard-hunted areas with a scarcity of antler-producing minerals and perhaps a skewed buck/doe ratio, any buck may be considered a great trophy! It isn't up to anyone but you to say that it isn't.

On the other hand, you may be fortunate enough to hunt an area that has decent genetics and a good buck/doe ratio. You might be able to hold out for a truly great buck, if not a genuine "Booner." Under such circumstances, you might set your personal standard for a mature buck of five and a half years or more, with fully developed antlers that have the points, the length, the mass, and the

Few animals in the world match the majesty of a really good whitetail buck—and none are more elusive. This buck is of the Dakota subspecies, one of the largest. (Photo by Ian McMurchy)

"character" that come with full maturity. Or you might not care about such things at all, and prefer instead to hunt for a younger buck for his tender venison. There's nothing wrong with that.

Whatever kind of buck you'd like to fill your tag, if you're hunting whitetail deer you're hunting one of the greats—and quite possibly our most democratic game animal. With the exception of a very few western states, the whitetail deer can be hunted from coast to coast. Across his broad range he can be hunted by nearly anyone, and he plays few favorites. It's true that there are expensive places to hunt whitetails, but merely paying money is no guarantee of a great buck. Great whitetails are where you find them. There are indeed fine whitetails on well-managed, exclusive ranches in south Texas, but there are bucks as good—or better—on timberlands in the South; national forests from the Appalachians to the Rockies; and small wood lots within sight of dozens of big cities. Many great whitetails are taken by beginners (there is something to beginner's luck!), but many others are taken by experienced hunters who work hard for them.

In succeeding chapters we will discuss hunting whitetail deer under a broad range of conditions—and indeed whitetail hunting spans an incredible diversity of habitat types and hunting conditions. Well it should, for whitetail deer range from the Amazon basin in South America almost to tree line in northern Canada—and from Atlantic to Pacific. First, though, it's appropriate to say a few more words about these deer that millions of Americans love to hunt.

Estimates place the total number of whitetail deer in the world somewhere between 15 and 20 million. It's been said so often that it's trite, but it's nevertheless true that there are more deer today than there were when the pilgrims landed at Plymouth Rock. Excessive hunting during European man's first 250 years on this continent nearly finished the whitetail along with much of our other wildlife, but the conservation efforts of this century have brought him back to unprecedented plenty. Although our hunter-backed and hunter-funded conservation success story is something we can all be proud of, the whitetail's population boom is partly a result of an accident of nature.

The whitetail, given protection and a chance to breed, is at his best an edge animal. He thrives where forest meets agriculture, where second growth brings out his best browse, where he has small wood lots and riverine growth for cover and cultivated crops for food. In other words, with modern controlled hunting practices he benefits from most of our activities—and that's why he is so incredibly abundant in the Northeast, the South, and much of the Midwest today. And yet he's an adaptable cuss. You can find him in the steamy South American jungles, in our southern swamps, in our southwestern deserts, and in the high mountains. He's been transplanted to such faraway places as Finland and New Zealand, and of course he thrives. These days he's even expanding his natural range in North America.

The excellent whitetails that eastern Colorado is now producing are a relatively new phenomenon, likewise those in eastern Wyoming. In Alberta the whitetails have expanded well beyond their former prairie habitat and today may be found in varying densities throughout the province. In Colorado and Wyoming they're pressing west; in Oregon and Idaho they're pressing east and south. Of the entire lower 48 states, only three have no whitetail population today: California, Nevada, and Utah. Chances are that may change by the turn of the century.

There's a real fear, and a justifiable one, that whitetail deer will eventually supplant mule deer throughout the West. Whitetails are indeed more adaptable, seemingly able, in time, to adjust to almost any conceivable habitat. Certainly they adjust better to life in proximity to people—and in fact thrive under such conditions. They are also far more aggressive.

Not many years ago it was considered impossible for mule and whitetail deer to cross. Today it's an accepted fact. Documented mule deer/whitetail crosses have been identified in locales as diverse as west Texas and Alberta. Interestingly, it is thought to be always the aggressive whitetail buck who mates with a mule deer doe. Today the ranges of the two species overlap across thousands upon thousands of square miles—much more than 20 years ago, and much less than will be the case 20 years from now. It isn't inconceivable that mule deer will one day vanish, unable to compete with the whitetail. Certainly many wildlife biologists in Manitoba, Saskatchewan, and Alberta attribute declining mule deer numbers to incursion by whitetails.

Just what is this wonderful beast we call the whitetail deer? Unlike the caribou, moose, and elk, all of which have close relatives in Europe and Asia, the whitetail (and the mule deer) are strictly Western Hemisphere animals. They and mule deer are of the same genus, *Odocoileus*—considered, in evolutionary terms, to be a more "primitive" form of deer than, say, elk and European red deer. But the biologists who call them primitive must not be deer hunters.

We speak of whitetail deer as occupying almost all of North America, all of Central America, and nearly half of South America. But we aren't speaking of one whitetail deer. Most hunters are aware that all record-keeping organizations have a separate category for the Coues or Arizona whitetail of the southwestern desert mountains; however, there are strong regional differences in whitetail deer, and these variations are just the tip of the iceberg. Biologists have classified fully 38 different whitetail subspecies. Eight of them are found in South America, while another 13, all smallish tropical subspecies, are found from central Mexico down through Central America. That still leaves a whole bunch of different whitetails—17 subspecies, to be exact—from northern Mexico through the U.S. and Canada, that huge expanse of real estate where millions of hunters pursue their whitetails annually.

Deer Hunting Coast to Coast

This is a book for hunters, and it isn't important to deer hunters to be able to recite all the different whitetail subspecies. It is important to understand that there are strong regional differences in coloration, antler conformation, and body size—especially when you traverse the range of several subspecies. It is also important to remember that these are subspecies, not species; they interbreed freely, and there are undoubtedly broad intergrade areas. Boundary lines are arbitrary, and even the great rivers that are sometimes viewed as the boundaries are readily crossed during winter freezeup.

The type specimen, or typical subspecies, is *Odocoileus virginianus virginianus*, a good-sized deer found throughout Virginia, West Virginia, and most of the Deep South. To the south are the Florida whitetail and Florida coastal whitetail (*O. v. osceola* and *O. v. seminolus*), both decent-sized deer, but not as large in body and antler as Virginia deer. Along the southeastern seaboard are a number of island subspecies, of interest if those are the deer you happen to hunt, but all a bit smaller than the Virginia deer. Smallest and rarest of the North American subspecies, fully protected today, is the tiny Florida Key deer, *O. v. clavium*. An adult Florida Key buck is said to weigh around 50 pounds.

The Avery Island whitetail, *O. v. mcilhennyi*, actually occupies a broad coastal belt from Mississippi to Texas. And yes, they're named for the family (of Brigadier General McIlhenny, USMC) that brought us McIlhenny's Tabasco Sauce. To the north lies the Kansas whitetail (*O. v. machrourus*), actually centered in Missouri, and to the west lies the Texas whitetail, properly *O. v. texanus*, which stretches from northern Mexico to South Dakota. On to the north lies the Dakota whitetail, *O. v. dacotensis*. The Texas whitetail is a small-bodied subspecies, but with proper nutrients can develop excellent antlers. The Kansas deer is much larger, but when you get to the Dakota whitetail you're starting to talk about the giants of the whitetail tribe. To the west of the Dakota whitetail lie the Northwest whitetail and the Columbian whitetail (*O. v. ochrourus* and *leucurus*); to the east lies the Northern woodland whitetail, *O. v. borealis*.

Collectively the northern tier of subspecies, stretching from British Columbia to Maine and New Brunswick, are our largest whitetails. This follows a biological principle called Bergmann's rule, whereby members of a warm-blooded species tend to be larger in body size the further they get from the tropics. This appears to aid in heat retention in colder climates. It seems to hold true: If a 50-pound mature buck is possible in the Florida Keys, then a 500-pound buck is possible in Wisconsin, Montana, Maine, or Manitoba. That's stretching a point, of course, but honest-to-God 400-pound bucks aren't all that uncommon. With a mature Texas whitetail rarely weighing over 150 pounds, it should come as no surprise that the northern deer occupy most of the top spots in the record books. But considering the disparity in body size, it is amazing how many Texas deer have reached record-class proportions!

Whitetail bucks come in all types of configurations, and number of points is just one dimension. This buck is the largest known 8-pointer, placing very high in the Boone & Crockett book.

Here's a typical 10-pointer, a real trophy buck in most whitetail country. This one was taken in some of south Texas' best big buck country—where such a deer is just average.

In the converse of that biological rule, the subspecies closest to the equator should have smaller bodies plus enlarged ears and tails to aid in heat dissipation. I haven't seen the deer of southern Mexico and Central America, and indeed few Americans have. But I have seen the Coues deer of northern Mexico and Arizona and their close cousins, the little Carmen Mountains deer (*O. v. couesi* and *carminis*) of northern Coahuila and the adjacent Big Bend region of Texas. They do indeed have outsized ears for a very modest body size, and the latter subspecies is locally called "fantails" in west Texas because of their incredibly outsized snowy tails.

Although there are 17 whitetail subspecies from northern Mexico to Canada, traditionally hunters have lumped together 16 of them and separated just one: the Coues whitetail. This tradition actually comes from an error: Back in the days of the Apache wars, when Army quartermaster (and naturalist) Lieutenant Elliott Coues identified the deer that bears his name, they were so different from the eastern deer he was accustomed to that he concluded they were a separate species. For the better part of a century we've known that they were simply a radically dissimilar subspecies, but the traditional separation has remained.

Yet this is the only subspecies separated out. This is probably a good deal for the Wisconsin sportsman, who hunts whitetail in a state that still holds the 1916-vintage world record, and three-quarters of a century later still takes more record bucks annually than any other state. For the hunter from Florida or the Carolinas, it's a different story: Florida has never produced a book head, South Carolina just one nontypical, and North Carolina one typical and no nontypicals.

Several years ago I was chairman for the Americas for the Safari Club International record book. A lot of members from the Southeast and hard-hunted states in the Northeast weren't happy about their bucks—in some cases the best bucks they could hope for from their areas—having to compete with deer from Montana, Alberta, and even south Texas. I played around with it for a couple of years, and ultimately the committee agreed to some additional categories for whitetail deer. But it was and is a real mess; there is simply no way to establish exact boundaries, nor is there anyone outside a laboratory who can positively differentiate one subspecies from another. Sure, anyone can tell a Texas whitetail from a Montana whitetail. But a Florida whitetail from southern Georgia and a Virginia whitetail from northern Georgia, well, that's getting tough . . .

We eventually came up with seven different categories for whitetail deer. They were drawn along very general geopolitical boundaries that attempted to follow the ranges of the primary subspecies. We came up with Northwestern whitetail, including the Dakota whitetail and those on to the north and west; the Northeastern whitetail, reaching eastward to take in the Northern Woodland whitetail; the Southeastern whitetail, which consisted of the Virginia deer and all the southeastern subspecies; the Texas whitetail, which actually included most of the Kansas subspecies; the Coues deer; and two "catch-all" categories: Tropical whitetails, North America; and Tropical whitetails, South America.

These last put all the Mexican subspecies (there are lots of 'em, and darn little known about any of 'em, excepting the Coues and Texas deer, which were already in categories of their own) and Central American subspecies into one category, and the eight subspecies south of the Panama Canal into another. The tropical groups had so few entries that no minimums were established. Coues deer, of course were next. Of the "regular" whitetails, only the Southeastern category had a significantly reduced minimum score, which is generally appropriate. The deeper I got into the project, though, the more it seemed we were creating a real can of worms.

It's obvious that trying to differentiate among that many whitetail subspecies is a record-keeper's nightmare. Can you imagine trying to sort out 38 subspecies rather than seven geographic groups? Fortunately few hunters care. A good whitetail is a good whitetail, period. And wherever he came from, if he's a good representative of the better bucks from his area, he's a great trophy. Period.

I think it's a terrible mistake to get wrapped up in record book measurements—that isn't what deer hunting is all about. It's fine to hunt for the best deer your area can produce, but it's just as fine to hunt for a buck for the freezer. Deer hunting is being out in the woods, hunting a magnificent wild creature on his own turf. In the case of whitetail deer, you're trying to outwit one of the best. As the seasons roll by you will eventually learn a good deal about him. But more importantly, in the process you'll learn a good deal about yourself.

CHAPTER II

EASTERN WHITETAILS—THE MOST DIFFICULT DEER

I t seems there is no end to the lessons hunters can learn from that great teacher, the whitetail buck. We were driving thru a small wood lot, a perfect hideout for a buck—and a place with absolutely no escape hatch if there happened to be a buck present. Or so we thought. The wood lot backed up to a big grain field, mostly harvested except for a small corner behind me. I was one of the standers in this little drive. The man to my right was over a little rise, but the man to my left was about 60 yards away, in plain view. Most of the ground between us was open, but there was a little swale of thigh-high brown grass leading out to the field. As the drivers approached, I glanced to my left, expecting deer to burst from cover at any second.

There was a buck belly-crawling through that brown grass, head down, and he was halfway between the next stander and me. I couldn't shoot, but I could admire the buck's nerve and count the points on his handsome eight-point rack. In that instant of recognition he made his move, not in a series of bounds but in one blurred rush that carried him into the only cover available—that tiny remnant of standing grain. Of course we reacted instantly, and of course we surrounded him as best we could. But that buck was gone, and nobody ever saw him again that season!

It's one of nature's ironies that some of America's densest whitetail populations coincide with dense human populations in our highly developed, highly industrialized Northeast. Intense hunting is required to keep the population in check, and it's a rare buck who survives past his first set of antlers. If he does survive, his first season gives him enough experience with people to make him virtually bullet-proof. The eastern whitetail is probably our most educated deer, and under normal conditions is one of the most difficult animals in the world to bag.

"Normal conditions" in the highly populated East mean short seasons that put a great number of hunters in the woods at the same time. The East, of course, is a huge area. I'm not speaking now of the virgin timber that covers most of Maine, and that still remains in remote corners of upstate New York and Pennsylvania. Big timber creates its own deer hunting problems, and we'll talk about that in a later chapter. Here I'm speaking of the small wood lots and creek beds interspersed with agriculture across so much of the country from Ohio up through New England.

Pennsylvania alone puts close to a million hunters in the field on opening day of deer season. It's true that under such conditions the season opener is extremely important. Hunters who stick with it throughout the season will find less crowded conditions later on and, undoubtedly, will enjoy a better hunting experience. But intensive pressure like that will make whitetails change their habits radically. They'll become almost entirely nocturnal, and they'll retreat to the thickest, most inaccessible brush they can find. Under the short seasons typical in this region it's a faint hope that deer will "settle down" later on in the season. They'll settle down, for sure—but probably not until hunting season is long since over.

Wherever deer are hunted, opening day is a ritual that must be attended. Where seasons are long and hunting pressure less intense, late in the season is often the best time to hunt—especially if it coincides with rutting activity. But under conditions that dictate a short season and intense hunting pressure, opening day is all-important. Even more important, though, is what you do before opening day. Pre-season scouting is critical in most deer hunting, but the greater the pressure on the deer herd, the more important it becomes.

What do you scout for? The usual, of course. Rubs, scrapes, extra-large tracks that might indicate the presence of a buck. Actual sightings of animals. Well-used trails and movement patterns. Preferred food sources, bedding areas. All of these things are important. But unless you are hunting under unique circumstances that give you absolute control over your hunting area, bear in mind that you won't be alone come opening day. And neither will the deer you've been scouting.

Traditional scouting determines where the deer will be come opening day. Smart scouting in anticipation of heavy hunting pressure should determine where the deer will move when that pressure arrives. Examine avenues of hunter access to the ground you plan to hunt, and figure out how you can get one step ahead. Consider putting your stand in the most horrible mountain laurel tangle you can find—not where the deer are now, but where they're likely to be when the orange-clad army arrives. In many, perhaps even most, areas, it isn't difficult to find the cover that deer—especially hunter-educated bucks—will escape to when the shooting starts.

I'm a western hunter, and although I've done a good deal of it, eastern deer hunting is foreign to me. I like to move and glass, and I'm used to hunting where I can do that. If you have the woods to yourself and the deer are relatively unpressured and behave normally, still hunting is a sound technique. But when hunting pressure is heavy and the deer are justifiably paranoid, stand hunting is safer, more sensible, and much more productive. The old adage in the eastern whitetail woods is: "He who sits still the longest gets the deer." It's true.

Early in the season, you know the woods will be full of hunters. You don't have to like it, but you know you have to deal with it. Do your scouting, but carry it a step farther. Figure out where less patient hunters will be moving the deer, get ahead of them, and wait it out. Personally, I hate to sit still. So I plan a deer stand that will be as comfortable as possible, and I either pack along or wear

Eastern whitetail hunting is often a waiting game—and he who waits the longest (and can sit the most still) is often the hunter who winds up with the deer.

Here's a good, heavy-antlered Eastern buck, taken with a shotgun. Much of the East is shotgun-only country, but the handicap is slight; a sighted-in 12 gauge is deadly to 100 yards. (Photo by Todd Smith)

enough clothes to be sure I won't get cold or wet. And that includes an extra jacket or pillow to sit on.

Where practical and legal, the stand you have chosen should be set up ahead of time. Before dawn on opening day is not the time to be making lots of noise—let the other guys make the noise. Permanent stands, screw in steps, and such may not be legal in your area, and hunting pressure may be so intense that it isn't practical to leave a stand in the woods. But do whatever you can to get into position quietly and quickly, and be there before it gets light. Then wait it out and hope for the best. Do your scouting and planning so that you know you're in a good spot, and stay there. When hunting pressure is heavy, it's the best chance you've got.

These days whitetail hunting has gone high-tech to an amazing degree. There are myriad scents, calls, and gadgets on the market—and most of them work under some conditions some of the time. During the mass panic of a high-pressure opening day, it's unlikely that deer can be called in, rattled in, or will respond properly to a scent or lure. But it makes sense to use a good cover scent that is natural to the area you're hunting. In the Northeast, where the red fox is common, a fox urine cover scent is one of the favorites.

Later on, especially in areas where the season runs long enough to coincide with rutting activities, every trick in the book is worth trying. Use of scent lures, hunting scrapes and creating mock scrapes, calling with a grunt call, and horn rattling have all been proven effective on whitetails everywhere, including the Northeast. One of the problems with all these techniques is human nature: the tendency to believe that, if a little is good, a lot is better. Whitetail expert Jerry Peterson, whose company offers a wide range of calls, artificial rattling horns, and other products for the deer hunter, believes in what he refers to as "social rattling." He doesn't use the hard clashing of dominant bucks fighting in areas with normal, relatively low buck/doe ratios. Rather he ticks the tines together very gently to imitate the sparring that all bucks indulge in to establish their social order. This gentle social rattling has been proven effective well before any actual rutting activity begins, so it is certainly worth giving it a shot.

Another option that's widely used in the East is the time-honored technique of driving deer. Especially effective in the smaller wood lots and coverts so common in much of the East, deer drives are often as organized as a military operation, with the same hunters participating throughout the season. Well-organized they should be; quite obviously they're extremely dangerous, and it's essential that everyone knows where he or she is supposed to be—and where everybody else is. Drives are simply organized by having drivers push the deer while blockers or standers wait at the ends and, if possible, along the sides. Most groups have one person designated to organize the drive. The leader's word must be law; he has to make certain that all know their positions and what direction will be safe to shoot. All participants must literally trust all other participants with their lives.

Drives may consist of as few as two or three hunters, or 20 or more. Spacing depends on density of cover; the idea is to push the cover thoroughly and attempt to block all the possible escape hatches. If there aren't enough people to cover a large area of cover it makes more sense to tackle pieces of it or simply work smaller patches. But even with the most efficient planning, whitetail deer generally don't want to be driven. They'll ghost between the drivers or out the sides, or wait until the last minute and offer a tough running shot when they burst from cover. Deer drives, obviously, aren't for the selective hunter: There's no way to predict who will get the shot, if there is one, or what kind of buck it will be. But it is an effective way to get deer, easily one of the best later in the season in hard-hunted areas.

A good deal of the East remains rifle country, but much of it has gone to shotgun-only, especially in the more populated areas close to large cities. Nothing can be done to make a shotgun effective for shooting across an open field, over a clearcut, or down a power line right-of-way. A shotgun with slugs, however, can be an extremely effective 100-yard deer gun—and that covers a good 90 percent of deer hunting situations, not only in the East but nationwide.

Shotgun slugs and shotguns that fire them have seen a lot of new development in the last few years, and there are a number of new wrinkles. The old hollow-base Foster slugs loaded by the major manufacturers are still available, but newer designs like the B.R.I. and Vitt-Boos sabot slug offer significant improvements in accuracy. New, too, are the rifled shotgun barrels available from several sources. They may not be legal in your area; it really depends on whether the regulations read "smoothbore" or "shotgun" for deer. If legal, such a barrel is worth the investment. It won't make a tack-driver out of your 12-gauge, but it will offer more than adequate accuracy for deer out to 100 yards, perhaps 125 or a bit more.

More and more shotgun hunters, too, are recognizing the need for good sights. My introduction to shotgunning for deer came in 1974 when I was first stationed at Quantico, Virginia. Shotguns were required, so I simply loaded up my Model 12 skeet gun with slugs and went hunting. I couldn't really sight the gun in, since there were no sights, but I did shoot several slugs to see where they went. By squinting down the rib and lining up the beads, I could hit a gallon can at 50 yards—and that was about it. We actually ate some venison that year, but I think it was mostly a miracle.

Every major manufacturer today offers slug barrels that have rifle sights and an open choke. That's okay as far as it goes; iron sights are better than nothing, and an open choke is better than a very tight one. But you never know how slugs are going to perform. In some shotguns, some brands work best through a modified choke, while others go wild in a choke tighter than improved cylinder. Just as you would a rifle, the best course is to head to the range with as wide a selection of slug loads as you can find and see what works best in your gun. Another smart option is to put a low-powered scope on your shotgun. You'll see better and shoot better with a scope, and whatever accuracy your shotgun is capable of, you'll maximize your ability to use it. There are sturdy, inexpensive scope mounting systems available today for most common repeating shotguns.

In later chapters, as we discuss differing areas and different types of deer, we'll make some general suggestions regarding good places to hunt. That's nearly impossible to do in the East. Big whitetail are where you find them, and in the East you find them in extremely unlikely places. Well-managed private land with restricted and controlled access is probably the best bet, but such hunting isn't available to all of us. The Adirondacks of New York annually produce a goodly number of huge bucks, but the deer density is not high there and the hunting is difficult. Southeastern Ohio may technically be considered more a midwestern than an eastern area, but has an extremely high density of deer. Maryland's Eastern Shore, known primarily for its waterfowl hunting, has a lot of deer and produces some exceptional bucks. Most of the land is private and access is difficult—a common problem throughout the East—but the deer hunting is superb. New Jersey is another sleeper, with access difficult but deer numbers very high.

One option we all have—but one from which eastern hunters particularly can benefit—is to take up bowhunting. Early and late bow seasons give access to less disturbed deer and less crowded hunting conditions, which is a tremendous advantage. More important, though, is the fact that many prime areas near cities with incredibly dense deer populations aren't open to any kind of firearms hunting at all. The bowhunter who does his homework and learns to shoot his bow has access to some of the country's very best whitetail hunting. During the bow season, too, the traditional whitetail hunting techniques—and the more modern methods—can be employed against undisturbed deer and have a much better chance of success.

I know a great many eastern whitetail hunters who simply don't bother fighting the crowds; they prefer to do their deer hunting up in the woods of Maine, the Deep South, Texas, or elsewhere. But I know a lot more who relish the challenge and look forward to every opening day. Some of them seem to come up with their bucks every year—and those who do are whitetail hunters without peer. Many of them rely heavily on opening day, but if it doesn't pan out, they have a whole repertoire of tricks, techniques, and places to try them—enough to carry them through the whole season. As in all hunting, persistence pays. Whether with bow, rifle, shotgun, or muzzleloader—or a combination of all—sooner or later the serious, dedicated eastern whitetailer will get a shot.

In much of the East permanent stands may not be legal—and may not be left alone by other hunters. But whether a permanent or portable stand is used, getting up off the ground makes sense.

CHAPTER III

DIXIE DEER

T he dogs were some way off, baying like crazy. All that splashing in the swamp just below the levee where I sat didn't come from canine feet. More splashing, even closer, and antler tips showed above the brush. I didn't move, but I got ready. When the buck gathered himself and launched into the rush that would carry him over the levee to the safety of the swamp beyond, my .270 rose to meet him. I had already dragged him out of the water and up onto the levee when the hounds splashed out of the swamp and gathered around.

He was a lovely buck, unusually large for the North Carolina swamp country. I would have called him a 10-pointer, or, by true western count, a 5x5. My hosts followed eastern point count to the letter and insisted he was a 14-pointer because of his "kickers." Whatever he was, he was a beautiful buck, and I was delighted to have him.

Hound hunting, the way I got that buck, is a tradition in much of the South. Today it's a tradition that seems to have fallen into disfavor. There are problems with it, to be sure. For one thing, it keeps the deer stirred up, and can indeed push them clear out of an area. For another, it isn't conducive to selective hunting. My big buck was a piece of luck; in general, if a legal deer comes by, the houndsmen are likely to give hell to anyone who doesn't shoot. Lack of control of the dogs is a legitimate concern. Just a couple of weeks ago I was sitting on a deer stand in Alabama when a lathered-up spike buck tore past. Not far behind were two big hounds—but nobody was running deer dogs in that part of the swamp.

Hunting deer with hounds goes back generations, to a time when deer were just plain scarce everywhere in the South except in the deepest swamps. It isn't my idea of an ideal way to hunt deer, but it is a way to hunt country that is almost impossible to hunt by any other means. When the hounds sound off on a hot scent, it's also tremendously exciting—and it's a way of life for those who practice it. A lot of folks today would like to see it outlawed altogether. I wouldn't go that far; a sensible compromise seems to be to designate either parts of the hunting season or particular areas for dog hunting and no dog hunting—and that is happening in much of the South today.

The days when it was necessary to penetrate deep into the swamps to hunt southern deer are over. In fact, for a westerner like me accustomed to drawing for a tag to hunt one deer, southern hunting regulations seem absurd. South Carolina opens some hunting areas in mid-August and there are still some areas open in January. Alabama opens her rifle season in November and leaves it open to the last day in January. Sixty-day rifle seasons are commonplace in the South, and bag limits seem unbelievable. Alabama, for instance, allows a buck a day throughout the season—and in high density areas, some counties have "buck and doe days" when a hunter can legally harvest a buck and a doe daily. Even in the South, that's unusually liberal—but restrictions such as three-deer areas and five-deer season limits aren't unusual.

This is nothing new, and certainly not news. The South's whitetail deer explosion has been making headlines in the outdoor magazines for a decade and more. What isn't widely understood is the magnitude of the population growth. Mississippi has close to two million whitetail deer today; neighboring Alabama something close to 1.5 million. Virginia, West Virginia, Georgia, and Florida all have deer herds comfortably over the half-million mark—approaching a million in Georgia's case. Louisiana and North Carolina are approaching the half-million mark, while South Carolina's herd is something over 300,000 and still increasing.

What deer populations were like in the South a century ago isn't known—but it is known that the whitetail deer was nearly extinct in the South just after World War II. It's believed that just 3,000 deer remained in Alabama in 1950, and the situation was just as grim in much of the South. Restocking and habitat management turned the situation around in the late 1950s and 1960s, and the early 1970s saw an amazing population explosion of deer. Today it has leveled off in much of the South; deer herds have nearly reached maximum sustainable levels in many areas, and have actually required reduction in some places. That restocking, incidentally, was clearly both necessary and beneficial. However, some of the transplants were of northern deer, so that genetically, today's southern deer may or may not be the native subspecies.

The next whitetail population explosion—and it's happening right now—will be in the states that were "border states" in the Civil War: Kentucky, Tennessee, Arkansas, and Missouri. When I was a kid, I hunted deer in both Arkansas and Missouri. It was pretty rare for anyone to see a buck, let alone get one—but at least they had deer hunting, which my own state of Kansas did not. Today it's a whole different world, with longer seasons, multiple deer limits, and incomparably higher success. And in those border states it's going to get better.

In the Deep South proper, right now it's probably darn near as good as it's going to get. And it should stay good for quite some time to come. From the outsider's viewpoint, especially for an outsider accustomed to short seasons and one-buck limits, it would appear that all you have to do is show up in the southern whitetail woods and bring lots of shells. It isn't quite that easy. Southern deer are indeed plentiful, but they're still whitetail deer. And they're subjected to quite enough hunting pressure to have acquired all the cunning of their crafty breed. Many dedicated and persistent southern hunters do indeed take multiple deer—sometimes, in buck-a-day states like Alabama, into the dozens. In a recent Mississippi season the deer harvest actually exceeded the number of hunters

Sports superstar Bo Jackson proved that he's good at just about anything he does with this outstanding Alabama buck—a typical 10-point frame with four extra "cheater" points.

North Carolinians Bud and Brian Long, father and son, took these near-matching Alabama 8-pointers within minutes of each other—but from different treestands some distance apart.

afield. But that mustn't be interpreted to mean that everybody got a deer; some took more than one, and many were unsuccessful. In a good season, hunter success throughout the South averages somewhere between 20 and 25 percent, with a few states below that and a few occasionally running close to 50 percent.

As whitetail hunting goes, that's outstanding—but it does indicate that, just like deer hunting anywhere, you must know what you're doing to be successful. But Lord, the deer are there. I recently spent a week hunting near Montgomery, Alabama—farmland broken by swampy bottomlands and stands of thick timber. It was the last week of an intensive season, and some 250 bucks had already been harvested from the country I was hunting. In spite of that, I could literally have taken my allotted buck per day. That I didn't is simply due to the fact that I would rather have one nice buck than half a dozen little guys—but the deer were definitely there.

The big bucks, the kind of deer I was looking for, are in that country, too. That particular hunt was the Buckmaster Classic, an annual event that brings together various sports figures and celebrities and a few writers. In the course of a week some 30 bucks were taken, and better than a third of them were wall-hangers. The best was a really beautiful, heavy-racked 10-pointer with some cheater points, taken by Bo Jackson. It wasn't close to a Boone & Crockett head, of course—the South isn't the place to look for such a buck—but it was a very fine deer.

If there's a drawback to southern hunting, it's the simple fact that it isn't the nation's best trophy country. Lots of deer, and good numbers of nice deer. But historically, the monsters aren't there. North Carolina recently produced its first Boone & Crockett head, a typical, while South Carolina has produced just one nontypical. Florida has yet to produce one. Alabama and Mississippi, with the South's highest deer populations, have produced fewer "Booners" than either Louisiana or Georgia. Both Kentucky and Tennessee, with much smaller harvests than other southern states, have been producing more than their share of book heads lately.

If I were picking trophy whitetail country, I wouldn't pick the South. But if I were forced to, I'd look at Kentucky's Land Between the Lakes; central Georgia; and the Black Belt region of west-central Alabama and adjacent east-central Mississippi. Whether it's minerals, genetics, overpopulation, heavy harvesting, or a combination of all these, the South just isn't the place for huge bucks.

I recently met an excellent whitetail hunter from North Carolina, Bud Long. We got to talking deer, and he showed me some albums of bucks that he'd taken. They were full of beautiful deer—eight pointers, 10-pointers, a super-rare albino 10-pointer, you name it. This guy knew his deer, and he annually took decent bucks with rifle, shotgun, muzzleloader, and bow. He had a great collection of fine deer, but he admitted wistfully that he felt he was taking the best sort of deer

This Alabama swamp buck is more typical of most southern whitetails. The big boys are out there, but forkhorns and 6-pointers are a much larger percentage of the harvest.

his area had to offer. If he wanted bigger deer, he simply had to start hunting farther from home.

Fortunately few of us are postgraduate whitetail hunters like Bud Long, and few of us will get to the point where we've taken the very best deer our area has to offer. For the average guy who lives in hard-hunted whitetail country with short seasons—or the guy like me who doesn't live in whitetail country at all—the South offers phenomenal whitetail hunting. I still have the mounted head of my North Carolina buck, and until very recently it was the only whitetail I'd had mounted. I thoroughly enjoyed that recent Alabama hunt, and I expect to do more hunting down there.

As mentioned, dog hunting is common through much of the South, and organized drives are practiced as well. A few really sneaky woodsmen have good success still hunting, but the preferred (and most successful) southern hunting technique—especially for decent bucks—is hunting from elevated stands.

Once I was out with Billy McCoy, world champion turkey caller, scouting some swampy country for a good place to put a treestand. I commented that I'd figured out the basic difference between eastern and western hunting. Out West I generally hunt for deer—the genuine, breathing article. In the eastern half of the country it's much more common to hunt for sign, and that's what we were doing. The sign was there, of course—good tracks in the soft ground where several trails converged, and several fresh scrapes scattered about. We put up a self-climber and anchored it with screw-in steps, then flagged a route so I could slip in quietly in the dark.

I have trouble staying on stand for hours on end, let alone days. I'm used to moving and glassing, and I just hate to sit still. If you have a good stand, though, sitting still is exactly what you should do—even if it takes days. I shot a nice buck on the second day of my vigil, then spent the rest of the week hoping for a big boy who never appeared. Colleague Nick Sisley watched a clear cut for five days, seeing nothing—and then shot a magnificent 20-inch eight-pointer at nearly 400 yards. Another writer, Tom Fegely, never saw a buck at all—but he was due. The year before he'd been on stand five times and had shot three bucks, all mounting-quality southern deer.

The real secret to stand hunting is, obviously, placing your stand in the right spot. The first step is to locate good, fresh sign. The next step is to read the prevailing wind, and then place your stand so you'll have a possible shot if and when a buck appears. All that remains is to get into your stand quietly and stay there. Southern hunting is pleasant in that it rarely gets really cold—but it can get wet, and there might be enough mosquitoes to carry you away even in January. A head net is probably a better choice than insect repellent.

I used Jerry Peterson's deer call, and was successful in "grunting in" a little buck, and I also used Gene Dismukes' locally produced scent mask and lure—and it worked! A six-point buck was chasing some does in a dense patch of cover behind my stand, and eventually the does broke and trotted underneath me. The buck followed until he came to the spot 20 yards in front of me where I'd sprinkled some scent. The little buck put the brakes on, sniffed and pawed, and stood stock still for a couple of minutes. It was his lucky day—I didn't want him.

What I'm getting at is that a good stand is essential, but you might as well make it even better by using every trick in the book. And these days there are more tricks than ever before. In some cases, as with that big buck that Nick shot, you can cover a large area from your stand. But you're more likely to be covering an acre or two of hardwood swamp, and a deer 75 yards away might as well be a mile off. You don't want to overdo anything, but get a grunt call and learn to use it. Use some good scent mask, and make certain it's natural to the area you're hunting. Try a little judicious rattling—nothing too aggressive, just a little "ticking" to imitate bucks sparring among themselves. I didn't used to believe in such things, but I've changed my tune.

Before you can pick a good stand you have to have a place to put it—in other words, a place to hunt. The South isn't as bad as most northeastern states, but it's far from an open ballgame. Most private land is posted, and these days an awful lot of the best private ground is leased out to hunting clubs or private individuals. Fortunately there is a fair amount of public land scattered throughout the South. It may not offer hunting as good as the best private ground—but it will offer whitetail hunting better than that found in many other parts of the country. Timber companies, too, have vast holdings that are generally open to the public for a very nominal fee which buys you a trespass permit.

There are also a number of excellent hunting lodges. Guided hunting isn't as it is in the West; generally speaking you'll be put on a good, pre-scouted stand, and the rest is up to you. On the other hand, the prices are quite modest compared with guided deer hunts elsewhere—and the southern cooking at such lodges is usually well worth the trip, as well as the cost. It takes a good deal of research for a nonresident to find his way into southern whitetail hunting—but that, too, is worth the effort.

CHAPTER IV

CORN BELT BUCKS

The year was 1964. The place was a river valley in central Kansas. We'd been hunting quail along the river, and towards evening we'd left the scattered covey to regroup and climbed up the low bluff to the truck. We dressed our birds there in the sunset, and just as the light began to fade he stepped out of the trees below us. In those days I didn't know a big buck from a little buck; I remember him as huge, but he might have been mediocre. I'll never forget him, because deer—any deer—were a rarity in the Kansas I grew up in. When I saw that memorable buck our first modern deer season was still a year away.

When Kansas' historic modern season opened, I drew a tag and was back on that ridge looking for that buck. I never saw him again, so he can be as big as I want him to be. It's quite possible he really was a monster; with an annual harvest of just a few thousand deer, the first 20 years of Kansas deer hunting saw 24 typical bucks and 15 nontypicals entered into the B & C records. These include a top ten typical taken by Dennis Finger in Nemaha County—on another farm where I grew up hunting quail. I never laid eyes on a deer there. Although it takes time for the records to catch up, the last few years saw even more record deer come out of Kansas, including several incredible nontypicals.

The Midwest is a difficult region to pin down. Certainly my home state of Kansas is part of it, but how far east, west, north, or south it extends depends on your local perspective. For instance, I'd call Ohio part of the East—but an Ohioan might think of himself as a Midwesterner. But if the Midwest defies exact description, America's "corn belt" is a little easier to pin down. You could say that it centers in Iowa, and you'd probably be close. From there, west to Nebraska, Kansas, and even eastern Colorado; south into northern Missouri; north into the southeastern Dakotas and the southern Great Lakes states; and on east into northern Indiana, Illinois, and northwestern Ohio. This is a region of intensive agriculture and, on the face of it, very little real habitat for deer.

Take a closer look, though. Remember that the whitetail at his best is an edge animal—and that's what the corn belt is all about. The habitat there is pure edge. Shelter belts, brushy fence rows, tiny wood lots—and thousands of miles of meandering waterways choked with brush. The habitat is ideal, assuming there is sound management and tolerance from landowners.

This is country that was settled well over a century ago, and in the settling and homesteading era the game was eradicated—first the buffalo, then the elk, and finally the pronghorns and deer. Some states had country remote enough or thick enough to retain a remnant population; a few deer remained in western Nebraska

27

and the hills of southern Missouri. Other states literally started from scratch. Deer were believed extinct in Indiana as early as 1893; in Kansas in 1904.

During the early years of this century deer herd growth, if any, was purely natural. A few deer moved into the farm country from wooded regions, following the waterways. By 1933 there were deer in Kansas again, no thanks to anyone's efforts at all. In the years following World War II many midwestern states got serious about their deer, and by then game management was becoming the science it is today. Indiana's excellent modern deer herd can be attributed largely to restocking efforts in the late 1930s and 1940s. Most of the corn belt's deer explosion came in the 1950s, but slow growth continues to this day. Eventually, much to even the local residents' amazement, there were enough deer to hunt.

I can well remember the summers I spent at a local Boy Scout camp in eastern Kansas. It was prime whitetail country, but I can't remember anyone ever reporting seeing a deer. Today they're everywhere in eastern Kansas; my old quail hunting buddies—who never thought of such a thing when I knew them—are all dedicated whitetail hunters today. By the mid-1960s virtually all of the corn belt was again occupied by deer, and was again being hunted. It was a good deal for local residents, but it was some time before the world became aware of this region's trophy potential.

Mel Johnson changed all that in a soybean field in central Illinois on October 29, 1965. On that day he arrowed a huge typical whitetail, a new (and still) world record for bowhunters and at that time the all-time number two typical in Boone and Crockett. One by one, the entire top ten for both typicals and nontypicals are being steadily replaced by corn belt bucks. In 1969 Jeffrey Brunk's northern Missouri whitetail almost broke the magic 200-point mark, and in 1971 Larry Gibson's Missouri buck beat it handily, replacing Mel Gibson's buck as the new number two. Dennis Finger's big Kansas buck came in 1974, the same year William Cripe broke 200 points with a huge Indiana buck. The nontypical category is much the same story. In or near the top ten you'll find Missouri, Iowa, Nebraska, Ohio, and Kansas—literally a roll call of the corn belt.

That's the good news, and there's a bit more of it: Whitetail deer are not particularly difficult to hunt in this kind of country. Their habits are relatively easy to pattern, since their escape cover is somewhat limited. No, I'm not knocking the Midwest's whitetails or whitetail hunters—but hunting river-bottom and shelter belt whitetails isn't exactly the same as hunting them in virgin timber. As examples, both Kansas and Iowa typically have hunter success rates of around 50 percent—incredibly high as whitetail hunting goes.

The bad news is that this is an extremely difficult region for an outsider to hunt. There are virtually no guided operations whatsoever, very little public land, and two of the best states—Kansas and Iowa—allow no nonresident deer hunting. There have been many, many very large bucks taken in this region in the past 25

Bowhunter success in Kansas is so unusually high that even dedicated archers may be a bit more casual than is customary in hard-hunted states. (Photo by Jon Blumb)

years. Yet the vast majority have been taken not just by local residents, but by very local residents, often hunting on their own or their neighbor's property.

There is hope, of course. Kansas is still on a drawing for rifle deer permits, but bow permits are now available over the counter. In the early years deer permits were hard to draw, but for the last couple of seasons there have been permits that went begging in some areas. It's time to let in the nonresidents, in spite of resident pressure against such a move. And it will happen—first nonresident bowhunters, then eventually a few nonresident rifle permits. You can bet I'll try to get one of those first nonresident permits. In the 1988 season archers took three monstrous nontypicals in Kansas, all of which should make the top ten in Pope & Young. It's my home state, so I may have a bias, but I wouldn't be surprised if Kansas produced the new world record typical whitetail that everyone is waiting for.

But for now deer hunting there is a resident's ballgame, as it is in Iowa. Illinois, Indiana, and Ohio all have superb whitetail hunting, and have produced monsters. However, the large human population, intense hunting pressure, and short seasons in these states make it tough for an outsider. Unless you have a connection with a friendly farmer, of course . . .

Northern Missouri has a bit more potential for outsiders; Missouri has had decent deer hunting for decades and is more accustomed to hosting nonresidents than most midwestern states. But even there it won't be particularly easy to find a place to hunt. It's the kind of thing that could take numerous pre-season trips, knocking on many doors, and much public relations work. And of course it's well worth the effort.

Nebraska has much more potential, but nonresident permits are limited. In general, the farther west you go in the state, the farther you are from population centers and, in theory, the easier it should be to find a place to hunt. The entire Platte River watercourse is magnificent whitetail country; its willow thickets have produced many fine whitetails, and will continue to produce many more. A friend of mine from Colorado took his barely-teenage boy up to Nebraska for his first deer. To be honest, he'd done a bit of scouting and knew it was a good spot. I actually feel sorry for the boy: His first deer was a typical whitetail that makes Boone & Crockett with room to spare—and where does a deer hunter go from there?

There is excellent potential for huge whitetails in areas not traditionally thought of as either corn belt or whitetail country. Eastern Colorado and eastern Wyoming are both, quietly and with little fanfare, producing monster whitetails right now. Tags must be drawn for, but are not hard to come by. Oklahoma is another sleeper. Historically she has produced very few truly big whitetails, but she shares a number of river drainages with Kansas. And Oklahoma, though mostly private land, isn't an inordinately difficult area in which to find a place to

This monstrous 8-pointer was taken along Nebraska's Platte River—from a duckblind during a break in a driving rainstorm. Who says luck isn't a part of the game?

hunt. Good whitetails—even great whitetails—do occur along drainages throughout northern Oklahoma.

Throughout this region the hunting is mostly river bottom hunting. Early and late, and during the rut, it's possible to catch the big boys away from the cover. It's also, on occasion, very practical to work two- and three-man drives through shelter belts or narrow stretches of riverine growth. However, stand hunting, based on careful pre-season scouting, would be my choice of technique. The cover is limited enough, and whitetail habitual enough, that the patient hunter should get an opportunity. And the hunter success throughout this region bears that out.

I'll never forget a morning spent in a duck blind on the Platte River in Nebraska. We were there to hunt ducks, but deer season was open and my host had a tag. So he propped a slide-action, open-sighted .30-06 against one wall of the duck blind just in case. Shortly after dawn a tremendous rain squall swept down the river. The willows on the opposite shore weren't 150 yards away, but for two hours the visibility was down to feet, not yards. Then the squall passed, and just as you might expect, deer started moving in its wake. The largest eight-point buck I've ever seen stepped from some willows across the river, and my host made the very nicest shot I've ever seen with open sights. There were some shallows, and we could drag that horse of a deer back to our position—but only with great difficulty, and it took all three of us. Oh yes, we shot some ducks as the day progressed—but what would I have given for a deer tag!

Kansas outdoor writer Michael Pearce took this fine 8-pointer along the edge of a grainfield. Kansas, with no nonresident hunting, is one of the best trophy whitetail states. (Photo by Jon Blumb)

CHAPTER V

ALBERTA'S MONSTER WHITETAILS

I 'll never forget the first whitetail buck I ever saw in Alberta. It was a beautiful Sunday in November. There wasn't a single cloud in a sky as blue as Paul Newman's eyes, and the temperature was an unseasonably warm 31 degrees. The countryside was at peace the way a Sunday afternoon is supposed to be in farm country. Lazy columns of white woodsmoke swirled from farmhouse chimneys, bundled-up children scampered about in the snow, and dogs napped on porches.

Western Alberta is grain country, and fields of winter wheat and alfalfa were set in among stands of aspen and thin conifers. Before people moved in, the land was a sea of trees that had to be cleared out to make room for agriculture. This has created the edge cover that whitetails love, the main reason the deer have expanded their range throughout this portion of the province.

Outfitter Lyle Dorey and I were driving the area, looking for deer and generally giving me a feel for the country we'd be hunting beginning the next day. As we passed one field about four o'clock, a doe trotted from a stand of trees near the road toward the center of the field, her legs a bit stiff at the knees and tail level with her backline. We stopped, and into the field came the most magnificent whitetail buck I've ever laid eyes on.

His main beams extended well past the nose before hooking inward just a bit. The back tines had to be 10 or 12 inches long, and the remaining tines were equally impressive. The eyeguards were thick and long, too. And the mass! He had some real weight in that rack, 12 total points, and a spread of perhaps 20 or 21 inches. Lyle and I both guessed him to be a buck that would score in the neighborhood of 180 Boone & Crockett points.

He strolled after his lady like the king that he was, regally taking his time, no thoughts on his mind except those controlled by his rutting hormones. We watched the pair for two minutes before they disappeared into the timber on the other side of the field.

I suppose it was fate that allowed me a look at such a monster buck on Sunday, a day when no hunting is permitted in Alberta. Lyle and I hunted that buck for five straight days, and of course we never saw him again. But it is a whitetail buck like that one that keeps sportsmen from throughout the lower 48 coming back to Alberta each fall. As a Texan who was on this same hunt said that night around the supper table, "I can shoot all the little whitetails I want to down home. I decided that this year I wanted to hunt me a serious buck."

Alberta has long been recognized as one of the best places anywhere to hunt trophy-class whitetail bucks, and rightly so. According to Brent Markham, an official with the Alberta Department of Fish & Wildlife, the prognosis for continued quality hunting is good.

"Generally speaking, our deer populations are down a bit from the mid-1980s, but that has been our intention," Markham said. "We gave out lots of additional antlerless permits in 1984-85, and that helped thin the herd. We continued giving out extra antlerless permits in scattered units up through 1988, but we've achieved our objective and will back way off on that practice beginning in 1989.

"What this has done for us is take a little of the resident pressure off the bucks in past seasons, as well as ensure that deer aren't going to overpopulate in these years of mild winters we've been having. We hope that by doing this we'll avoid a big die-off once our 'normal' winters return. We also think it will give the bucks the room they need to grow to maturity in many units."

Markham says whitetails are still expanding their range in the province, especially where timber is harvested. "In coming years, the northern portion of the province will be the scene of lots of this clearcutting. The deer are also expanding into the western part of the province, where new agricultural land is being opened up. The fringe forest and agricultural country north and northeast of Edmonton also holds a very good whitetail population."

Alberta holds a good population of trophy-class whitetails for several reasons. The opening up of new fringe habitat is certainly one of them, but there are others. The deer are Dakota whitetails (*O. v. dacotensis*), one of the largest whitetail subspecies, a fact reflected both in antler growth and body size. Mature bucks weighing 300 pounds on the hoof aren't uncommon. Along with these genetics, the fringe timber/agriculture country provides them plenty to eat as well as lots of escape cover. And obviously the minerals needed for the growth of big antlers are present.

"I believe that the only real limiting factor in growing record book-class bucks in Alberta is age," Dorey told me. "That's why the fringe country is so good to hunt today, as compared to the more open farmlands south and east of Edmonton, where most nonresidents hunt deer. That country still holds some monster deer, but by the time they reach maturity you can bet they've been shot at a time or two.

"In the fringe country, the deer have lots of trees, overgrown gullies and brushy creek bottoms to hide from resident hunting pressure when they're under three and a half years of age. That gives them an excellent chance to reach maturity at five and a half years old. When they get that old around here, you can bet they'll be the kind of buck most hunters would want to take a real long look at."

Hunting trophy-class whitetails in Alberta presents its own unique set of problems. For one thing, the hunter must be prepared to shoot at a deer anywhere from 40 to 400 yards away—and probably on the move. The greatest limiting factor in the hunt is time. The rule of thumb in hunting these northern whitetail

Alberta bucks are big-bodied, often weighing well over 250 pounds on the hoof. Robb shot this good 10-pointer at relatively short range—50 yards—as it lay in a bed at midday with two does.

Alberta holds some of the most phenomenal specimens of whitetail bucks in the world. Not every hunter tags one, but if a true book buck is your goal, this is the place to give it a go. (Photo by Ian McMurchy)

bucks is that, on the average, you'll have a total of five seconds to put it together: That means, see the deer, get on him, and shoot him. "If a true trophy whitetail gives you more time than that, you've got the one thing a trophy hunter needs more than anything else—the blessings of Lady Luck," Dorey said. "If two bucks give you more time than that in a single week, you really should be spending your time on the tables in Las Vegas, not hunting deer."

Mental preparation is critical to success. Because you may spend an entire week of hard hunting to see just one trophy-class buck, you have to be ready when opportunity comes knocking. If, by the fifth day, you haven't seen anything to speak of and your mental edge is dulled, you'll probably give a buck just that little extra leeway he needs to escape once you finally get an opportunity.

"You have to make the most of your chance, and if I've learned one thing in a lifetime of guiding whitetail hunters, it's that the chances don't always pop up when you want them to," Dorey said. "They like to wait until you're bored, reaching for the thermos, eating a sandwich, or just staring off into space. Then the deer appears like magic, you're not ready, he's gone before you can get the rifle up, and that's all you get for the week."

Decisions about whether or not to shoot must often be made in a split second, and that means you have to trust your guide and his judgment. "A good whitetail guide knows whether or not a buck is a taker at first glance, while the hunter usually doesn't," Dorey said. "The first reaction of lots of hunters is to throw up their binoculars instead of their rifle right off the bat." By the time such a hunter sees the deer through the glasses, decides he's a taker, and gets ready to shoot, it's often too late. If the deer is still in view, now instead of a 100- or 200-yard standing shot, you have a shot at a running deer at 300 or 400 yards.

"The guide has binoculars. Let him look through them while you get ready. That way, when he says shoot, you're ready. Part of what you're paying for on these hunts is the guide's expertise in trophy judgment. The smart hunter will use it."

My hunt with Dorey opened my eyes to several new whitetail tricks. For example, we spent lots of time just sitting in the pickup cab, glassing for deer. When I asked Dorey about this, he said that the deer are used to vehicles being parked all over the place in farm country, and aren't spooked by them nearly as much as they would be by a smelly human being crunching around on frozen snow. His point was proven one morning when a small 10-pointer following a doe came so close to our pickup blind that I could literally have reached out and grabbed his tail.

We also used hay-bale blinds, tried a little rattling, and did some walking. At all times we were looking for fresh sign. An open field that had a fresh scrape line, fresh rubs, or tracks in it was where we'd set up before first light and again in the evening in the hopes of catching moving deer. Midday is a virtual nothing in terms of deer movement—although, as Dorey said, "You never know. I encourage the guys to pack a lunch and stay with it all day, but quite a few choose to come back to the lodge for a nap. I've never had a hunter yet that shot a buck from his bunk, and you just might see a big old buck wandering around in the middle of the day. It's happened to me on several occasions."

During the November season, the deer are quite unpredictable. One day you might see lots of deer, does and bucks alike, scampering about everywhere. The next day it might shut off, and the only reason you know there are still deer around is by the fresh tracks in the snow. You just have to stay with it.

That's the way it was for me. On the fifth day of my hunt, I shot a nice 10-point buck that scores right at 150 Boone & Crockett points. I had seen a nice 10-pointer the first morning, too, but passed him hoping to see that monster we'd stumbled onto on Sunday. I did see bucks every day, but the others were little guys.

One of the Texas boys had much better luck, at least in seeing bucks. He saw three very shootable bucks in six days. His guide told us that one they just didn't have a prayer of getting on, one they had a prayer shot at and missed, and one they had dead to rights and flat blew the shot on. That old boy went home deerless, but his hunt was certainly a successful one. Overall, you can expect success rates on these hunts to run at right around 50 percent.

The nonresident whitetail picture has not been without its problems. The past decade has seen the emergence of more than a few fly-by-night outfitters, rip-off artists that take your money and provide little in the way of quality hunting. Because of this, the province is looking at several regulation options, two of which include assigning exclusive guide areas to long-time outfitters, and giving existing outfitters a limited number of whitetail permits. Brent Markham said that no changes were expected for the 1989 season, but after that the implementation of the permit system was a real possibility. "We hope that will help regulate hunting pressure and harvest in each unit of the province," Markham said. "In so doing we hope to help ensure that the nonresident will have a quality experience when he comes to Alberta."

The outfitters themselves have taken the matter seriously enough to form the Alberta Whitetail Outfitters Association with the intent of self-regulating the business. Membership criteria are stiff, and the association will provide a list of its members to interested parties. Lyle Dorey is president of the association, and for information you can write to him at P.O. Box 1463, Rocky Mountain House, Alberta, Canada T0M 1T0. By law nonresidents must use an outfitter to hunt whitetails in Alberta, and it's very important to research prospective guides before booking a hunt. Information on both outfitters and hunting in general can be obtained from the Alberta Department of Fish and Game, 9915 108th St., Edmonton, Alberta, Canada T5K 2C9.

Whitetail hunting in Alberta was extremely exciting to me. Just knowing that around the next corner, behind the next tree, or in the next field I might see a true monster buck kept the adrenalin level on high all week, a tingle that didn't go away even after a day of seeing no deer at all. And while I took a very nice buck, I'm looking forward to making the trip again, perhaps topping him with the "Sunday buck."

I like it when I tingle like that.

Fresh rubs are a good indicator that bucks are working a specific area right now. Finding rubs still dripping with sap indicates a good area to set up a stand at first or last light.

Classic Alberta whitetail country looks like this—open grain fields with adjacent escape and bedding cover. Glassing from afar is the preferred hunting method.

CHAPTER VI

BIG TIMBER BUCKS

F resh snow fell in the night, four-inches of soft powder that blanketed the crusty old snow. It was an answer to a deer hunter's prayer. For a week I'd been battling the "crunch, crunch, crunch" of hard-frozen snow, and it had been hopeless. Now the woods were quiet, and while I'd never been on equal footing with a whitetail buck in his home territory, at least I had a chance.

I picked up the tracks along the edge of a creek, big toe-dragging tracks like cross-country skis. I know it's said that you can't sex a deer by its tracks, and that's partly true. But in the northern timber, a big buck approaches the size of a spike elk—and no doe leaves a track of that size. This was a deer traveling down the creek alone, meandering in and out of thick cover—and I knew it was a buck. The soft powder snow was still falling, big fluffy flakes like cotton balls. These tracks had been snowed into but little, and there was almost no wind. I knew also that I could catch this buck. The question was whether or not I would see him when I caught up to him.

I moved slowly, hardly more than a step at a time. The buck could be anywhere, but I felt he was just ahead. Under such conditions you can't make a single mistake—and the slightest noise in the silent, snow-laden trees is a big mistake. You take a step, pause and scan the trees ahead, look down and plan where to plant your feet. You step slowly, bringing your weight down gradually to feel what lies under the snow. There's a rhythm to it, but it's agonizingly slow and must not be rushed unless you have extremely good visibility ahead. And in the timber you almost never do.

The tracks led into thicker evergreens on a little bench just above the creek bank, and now there was no snow in them at all. They were meandering more aimlessly now, winding back and forth through the jackpines. Aimless to me, but not to the buck: He was looking for a place to bed. He found it on the far side of a tiny rise, well sheltered by a deadfall and two bushy evergreens. I saw his antlers first, just the top tines projecting above that slight rise. He was less than 20 yards away and unaware of my presence. I couldn't help the elation that soared through me; beating a whitetail at this game in this country is like finishing a marathon or breaking 100 straight in handicap trap. But with the elation came bitter disappointment: The buck was a nice eight-pointer, but he wasn't what I was hoping for.

I circled to the right, moving by inches until I had a clear view. He was lying down, head to one side, and his coat was that peculiar grayish tan of the big northern whitetail. I hadn't been wrong about his antlers, either—a good eight, but not the monster I had come to that country to hunt. Time was growing short, and I was undecided. I brought the .338 to bear, and that movement finally gave me away. Astonished, the buck swiveled his head and stared at me for a long instant as if he knew he'd been had. The crosshairs were steady on his white throat patch; the safety was off. The spell broke when I lowered the rifle; in one bound the buck was off through the trees.

The kind of deer I was looking for was indeed there, a true monster that would beat the elusive—almost unreachable—Boone & Crockett minimum of 170. I didn't get him that trip, but we saw him later that same day. We found his outsized tracks leading into a little patch of timber ringed by clear cut, and we surrounded him fair and square—as well as you can surround a truly great whitetail with the wisdom of a half-dozen hunting seasons. When the buck made his move, one of my hunting partners had him at 20 yards—but that was the one man who had filled his tag, and thus the one man who couldn't take the shot. What was that buck? I hesitate to say, because I don't want to be called a liar. Let's just say he was a high, heavy-horned typical 12-pointer with an outside spread in the high twenties. Where was he? Let's just say he was in timber country in western Montana . . .

From Maine and New Brunswick all the way west to eastern Washington and British Columbia live the largest of the whitetail deer. They aren't of the same subspecies: They might be Dakota whitetails, Northwest whitetails, Northern woodland whitetails, or even Columbian whitetails—but they'll be the largest of their breed. Until the emergence of the corn belt as a whitetail hotspot, these big northern deer dominated the record books, and well they should. It stands to reason that a buck with a body weight of 400 pounds has a better chance of having big antlers than a buck weighing 150 pounds on the hoof! In days gone by the mobile hunter who wanted his name in the record book headed to wood lots and creek bottoms of southern Saskatchewan. The late Elgin T. Gates, for example, shot a monster buck there in 1958—making him darn near the only internationally-known big-game hunter with a Boone & Crockett whitetail to his credit.

The open country of southern Saskatchewan was much like the corn belt—and in fact is the same type of hunting, except that it was uncomplicated by human populations and access problems. It was quite possibly the only "easy" place for the outsider to take a monster deer—easy meaning at least possible, instead of practically impossible. Virtually all of the areas that were producing Saskatchewan's best heads were closed to nonresidents a number of years ago. Things are loosening up some today, but it's a slow process.

And yet the big deer are there, and they can be hunted. But not in the easier, open areas. They can be hunted in the virgin timber farther north—and west, and east, and south. It's the timber country that, in my view, produces America's best whitetails. But it doesn't often hold great numbers of deer, and the hunting is

This 9-pointer is a small buck in western Montana, what the locals would call a meat deer rather than a trophy. The deer aren't plentiful, but they grow huge.

Only two things give the hunter a significant edge in big timber country: the rut, and a good, fresh tracking snow that keeps the woods quiet. When they combine you're in business!

some of America's most difficult.

I've already said I wouldn't be surprised if the next typical world record came from Kansas. I'll hold to that, because if such a buck exists there's a good chance that he can be shot. On the other hand, I know bucks in that class exist in the forests of western Montana, northern Manitoba and Saskatchewan, and possibly the Great Lakes states. It's well-known that the 1916-vintage world record typical came from Wisconsin, but it isn't as widely known that Wisconsin still leads the country in producing Boone & Crockett heads. In a recent three-year period, 14 typical Wisconsin heads made the book, plus nine from Minnesota, seven from Michigan, and seven from Maine. In the same period no Montana heads were entered, and only five from Alberta and four from Saskatchewan. Manitoba had just one.

Interesting figures? You bet. In spite of heavy hunting pressure, the forests of the Great Lakes states continue to produce their share of big bucks, and Maine doesn't look too shabby. But these areas, for the most part, are a resident hunter's ballgame with short seasons and difficult access. A guide may be required in Canada, but there's little hunting pressure in the huge forest belt—and whether the deer are being taken or not, they're there. Montana, too, is fairly accessible to nonresidents, with vast tracts of public land open to hunting. The whitetail have received some publicity, and are being hunted some today—especially in more open eastern Montana. By and large, though, Montana's whitetail, especially in the forested west (where the biggest deer are), are still overlooked in favor of mule deer. The light resident pressure that exists is generally directed toward filling freezers for winter rather than toward the trophy-class whitetail bucks.

The hunter who lives in or near the northern timber may have America's biggest whitetails practically in the backyard; the nonresident will have to travel, and won't be welcome everywhere. An interesting thing about big timber whitetail, however, is that it isn't so critical where you hunt them; Montana differs little from Maine or New Brunswick. All of the northern forests produce big deer, and all produce bucks with monster racks. And all the northern forests yield these bucks only grudgingly.

Wherever you hunt these forest deer, you're going to find some of the most difficult whitetail hunting there is—and also, if the conditions are right, some of the purest hunting in the world. In general, coniferous forest doesn't support large numbers of deer. Nor does mature hardwood forest. Remember, whitetails thrive in edge habitat. However, deer do live in virgin timber—and bucks can grow old there, producing the best antlers they're genetically capable of. Where there's been lumbering, you'll find the deer feeding out in the clear-cuts and second growth—although usually only at night. The big tracks will tantalize you where they've left deep, clear impressions on logging roads. On occasion you'll even see a big buck from a county road, and getting him will seem so simple.

When you go into the timber after him, it's a different story. You can still hunt these timber bucks in the open forest, and in the denser growth along watercourses. Most of the time your reward will be deep-cut running tracks, only occasionally accompanied by a crashing of brush and, even more rarely, the flash of a white tail. The truth is that big timber bucks are darn near unkillable—which makes hunting them so much fun.

Stand hunting is a sensible option. This is the technique of choice among the better New Brunswick outfitters, and is echoed in Manitoba, Wisconsin, and, in truth, most of the big timber region. Just as it does everywhere else, the success of stand hunting depends on two primary factors: good scouting to determine an appropriate location for a stand, and the patience and determination of the person sitting in that stand.

A good friend of mine is desperate for a big northern whitetail, and he has decided New Brunswick is the place to get one. The guy he's hunting with believes in stand hunting, and he places his stands with the greatest possible care. My friend has stayed in a tree stand in the New Brunswick forest from dawn to dark for 14 days now, spread out over two seasons, and he hasn't yet seen a shootable buck. On the other hand, a guy that went with him one fall shot a perfectly acceptable heavy-horned 10-pointer on the first day of their hunt. And so it goes.

I believe that the movement patterns of timber whitetails are more erratic than those of deer in other habitats. The unbroken forest is just that—unbroken forest. The deer are not channelized by the terrain, nor are they obligated to follow specific movement patterns. It's much the same with Coues whitetails which, in their big country, appear not nearly as habitual as typical wood lot eastern whitetails. On the other hand, with no snow and under pre-rut conditions, there's really no sound choice other than stand hunting. Still hunting can be attempted, but there is little chance of a shot and less chance to determine exactly what you're shooting at. Drives aren't a good option, either—remember, we're talking about unbroken forest, with a very low deer density. So stand hunting is the best choice, at least before the snow flies—and that stand must be sited with the utmost care.

There will be deer trails, particularly along watercourses and at stream crossings, and there will be clearings—natural or man made—that are prime feeding areas. They will tend to be less reliable than in areas with limited bedding and cover, but they still make natural stand locations. Under typical timber conditions, where there are relatively few deer, scouting has to be thorough and careful. Tracks are important, of course, but more important are rubs and scrapes—and with few deer, they'll be harder to find.

Find them, though, you must. Unless you're hunting some hard-hunted timber where hunting pressure is sufficient to move the deer around, a deer stand location based on nothing will result in just that—nothing. Optimally you will find not only some tracks and perhaps a huge rub, but also determine what foods the deer are going for, and then you start to have a faint chance. Once you have a decent idea where to hunt, patience and persistence are the keys.

It's worthwhile, too, to employ all the modern tricks available to you. Cover scents, of course. Later on, when rutting activity is getting underway, sex lures—why not? Experiment with a grunt call? I have . . . and they work! Most of all, accept that not seeing a lot of deer is normal in timber country. But accept also that a buck, if you see one, has a good chance of being well worth seeing!

Then the snow flies, and it becomes a whole different game. The leaves are down, and the deer's natural camouflage isn't so sight-proof against the blanket of white. It's quiet in the woods; every sound is muffled by the soft powder. And every creature that moves leaves tracks . . . and all creatures must move to feed. Make no mistake, the odds still favor a hunter-wise old buck—but his margin has decreased immensely.

Under such conditions stand hunting remains a viable option, but now the still hunter has a chance. How good a chance that is, well, that's pretty much up to the hunter. If still hunting means strolling through the winter woods, then that chance remains quite slim. On the other hand, if it means being what my teacher at this game, Montanan Ed Nixon, calls "catty," then you might pull it off. "Still" hunting, of course, doesn't mean being still in the sense of stand hunter. But it does mean moving and stopping, moving and stopping, so that progress is very slow, and the hunter misses nothing—and sees game before the game sees him. It's extremely difficult, requiring total concentration and superior powers of observation. Very few people are good at it, and I won't claim to be one of them.

Old Ed Nixon is a master at it. Hunting like this is a one-man game, so I've never seen him still hunting. But I have seen him walk into the woods, and he does indeed remind you of a cat stalking a bird. We'll go along hunting for several days, but on the day Nixon announces that he'll "get on the trigger," you can count on venison—and the venison will usually come from a lovely buck. Ed isn't alone; there are good hunters all over the country who successfully still hunt whitetails—especially after the snow flies. Larry Benoit and his clan are legendary in the eastern woods, and have been featured in numerous national magazine articles. They are exclusively still hunters, relying primarily on good tracking snow.

There is a difference between still hunting and tracking, but it's subtle. When you're tracking you are still hunting, and you know that whatever left those tracks lies ahead. Still hunting without the tracks is a bit different; you don't know what's ahead, nor from what quarter your game might appear. You must constantly search the trees ahead, to the sides, and even occasionally take a careful backward look. The hunter who has ahead of him tracks should do this as

Manitoba outfitter Don McCrea picked up this matching set of sheds near his cabin, right at the southern fringe of Manitoba's forests. The deer still lives, but Don's never laid eyes on him.

In timber country this is the still-hunter's dream. It is possible for a man on foot to outwit a whitetail buck at his own game—but you have to be "catty." (Photo by Nick Sisley)

well; if he's concentrating too much on just the tracks, he's making a mistake—those tracks could angle in any direction just beyond his vision.

Snow is a near-essential ingredient for successful still hunting in heavy timber, and it means there will probably be tracks. You may or may not want to follow the tracks—that depends on their size and freshness—but they will keep you posted on deer movement. There's little advice that can be given that will be of genuine assistance in hunting big timber whitetails; it's something you just have to get out in the woods and try. The chances of success are not good, especially on the mossy-horned, old record-class bucks. But they're there, and that alone makes it worth trying.

It's best to plan such a hunt very late in the season, so that the chances of getting a good fresh snow are the best. Obviously this varies; in Montana the end of the season is around Thanksgiving. By then you can generally bank on some good snow—and you just might hit the rut perfectly. Plan, also, for as long a hunt as you can manage. It will take a couple of days to start to figure deer movements, as it does with most hunting situations. But in the timber I've found that it takes me a couple of days to get my movements in tune with the country—to slow down, be alert, and be "catty."

A final word about equipment. The north woods in winter can be extremely cold, bitter cold. Which is one reason why stand hunting becomes very difficult—at minus 30 degrees it's tough to sit still for hours on end. If you plan to stand hunt in such weather, the very best of the modern high-tech clothing is for you. On the other hand, if you plan to still hunt, above all you must choose your clothing for quiet. Even at temperatures well below zero I wear a couple of sets of good long underwear, heavy wool trousers with suspenders, a wool shirt, and perhaps a wool sweater either over or under the shirt. Sorel pacs with felt inserts have always done a good job for my feet, and I wear a knit wool cap, with or without a silk bandanna over my face. The modern fabrics are wonderful, but they aren't as quiet as good old wool, not yet anyway. Polar fleece in snow camo would certainly be an option, but you'd be amazed how well gray wool blends in. And how warm it will keep you even at unbelievable temperatures.

Frostbite is, obviously, a serious hazard in these types of conditions and one should take sensible precautions. Keep exposed skin to the very minimum. Don't underestimate the wind chill factor and test your digits for numbness occasionally. Wear a pair of mittens over your gloves and do not take either off unless you absolutely have to. I carry a space blanket with me at all times for emergencies.

In that kind of country, incidentally, I carry a .338 with a low-power scope—and I'm not overgunned in the least. In Montana there's always the chance of running into a big bull elk, and for that matter some small chance of a close encounter with grizzly. More to the point, though, is that you're hunting very large deer, and whatever shot you get probably won't be the best angle you could pick. In the little Montana community where I've been doing most of my timber whitetail hunting, life is fairly slow. There hasn't been electricity for too many years, and phone numbers just recently went from four digits to seven. I imagined it to be traditional .270 and .30-06 country, and I expected to get a hard time when I showed up with my .338. There's a .30-06 or two left in the valley, but the .270s are all gone—replaced almost universally by .338s. Even the locals have a lot of respect for those magnum-sized big timber whitetails!

CHAPTER VII

HILL COUNTRY WHITETAILS

T he Lone Star state has a unique, distinct character, an individuality not found in the other 49 states. Perhaps it's the vastness of Texas. Perhaps it's the fact that this state alone stood as an independent republic before joining the United States. Most likely it's a combination of many factors. The sociology of Texas is far beyond the subject of this book, but it does affect the attitudes of both Texans and non-Texans toward deer hunting in that state. To most Texas hunters, whitetail hunting is a way of life—and Texas deer hunting is quite simply where it's at. Non-Texans who live in good whitetail country get tired of reading about Texas whitetail hunting, or so the mail I receive seems to indicate. And non-Texans who don't live in whitetail country view the Lone Star state as the place to go.

All these attitudes are based on a good deal of truth—and some untruth. With a deer herd conservatively estimated at some 3.5 million, Texas does indeed have some of the world's finest deer hunting, and Texans should be justifiably proud of their state's hunting potential. Over the years the state has received more than its share of publicity, and there are reasons for that, too.

For the last 40 years some of America's most respected hunting writers have been Texans, and they've written prolifically and eloquently about Texas deer hunting. Such a list would include John Wootters, Bob Brister, Byron Dalrymple, Russell Tinsley, Hal Swiggett, and more—even Colonel Charles Askins chose Texas when he retired from the Army. With so many good writers there, it's natural that Texas deer hunting should receive so much press. And it's justifiable, too, in that Texas' long season, generous bag limit, and varied hunting conditions give a scribe a lot to write about. It's possible, even likely, that the number of writers based there have given Texas more than its fair share of limelight—but until a new generation of equally skilled writers crop up in another part of the country, that situation is unlikely to change.

Texas writers, as you might expect, have written of their state's deer hunting with that special pride that seems ingrained in Texans from birth. It's even possible that, as a group, they've indulged in Texans' famed propensity for exaggeration. Certainly they've sparked a fair measure of envy among whitetail hunters elsewhere, and a burning desire to hunt in Texas among deer hunters nationwide.

The envy is justified, and so is the desire. I've hunted in some parts of Texas more or less annually for at least a dozen seasons, and the hunting is spectacular. But there is a whole bunch of things that the outsider must understand before contemplating a Texas whitetail hunt.

Deer Hunting Coast to Coast

First, Texas is vast. With a land mass in excess of a quarter-million square miles, her deer density is far lower than that of most southern states and many eastern states. There are scads of deer—but not everywhere in Texas. There are also vast differences in topography, and tremendous regional differences in both deer numbers and trophy quality.

Second, Texas is something like 98 percent privately owned. There are a few public parcels of land that offer deer hunting, but they're widely scattered and, as you might expect, they receive more than their share of hunting pressure. Since Texans love their deer hunting, and since their deer hunting is quite famous, Texas landowners have come to realize that deer have significant value.

The bottom line is that there's no free lunch with Texas deer hunting. It's good, but you'll generally pay for the privilege. And the better it is, the more you'll pay for it. Texans who like to hunt either own their own land or have friends and relatives who do. Or they put together a group of friends and lease the hunting rights to a parcel of land. They didn't grow up with "free" hunting the way so many of us did in other parts of the country, and they think nothing of shelling out a substantial portion of their recreational dollars for deer hunting. Nonresidents must expect to do the same.

The bad thing about this system is that Texas deer hunting is for those who can afford it—and depending on the quality of the hunting, the costs can be very substantial. The good thing, and it's very good, is that an increasing number of Texas ranchers manage their deer with almost a religious fervor. Well they should, since deer are virtually a cash crop, and the better quality the deer, the more the cash. Texas deer, like deer everywhere else in the country, are subject to state-controlled seasons, licensing, and bag limits. But within those parameters, Texas deer on private land are pretty much hands-off to Texas Parks and Wildlife personnel. Landowners can harvest does, improve habitat, and cull genetically inferior bucks to their hearts' content to produce the best bucks their range is capable of—and many do just that.

Much of Texas' finest deer hunting is just plain not available to nonresident hunters. Many prime ranches simply aren't hunted except by the owners' family and friends. And even more acreage is tied up in seasonal leases. But there are outstanding opportunities remaining for nonresidents, including some of Texas' finest deer hunting. For the outsider with no connections, Texas deer hunting normally takes one of two forms: hunting on a private ranch where the owner runs his own hunting operation, either guided or on a short-term lease arrangement (including day-hunting for a fee); or hunting with an outfitter. In the latter case, the outfitter will normally obtain season leases from several ranchers, sometimes on a per-acre basis and sometimes on a per-buck basis.

To the nonresident, there is little difference between the two routes. The outfitter, of course, must obtain his leases, then provide his services, and finally

The tripod stand is a way of life with Texas whitetail hunters, where climbable trees can be scarce. Stands like these are generally high enough for the Texas brush.

Thin-antlered 8-pointers like this are the norm for Texas Hill Country whitetails. It's possible to find a better buck—but you'll look at a lot of deer like this first.

figure in his profit—so outfitted hunts where the outfitter is not the landowner may average a bit higher. On the other hand, the outfitter has his reputation at stake, and if he's honest he'll put you on a ranch that he knows has the kind of deer you're looking for, in keeping with the price you paid for the hunt. The rancher running his own operation can obviously offer only the quality of deer he has on his own ranch, whatever that might be. Selecting a Texas hunt can be very confusing, and just as in planning an outfitted hunt anywhere, the best course is to demand references and call them, don't write, quizzing them carefully with pointed questions.

Confusing as it is, the good news is that Texas' system has pretty much established a market value. Bargains are most unlikely and should be suspect, and you'll find that there are two distinct classes of Texas hunts. The first is what I call "fun hunts"—lots of deer, lots of shootable eight-point bucks with the occasional small 10-pointer, and generally some potential for turkeys, javelinas, and does thrown in or available at a small additional cost. Depending on where you come from, the bucks available may be mountable quality, but a real monster will be most unlikely and should not be expected. There are hunts of this nature that still cost well under $1,000 for three days or so, and such a hunt shouldn't cost more than $1,500, at this writing.

Then there are the real trophy hunts, hunts where there is genuine potential for wide, heavy-horned deer that anyone, anywhere would be proud to hang on the wall. Such hunts are expensive; if the asking price were less than $2,500 in today's Texas, I'd question the trophy potential. A full $3,000 and up is actually more realistic. We'll talk about Texas trophy hunting in the next chapter, but for now let's look at the fun hunts.

The so-called Hill Country of central Texas spreads westward like a fan from about San Antonio. Technically it's called the Edwards Plateau, and if you drew a line from Kerrville west to Ozona, then looked about 50 miles north and 100 miles south of that line, you'd have a rectangle that enclosed some the densest deer populations in Texas—and thus in the whole world. When I was growing up, it was this region that drew most of the attention in national magazines. We all remember hearing about the famed Y.O. ranch with its eight-point guarantee, and as a kid I remember dreaming about hunting the Y.O.

It's still there, near Mountain Home, Texas—and it still makes good its eight-point guarantee. And of course there are many more. The Hill Country/Edwards Plateau is beautiful country—rolling oak hillsides, deep canyons, meandering streams, pockets of heavy brush. And there are lots of deer.

My first Texas deer hunt was on Steve Wilkins' Flying W ranch near Ozona, towards the western edge of this region. The Flying W is still in operation, and is typical of the inexpensive (relatively speaking) "fun" hunts that the Hill Country is all about. It's country where you can stand hunt or still hunt, and you'll see a

A big 8-pointer like this one, with decent mass, spread, and point length, is about as good as you can hope for in most of the Hill Country—good hunting for nice deer, but few monsters.

ton of deer. On that particular hunt, I recall that I also shot a javelina and missed a wild turkey—and that's also part of the game. The bucks we got were typical Hill Country bucks—basket-racked eight-pointers. Nice, representative whitetails for that part of the world, but no world-beaters.

I saw a good deer, a lovely yellow-horned 10-pointer, and he gave me a quick running shot as he streaked along a brushy creek bottom. I didn't get him, but if I had connected, I'd have had a monster for that region. They're there, but they aren't common. That should come as no surprise. The Edwards Plateau region has produced a couple of Boone and Crockett heads over the years—but thousands upon thousands of small, mediocre, average, and even above-average bucks have been taken in that area. So many bucks have been produced there that it stands to reason that one or two monsters would show up. With extremely careful management, the Hill Country is capable of producing good deer—but a record-class head is pretty much a fluke, and should be considered as such.

A record head isn't what you go to that area for. You're better off either to look elsewhere, or put it out of your mind. Instead, go to the Hill Country to have a nice deer hunt and a good time. If the conditions of your hunt allow for two bucks, take a nice basket-horned eight-pointer, then look for a better one. If you're allowed just one buck, look for something a bit better—but don't look for a monster that isn't there. And if your hunt allows you to take a doe (or two), by all means take them. The real problem with Texas' Hill Country today is there are too damned many deer, and the does on many ranches need harvesting badly.

I'm not knocking Hill Country whitetails, not at all. If you've never taken a whitetail deer, you can find a buck to be proud of there. And if your whitetail hunting is done on public land in heavily hunted regions, you can be in for a real treat—as well as finding bucks better than you can hope for at home. But the neat thing about the Hill Country isn't the size of the deer. Rather, it's the fact that deer hunting there is so doggone successful—and there's nothing wrong with that.

I live in California, a long way from any whitetail country. Last year a bunch of guys from my local Safari Club chapter went to Texas and hunted the Flying W ranch together. These were all guys who had hunted a variety of game from Africa to Alaska and back, and some of them have taken very fine whitetails in different parts of the country. They didn't go there expecting huge bucks; they went to see lots of deer, have a great time, and bring home some venison. They're still raving about the trip, and I wish I had gone with them.

Sometimes, of course, it isn't all that easy. Even in the Hill Country, a whitetail is a whitetail—and when he wants to be scarce, he can be. I spent more than a week on a super ranch near Mountain Home trying to find just an average, garden-variety whitetail—and didn't get a shot until the very last minute. Well, that's not true. Early in the hunt I saw a very fine 10-pointer chasing some does on a bald ridge about 300 yards away. I was shooting an accurate .270, and to

Texas' Hill Country is centered about a hundred miles northwest of San Antonio. It's beautiful, rolling country with one of America's densest concentrations of whitetail deer.

Part of the fun of Texas hunting is the incredible variety of game. The bucks may not be huge in the Hill Country, but it's possible to hunt turkey, javelina, and wild hogs on the same hunt.

this day I don't know why I didn't take the shot. For some odd reason I thought I could get closer, and I made an elaborate stalk with the wind just perfect. Needless to say, I never saw that buck again. A week later I settled for a basket-racked eight-pointer, the most typical Hill Country deer you could ever find!

Hill Country deer can be successfully hunted by a variety of means, from stand hunting to still hunting to horn rattling during the rut. Considering the numbers of deer and the relative openness of the country, I've always preferred to still hunt in this area; you can just sort of mosey along, and there is usually enough relief to allow good glassing. Texas is a funny place, though. Some of the favorite local hunting methods would be called unsporting or be downright illegal in much of the country. Baiting, for example, is legal in Texas. Corn feeders with timers are a fixture in front of many Texas deer stands. On private land, too, it's perfectly legal to shoot from a vehicle. I wouldn't be surprised if most Texas deer were shot by cruising ranch roads—what Texans like to call "safari style hunting." No, I'm not knocking it, not really. It's not only legal, but a way of life in a state where deer are managed as a cash crop—and are often overpopulated to the point where they must be harvested.

The Hill Country is a great place to start Texas deer hunting, and it's a perfect place to be introduced to whitetail deer. The hunting will be enjoyable and successful, and the country is gorgeous. But if you're looking for monster deer, you'll need to look elsewhere.

CHAPTER VIII

TEXAS' BIG BUCK COUNTRY

There are great whitetail bucks in Texas, but to find them you have to travel away from the Hill Country. You'll go to country where the deer aren't nearly as plentiful, nor is the hunting generally as easy. You'll work a great deal harder for your deer, and you may come away empty-handed—but you could well take a truly great whitetail.

South Texas is the most famed trophy zone, and indeed it's very good. When you think south Texas, you're probably thinking of the brush country, that flat sea of dense brush centered around Laredo. It extends well south into old Mexico, and it's here that you find the famed big buck-producing counties such as Webb, La Salle, Jim Hogg, and Dimmitt. However, south Texas isn't all black brush. To the east, as the soil becomes sandy, lies a belt of more open country of oak thickets interspersed with clearings—the oak motte country. And farther east still, right along the Gulf of Mexico, there's a narrow coastal plain. These areas, too, produce fine whitetails.

These days, it wouldn't be fair to the Lone Star state to single out south Texas as the only big buck region. The piney woods country of east Texas has been coming on strong in recent years, and is producing some exceptional bucks. The deer of east Texas, incidentally, are not of the Texas whitetail subspecies (*Odocoileus virginianus texanus*), but rather are Kansas whitetails (*O. v. macrourus*). This whitetail is larger in both body and antler, and this is reflected in east Texas deer now that the population is swinging upward. The bad news is that there is relatively little opportunity for nonresidents to hunt the piney woods. One exception would be the Hawkeye Hunting Club near Center, Texas, an excellent bird-hunting operation that has recently added limited guided whitetail hunts.

The farm country of northern Texas, too, is producing some outstanding whitetails—but this region is even more difficult for the nonresident to get into. Texans in the know are getting some great whitetails in some surprising corners of the state these days, but for the outsider south Texas remains the region of choice for trophy whitetails.

At this point it's only fair to attempt to qualify just what comprises a trophy whitetail in Texas. Because of all the press Texas hunting has received over the past few decades, most outsiders who journey there for the first time have unrealistic expectations. First off, there are Boone and Crockett-quality whitetails in south Texas, and probably in east Texas as well. Texas has long been a leader in producing record book deer, falling just behind Saskatchewan and running neck and neck with Wisconsin and Minnesota in total numbers of book deer taken. The big buck country of south Texas has the nutrients and the genetics needed to produce big bucks, and a combination of trackless brush, good management, and very light hunting on many large ranches combine to allow bucks to live to their maximum antler-producing potential.

Texas is also one of the top producers of whitetails in sheer numbers of deer harvested—and that doesn't hurt. Given decent browse and good genetics, producing record book heads is something of a numbers game. A Boone and Crockett buck is so abnormally huge that he's actually almost a freak of nature, as unusual as a seven-foot man. Texas has produced many of these huge bucks, and without question there are Boone and Crockett bucks living in Texas today. But you aren't going to get one, and neither am I.

That's a cryptic statement, so let me qualify it by saying that it is possible, just as getting struck by lightning is possible. It isn't much more likely than that. Consider that my good friend John Wootters, perhaps America's best-known whitetail fanatic, has spent 40 seasons hunting some of Texas' best trophy whitetail country. He has never had an opportunity at a Boone & Crockett buck. Well, maybe he's unlucky. Another friend of mine, outfitter Robert Rogers, has handled hundreds of hunting clients over the past decades, and he's hunted them in some of the best country—country that has produced "Booners" and will produce more. He has yet to put a client onto a record buck. The huge Kenedy Ranch in the coastal plains, unhunted for generations, was recently opened. This, too, is country that holds Boone and Crockett deer. But so far no client has gotten one.

The nonresident hunter plans to hunt for a specified number of days at a certain predetermined time in the season. This alone limits his chances; even with the very best planning, the odds are against his hitting the exact, limited peak of the rut that will see the most movement among the biggest bucks. And then the elemental luck factor comes into play—and the odds are strongly against any one hunter catching sight of that ultra-rare record buck. He exists, but at best he's one in many hundreds of bucks, and he roams in very big country. Every Texas outfitter, every season, has hunters who show up demanding to shoot Boone and Crockett deer. The beginning outfitter is dismayed and concerned; the veteran is merely amused. It ain't gonna happen!

On the other hand, with realistic expectations the nonresident hunter can take a magnificent buck home from Texas. Keep in mind that the Texas whitetail is a small deer. Most bucks from the Hill Country will field-dress under 100 pounds, and an eight-pointer with a 15-inch spread is a pretty good Hill Country deer. In the brush country, mature bucks that field-dress 140 to 160 pounds are normal. Farther east, toward to coast, the deer are about midway between these extremes; dressed weights from 110 to 130 pounds are pretty normal. Eartip to eartip spread on a coastal whitetail is just 13 inches, so a deer with a spread significantly

Outfitter Robert Rogers with a huge whitetail from northern Mexico. Essentially an extension of South Texas' Brush Country, well-managed Mexican ranches hold a few wonderful deer.

Horn rattling is said to have originated in South Texas, and it's still the favored method there when any rutting activity whatsoever is underway. It works, but isn't foolproof.

wider than the ears looks extremely impressive—but may only be 18 inches or so.

The heart's desire of most Texas trophy hunters is a 10-pointer with a 20-inch outside spread. That is indeed a very possible goal. Depending on mass and point length, such a buck could score anywhere from 135 to 160 Boone and Crockett points, but will certainly fall well short of the 170-point B & C minimum. Such a buck, too, will be hard to judge—especially in areas producing small-bodied deer. In the brush country, where the deer are significantly larger, a buck with antlers spreading well outside the ears will be a "keeper," depending on points, mass, and what you are looking for. On the coast you'll need to look more closely; those small deer with narrow eartip spreads will fool you time and again.

Of course, antlers take innumerable forms. Nontypicals aren't particularly uncommon in south Texas, and "drop points" do occur with surprising frequency. On the other hand, I've never laid eyes on such a buck! Typical 10-pointers are common, and typical 12-pointers can be found that may or may not be larger than a big 10. Likewise there are some huge eight-pointers running around. In the oak motte country and coastal plains, a hunter will have a chance to look over a number of deer and perhaps make a sensible choice. In the brush country few deer will be seen; opportunities won't be many. But anywhere in Texas, just as with whitetail hunting everywhere, when the opportunity comes to take a great whitetail, the hunter must be able to recognize him instantly and shoot. The really big boys won't wait around, and they aren't prone to giving second chances!

The famed south Texas brush country is a different sort of deer hunting. It's literally an ocean of so-called black brush, level country that stretches for miles without a break. It doesn't support many deer, but when you see, it you'll understand why it holds some wonderful bucks. I'll be perfectly honest and tell you that I don't like it. I recognize its trophy potential, but it doesn't suit my personality or the hunting methods I prefer. You can't glass into it, and it's far too thick to still-hunt effectively. In fact, there is really just one hunting technique that works, although it has several wrinkles. It's country for stand hunting, pure and simple.

The brush country is comprised of very large ranches, and for access these ranches are broken up by bulldozed rights-of-way, called senderos. These stretch for miles upon miles, and in most areas they're the only places open enough for a hunter to see a deer, let alone judge antlers and make a shot. The hunting technique, then, is obvious enough: find well-used crossings, plunk down a high stand to give maximum visibility, and wait. It takes patience, which I'm short of, and it takes faith in the presence of a deer worth waiting for. But it works. With proper scouting to determine the location of a buck, a hunter who stays on a good stand for the duration of his hunt will probably get an opportunity.

The deer he gets an opportunity at will probably be worth the wait, too. I will never forget a heavy-antlered 10-pointer that stepped into a sendero in Webb County one evening. He was high, wide, and massive, and he was master of that area. But it was the day after the season, so all I could do was look.

The big buck country of northern Mexico is much the same, neither better nor worse in terms of trophy quality or hunting possibilities. The idea, of course, is to find a ranch that has been well-managed and has had little hunting pressure. That's more difficult in Mexico, but such places do exist. The problems are the same on both sides of the border—big country, heavy brush, and relatively few deer. There are bucks in that country well worth the taking, and thus worth trying for. However, nonresident hunters who want to give the brush country a shot should understand that their chances for success aren't much better than 50 percent—especially if they're looking for good deer.

There are some variations of stand hunting that should be mentioned. Remember, shooting from a vehicle is legal on private land. It isn't uncommon for Texas hunters to put high seats on the back of a Jeep or pickup truck; such high seats give some a few additional yards of visibility into the brush. I'm not personally comfortable with such an arrangement, but obviously it works. The other technique was made famous in the brush country first, and in recent years has proven effective on whitetails nearly everywhere. It is, of course, horn rattling—imitating the clashing of antlers in a mating duel. It's particularly well suited to the brush country, where visibility is extremely limited and the buck/doe ratio is high, which creates competition among the bucks for the available does.

Horn rattling does have some drawbacks, especially for the nonresident. First off, it works best in the early stages of the rut, not so well during the middle portion when the better bucks are with does, and then works well again after the majority of the does are out of season. The rut can vary by several days from one year to the next, so it takes a bit of luck for a nonresident to time a hunt just right. Most experts agree, too, that the very best bucks are unlikely to come to the horns. However, it's a technique that does work, and in the brush country it's worth trying if there's any rutting activity going on at all.

Farther to the east, where the country opens up into scattered oak mottes, deer hunting is a different game. I'll never forget my first look at this country. It was just after the deer season closed; I'd been hunting south Texas for a week with Robert Rogers, and on the way home he wanted to spend a day looking at a potential new lease near Falfurrias, north of McAllen. It was one of those perfect midwinter days, frosty cold in the morning, but fresh warmth in the bright sun. The deer were rutting heavily, and we saw a number of decent bucks—certainly enough to make the lease worth the asking price.

More importantly, though, it was country you could hunt, and it was rich with game. I've never seen more wild turkeys in a single day, and there were plenty of wild hogs and a few javelina. It was the kind of country that an outfitter dreams of, because there was no way a client could leave unhappy. Since that day I've enjoyed several fine hunts in the oak motte country, and it's an area I'd go back to anytime. It has good deer, too. Twice during open season I've seen the kind of Texas buck a man should shoot, but I didn't shoot either one.

The first time it was nobody's fault; I'd arrived late the evening before and couldn't find a hunting license. Inevitably, early the next morning on the way to buy a license, we saw a golden-antlered 10-pointer—high and wide if not overly heavy. He paraded back and forth just off the road a couple of miles from camp: He knew he was safe. Later that day, with the license safely stowed in my pocket, he wasn't quite so safe—but he knew that, too. I never saw him again.

The next time I saw such a buck, it was my fault I didn't get him. This was on another ranch near Raymondville, a stone's throw from the Gulf of Mexico. The buck had been seen before, a chocolate-horned typical 12-pointer, and we went looking specifically for him. Of course he wasn't exactly where he was supposed to be—they never are. We jumped him in a little clearing between two thick patches of oak brush, and he wasn't a deer you could mistake. His antlers were as dark as bitter chocolate, and he was a typical 12 with a 22-inch spread, plus or minus, and decent point length. I don't attempt to guess Boone and Crockett scores on live deer; perhaps I should, but it doesn't seem so important. In any case, there wasn't a lot of time on this guy, and all I have is an impression. He wasn't a book deer, or at least I don't think he was. But he was a good solid 160-pointer, and beyond that, who knows?

We came around the edge of an oak thicket, and he streaked for the nearest brush with no hesitation, headed straight away from us. I got the rifle up, and my impression of his antlers was obtained through the crosshairs while I waited for him to turn and give me something more to shoot at. He never turned, and I never got the shot off. To this day I don't know why; he was the best whitetail I've ever had in my sights, and at 30 yards the .280 I carried was enough gun—even for a straight-on rear-end shot. But I hate the so-called Texas heart shot, and I waited for a better shot that never came. We hunted for him hard after that, but of course never saw him again, either. Nor has anyone else to this day . . .

Unlike the true brush country, the oak mottes and the coastal plains they run into can be effectively glassed and still hunted. None of these areas has the density of deer that the Hill Country enjoys, but the oak mottes and the coastal plains do carry more deer than the brush country. Don't misunderstand me; the average buck in such country is not huge. You'll weed your way through a great many eight pointers, and small 10-pointers about the quality of the better Hill Country bucks, to find a dandy.

One year, near Falfurrias, Robert Rogers and I tried everything to get a really good deer. I don't know how many we passed, but finally the last day of the season arrived and we were out of time. We decided on this day we would just

Gary Ohls took this lovely drop-point buck on the Kennedy Ranch. Drop-points are a rare antler configuration that Texans especially prize.

Here's a beautiful typical 10-pointer from the coastal plains, a very normal mature buck from this region. He's a good buck, but his small body makes him appear larger than he is.

cover ground, and we'd shoot the best buck we could find. I know we looked at more than 50 eight-pointers and small tens. The buck we finally settled on wasn't what the country could produce: He was a 19-inch-spread nine-pointer, a good last-day buck. After we took him, we hunted 'til black dark hoping for a better one, but never found him.

My most recent Texas deer hunt was on the huge Kenedy Ranch south of Corpus Christi, newly opened to hunting by a group called Sarita Safaris. The Kenedy Ranch was established about the same time as the famed King Ranch, which it adjoins. It runs from oak motte country into coastal plains and sand dunes, and occupies a long strip of the Gulf Coast itself. I expected to find a paradise, and indeed I did.

The deer densities are relatively low in much of this country, but the buck/doe ratio must be very close to even. And if there aren't deer to look at, there are turkey, javelina, wild hogs, and the big nilgai antelope from India that have roamed the coastal plains since the 1930s. It's country that you can glass, still hunt, horn rattle, or just mosey through looking for something interesting. Eventually you'll find it. Perhaps not the record-class bucks that are undoubtedly there, but at the very least a lovely buck that anyone can be proud of.

I saw the best buck of the hunt at midmorning on the first day, a wide, heavy-antlered 10-pointer. He was bedded in a little patch of oaks 30 yards from me, and he wasn't the least bit concerned about my presence. I knew I should shoot him, and I knew I'd regret not shooting him. But too much country and too many possibilities lay ahead. We left him, and the buck we eventually got wasn't his equal.

On the other hand, the one we collected was a perfectly beautiful, perfectly symmetrical 20-inch 10-pointer. After playing tag with him in a patch of oaks for quite some time, I shot him at a little over 300 yards when he finally left the cover. In the time that remained on the hunt, I stalked and shot a big turkey gobbler, and we looked around for a long-tusked wild hog that we didn't quite find. That, too, is part of Texas deer hunting. There may not be record book bucks behind every bush, but well-managed ranches in Texas do offer one of America's most enjoyable hunting experiences.

CHAPTER IX

PRAIRIE WHITETAILS

After 36 straight hours on the road, my backside was killing me, and my eyes felt as if I'd spent the entire trip with my thumbs stuck in them. But the weather from Los Angeles to Jordan, Montana, had been good, the road clear, and we'd arrived at last.

I had come hunting with friends originally from Montana, and when their family met us at the old abandoned church that would serve as our camp, we had quite a crew. Most of the Montanans were out to put deer and antelope in the freezer for the winter, but I was looking for some antlers.

That was back in the mid-1970s, and at that time if you were lucky in the tag draw, you could have one buck and two doe deer tags, and one buck and four doe pronghorn tags. Game populations were at a peak in the cycle, and that flat prairie country was full of animals.

Having spent all my life hunting mule deer, I was more interested in the strange creature called a whitetail that I'd read so much about in the sporting magazines. When the boys told me there were whitetails here, I knew immediately what I wanted to hunt, even if I wasn't quite sure how to go about it. While my friends were out searching the breaks for muleys and the open grain fields for pronghorn, I was poking along the creek bottoms, and peeking among the willows for a whitetail buck. The first three days weren't very productive, though I saw a few does and rousted out a cackling rooster pheasant or two. But I just knew there were some bucks in there. The question was: What was I going to do about it?

The answer on that trip was a sort of modified drive. Two of my buddies had filled all their big-game tags by the end of the third day, and they had decided that it was time to shoot a few pheasants and a sage grouse or two. So I dropped them off with the dogs in the creek bottom where I'd been hunting deer, and drove upstream a half-mile. Daylight was just creeping over the eastern horizon, the reds and oranges and purples of the new day promising clear skies. I huddled into my jacket and took a stand, hoping to glass some deer movement at first light.

It was deathly quiet, so still that when the first rooster broke from the berry tangles a quarter-mile below, the cackling seemed very much out of place. The two Labradors barked, and then two shots dropped the bird in a shower of iridescent feathers.

I watched the bird fall, turned back to look over the edges of the creek bottom, and just like magic he was there. A nice whitetail buck was coming out at a canter, moving up into the flat of the adjacent grain field and trotting away from all that ruckus. He was about 300 yards off, but I quickly got a rest, found him in my scope, and squeezed the trigger of my old Browning BBR in .25-06. At the shot, the deer kicked his heels high and raced for the center of the field. He piled up not 75 yards later.

He was an old buck, not overly large in the body but with heavy-based antlers with three prominent tines per side, forked eyeguards, and a spread of 15 inches (At the time, I remember thinking that *all* whitetail bucks must have forked eyeguards!). I sat and admired that deer for at least a half an hour, stroking his reddish coat, checking out that funny tail, looking at those small ears. This buck had been shot the year before in the left front leg, and though the wound had healed, he had never regained full use of his leg. The hoof on that leg had grown out to a length of perhaps four inches from lack of wear on the ground, much like a fingernail that's never clipped. I admired the old three-legged buck for being so fat and healthy-looking despite his handicap.

That was my introduction to hunting whitetails, and I was hooked. I made the same trip five years running, and took a whitetail buck from that prairie country each season. Then I got off on a tangent and didn't return until 1984, when I hunted in an outfitted camp run by Jack Atcheson, Jr., the Butte, Montana hunting consultant. Jack and I hunted for a whitetail every evening along the Musselshell River, and on the fourth day I got very lucky and shot a quality 10-pointer that scored 155 Boone & Crockett points. We found that buck not in the creek bottoms, but instead in the adjacent sagebrush flats where he had obviously gone to get away from the hubbub of another hunting season.

Flat, wide open prairie country is not what most of us think of first when campfire chatter turns to whitetail deer. The terrain isn't anything like heavy north country timber, thick southern swamps, or even brushy Texas. At first glance it looks more like a good place to shoot pheasants or quail, or maybe set up a stand near a prairie dog town. Unless you'd heard about it before the thought that some good deer hunting could be found among the fields of wheat and corn and alfalfa that break the virgin prairie would make about as much sense as walking barefoot in a cactus patch.

In reality, the prairie country that comprises eastern Montana, eastern Wyoming, the Dakotas, and Nebraska offers some excellent whitetail hunting. In most of this country (except eastern Montana, where bluetongue has taken a toll on whitetails in recent years), deer populations are either stable or increasing. The animals find farmers' crops a highly nutritious diet, and water isn't usually a problem even in drought years. Although the cover appears to be sparse, there are, in reality, quite enough spots for a buck to sneak off into.

The number of hunters who have discovered prairie country whitetailing continues to grow, a fact that has helped to educate an already tricky animal. Even 15 years ago, when most eastern Montana hunters came for the mule deer and left the whitetails alone, the bucks weren't dumb. Today they are as tough to find as any whitetail on earth, even in the seemingly wide open spaces they call home.

This typical 8-pointer was taken by Robb as he waited along the edge of a creek channel as pheasant hunters worked a half mile below. The buck bolted into an open wheat field.

Unlike heavy-cover eastern hunting, successful prairie white tailing requires a combination of western long-range glassing techniques and a knowledge of general whitetail behavior. (Photo by Todd Smith)

Deer Hunting Coast to Coast

One example of this is a story that a very serious South Dakota whitetail hunter told me recently. He likes to walk and glass, and had seen a pretty good 10-point buck bedded down in a small patch of sagebrush. Because he was hunting with his bow, he had to get close, and this he did—to about 40 yards. The sun was up, and the deer was enjoying the warmth in the 10 degree temperature. My friend had time on his side, so he took a reading with his rangefinder and quietly settled in to wait for the deer to stand up and present a decent shot.

Suddenly, the buck lay on his side, head sideways on the ground and antlers dipped below the 10-inch-high brush. Two minutes later Mike heard a truck, and a minute later it came into view on a dirt road not 100 yards from where hunter and deer crouched out of sight. Two minutes after the truck was out of hearing range (it was out of sight minutes before), the buck cautiously lifted his head up again and went back to chewing his cud. The scenario was repeated several times in the next four hours as road hunters continued to cruise the country.

Mike never did kill that buck, missing the shot at 45 yards when the deer finally did stand. His poor shooting isn't the point, however. The point is that in the open prairie country—and maybe all country where bigger bucks live—the animals have learned that a vehicle means trouble. They begin hiding when they hear one coming, or maybe when they feel the vibrations as it clumsily rumbles along; they don't have to visually identify the problem. You have to be just as "catty," as Ed Nixon would say, to hunt the bigger prairie whitetails as you do to hunt them in the timber.

Still, many of these whitetails like to hole up in places that are a bit more obvious to the deer hunter than the open fields and sage flats. Some areas of the prairie region still hold relatively good-sized patches of timber, and there always seem to be whitetails hanging around these. The shelter belts planted to protect crops from the gale-force northern winds that ravage this country in winter are also likely spots to find a buck. Scattered islands of woody cover and thick creek bottoms may hold deer, as may gullies, cuts, and small breaks in the flat terrain. Fields of tall crops make excellent hiding places, and provide more than enough to eat. And then there are the numerous overgrown fence lines, small patches of brush, tule-lined potholes, and the like to offer cover from the prying eyes of sportsmen. I once saw a small eight-point whitetail buck sneak right into the middle of a tule patch centered in a shallow pothole not as large as the average swimming pool. He saw some hunters coming, and lay down right in the water! If I hadn't seen him go in there I would never have known he was anywhere in the neighborhood.

One group of friends from eastern Montana call their whitetail hunting "modified pheasant hunting": They drive small pockets of "pheasant cover" in open fields. The only difference is that they carry rifles instead of shotguns; they expect their shots at a speeding buck to be on par with a flushing rooster. They take their share of whitetails each fall this way. But by and large, unless you're hunting the rut, prairie country can best be hunted with a modified spot-and-stalk technique.

To use it, find a high vantage point in open country and get comfortable well before first light. Set up your optics, and glass everything—open fields, creek bottom brush, fence lines, small isolated pockets of cover—for feeding and traveling deer. If you're lucky, you'll see something you can move in on before it heads to an impenetrable creek bottom or shelter belt for the day. If that isn't possible—and it often isn't, the deer being a mile off and the cover for a quick stalk not available—then I like to try and pattern the buck. Does he feed here only in the morning, or both morning and evening? Where's the closest cover I can use for a blind? Is the blind in a position where the wind won't be a disadvantage in morning, or in the afternoon? How can I sneak into the blind without disturbing anything, or being seen?

If I can pattern him, I'll be in my blind at least two hours before daylight for a morning hunt, or just after high noon for an evening hunt. If I have to move into position during the day, I do my best to do so as if the deer were in fact standing right out in the open. You never know what's in the shadows of a bedding area peeking out at you in the bright sun. You can rest assured that if a buck sees you move into the blind near his feeding area, he'll change restaurants.

Never randomly drive around and expect to kill a really good buck. It can happen, but the odds are against it and besides, what's the fun in that? Really dedicated prairie hunters won't even set foot in an area where they know a good buck lives unless conditions are exactly right, including wind direction, thermal currents, ground conditions (crunchy, frozen ground keeps them on spotting stands), and so on. Those who take a stand near heavy cover get into the stand at least two hours before daylight, then stay there until an hour after dark, using rubber-soled boots and cover scents to reduce human pollution within the hunting area. If drives are to be used, setting up shooting stands with the wind in the shooters' faces and getting these shooters into position undetected is critical.

What can you expect if you travel to the prairie lands for whitetails? Here's a brief state-by-state rundown.

Eastern Montana

Extensive grain country and sagebrush habitat support both mule deer and whitetails. Generally speaking, the whitetails will be found close to the creek and river bottoms, and that's where to center your hunt. I like to find thickly-bordered creeks and streams away from road access yet adjoining wheat or alfalfa crops. There's quite a bit of private land, but many farmers will allow hunting because the deer often ravage their crops. There's also a good deal of BLM land checkerboarded in among blocks of private ground. As mentioned earlier, a bluetongue epidemic hit the whitetails a good lick here in the late 1980s, and populations are down at this writing. There are still some good bucks to be found, though, and when hunting here, you can also try your hand at pronghorn, sage grouse, sharptail grouse, and pheasant hunting.

North Dakota

Good whitetail hunting can be found throughout the state, where these deer live in proximity to mule deer. Finding a buck that would meet the Boone & Crockett Club minimum score of 170 points would be rare; while there are a a number of North Dakota bucks in the book, few have been taken in recent years. Some of the best bucks are found in the grain-growing Coteau Hills region, located in central North Dakota, east of the Missouri River and extending north to the Canadian border. The strip farming area of the slope unit in the southwest includes all drainages that flow into the Missouri River from the west, and good hunting can be found here as well as along the banks of the Little Missouri River.

South Dakota

South Dakota has kicked out some dandy whitetails in recent years, and the chances of getting a fine buck are as good here as anywhere in the prairie region. West of the Missouri River most habitat consists of grasslands and cultivated crops outside the Black Hills, with scattered areas of woody cover, shelter belts, and brushed-over stream cover the best bets for whitetails. The Black Hills area itself, about 100 miles long and 40 miles wide on the southwest border of the state, has the highest deer densities anywhere in South Dakota. Both mule deer and whitetails are plentiful, with bigger whitetails preferring riparian habitat along major waterways. As a footnote, South Dakota receives very little nonresident deer hunting pressure, and could be one of those places that we'll be talking about 20 years from now as a "good old days" spot to hunt big whitetail bucks.

Nebraska

The No. 1 Pope & Young nontypical whitetail came from Nebraska, a monster scoring 279-7/8 points, and more than two dozen other nontypical bucks have made the book. Obviously, there's good trophy potential in this food-rich state. The eastern half of the state, comprised largely of irrigated farmlands interspersed with numerous Missouri River tributaries and lots of shelter belts, offers the best hunting. Western bottom land drainages also hold some good whitetails. This is another state not often connected with huge bucks, but it should be. They're more plentiful here than in many other better-known whitetail areas.

Wide, shallow rivers like the Platte dominate much of this country. Whitetails love the heavily-brushed river-bottoms, often taking shelter on mid-river islands. (Photo by Todd Smith)

This quality 10-pointer was found out on a huge sage brush flat. Prairie whitetails will go where human pressure is lightest, and that's often where you least expect them to be.

Deer Hunting Coast to Coast

Eastern Wyoming

Very few whitetails make the book from Wyoming, but that doesn't mean there isn't good hunting available. In fact, while mule deer tags sell out here annually, there are always extra whitetail permits available in the eastern regions. The best whitetail hunting that occurs in the Black Hills is in the state's northeast corner, where there's plentiful public land and hunter success rates run right at 60 percent! Most whitetail seasons are open in November at the peak of the rut, too. The chances at a book-class buck are rare, but some dandies are shot each fall.

Prairie whitetail hunting is a best-of-both-worlds situation for a westerner like me. It's a hunt that lets me have my cake and eat it too. I can hunt the fabled whitetail deer just like all those fellows I read about in the sporting journals for so long, and yet also hunt the way I like best, spotting and stalking. There's almost always some good bird shooting nearby, too, and if I plan it right, I might also fit in a few days of pronghorn hunting. There aren't many better ways than that to spend a fall week or two.

CHAPTER X

DESERT WHITETAILS

T he desert mountains of the southwest have a special charm, a beauty all their own. They're tough and unforgiving mountains, to be sure. The steep slopes are covered with rotten, crumbling granite and loose shale, and plants without cruel thorns are few and far between. But a golden sunrise over the mountains of southern Arizona is worth whatever it takes to see it. The colors change gradually, bathing the slopes in hues of red and gold. When the light comes, you want to be deep in those mountains, binoculars ready. It's simply amazing how much life these arid mountains support, and you never know what you might see.

Off on a far prickly pear-dotted slope, you'll pick up the pepper-and-salt smudges of a dozen javelina. You may see the long-tailed coati mundi, and of course you're likely to see coyotes and perhaps a bobcat. If you perform the glassing ritual often enough, sooner or later you may even see a mountain lion gliding along in search of a meal. You'll also see the animal that brings you to these mountains, the pretty little Coues whitetail.

The Coues deer, also called Arizona or Sonora whitetail, is a small whitetail well adapted to life in the harsh desert mountains. Iron gray in color with a muted, almost nonexistent white throat patch, the Coues deer has both an outsized tail and ears to aid, it's said, in heat dissipation in hot climates. Body size isn't impressive: Few Coues bucks will field-dress over 80 pounds. Nor are the antlers impressive. A petite eight-point rack is common, with only the occasional buck reaching 9 or 10 points. The antlers are distinctive, too, to hunters who have studied these little deer. The beams and points rarely flow in exactly straight lines, but have little kinks and irregularities that seem to reflect the stress of the little deer's environment.

Of the 38 whitetail subspecies that exist from the Arctic to the Amazon, only the Coues whitetail has traditionally been given its own record book category. This tradition can be traced back to a biological error. During the Apache wars, U.S. Army quartermaster Lieutenant Elliott Coues identified the deer, which still bears his name. It seemed so vastly different from the familiar Virginia whitetail that it was initially recognized as a separate species. It wasn't many years before its true status as a whitetail subspecies was acknowledged, but its separate classification by sportsmen has remained.

Biologically accurate or not, from a hunter's standpoint the Coues deer is different from the other whitetails. I'm looking over my shoulder at two mounted heads—a Virginia whitetail from North Carolina, and my first Coues buck from Arizona. The differences are so striking that indeed they look like totally separate species. And the Coues deer is hunted in country totally different from that inhabited by most North American whitetail deer.

I'll never forget the day a well-known deer hunter showed a "Coues deer" rack at a sports show in Arizona. The rack appeared to be from a pretty decent Hill Country whitetail—also a distinctive antler conformation. I suppose it could have been a Coues deer, but at least half a dozen serious Coues deer hunters were walking around shaking their heads—it sure didn't look like any Coues deer any of us had ever seen.

The Coues deer is found in southern Arizona, extreme southwestern New Mexico, across much of Sonora, and perhaps western Chihuahua. In Arizona the little deer have been extending their range north and west; today they're found north to the Mogollon Rim and west virtually to the Colorado River—which leads one to speculate that perhaps we'll hunt them in California someday! Their range extends very deep into old Mexico, but remains quite limited in southwestern New Mexico. There are some confusions that should be cleared up. Eastern New Mexico has some superb whitetails of the Texas subspecies, and they mustn't be confused with Coues deer. There are also no Coues deer anywhere in Texas; the little "fantails" of the Big Bend region aren't Coues deer, but rather Carmen Mountains whitetail, another subspecies altogether.

Although their range is large, Coues deer are hardly found throughout this region. They are not a creature of the desert floor, but rather of the numerous mountain ranges that dot the Southwest. The bulk of their population will be found from 3,000 to 7,000 feet in elevation, usually in a vegetation belt that includes scrubby oak thickets.

There are indeed some fine Coues deer in Sonora, as we'll discuss in the next chapter. But Arizona's estimated 50,000 Coues deer represent the bulk of the world's population, and Arizona has always dominated the record book listings. Adjacent New Mexico, with light hunting pressure and a whitetail herd that seems to be expanding, nevertheless offers excellent opportunities—especially for experienced whitetail hunters.

Hunters journey to the Southwest's deserts in search of Coues deer for many reasons—to fill out a collection of deer; just for something different; perhaps to enjoy the sunshine. I don't think it's unusual that Jack O'Connor's writings led me to the Coues whitetail. O'Connor was an Arizona native, and he had a special feeling for the petite little desert deer. He was also, in my view, the finest hunting and shooting writer that America has produced. O'Connor was one of the most persuasive; he virtually created the mystique of sheep hunting, as well as a generation's allegiance to his favored .270 Winchester cartridge. He often wrote of hunting Coues deer, especially in his earlier years. I could never experience the kind of freewheeling desert-sheep hunting that O'Connor enjoyed—but I could hunt Coues deer. Eventually I did.

Boddington shoots while Duwane Adams spots. Shots can be long in the desert mountains and the deer are very small. Powerful rifles aren't needed, but accuracy is essential.

Duwane Adams and Frank Morales, Coues deer guides out of San Manuel, Arizona, in a comfortable dry camp in the Galiuro Mountains. This is the end of the road; it's uphill on foot from here!

Deer Hunting Coast to Coast

That first hunt was in Arizona's Peloncillo Mountains, down in the southeastern corner. Guiding me were the father-son team of Marvin and Warner Glenn, Arizona ranchers with a half-century of guiding lion and deer hunters between them. I got a pretty nice buck on that trip, a short-beamed, heavy-antlered nine-pointer that I'm still proud of. But more importantly, I fell in love with the desert mountains and these pretty little deer. So much so that a Coues deer hunt has been an annual rite for the past dozen years.

I've been lucky, too; I live too far from Coues deer country to ever be truly knowledgeable about them—but I've come to know some of the real experts. Greatest of them all was the late George Parker—Arizona rancher, decorated World War II hero, border patrolman, international hunter, and Coues deer king. I didn't get to know George until his last few years, but there's a story there. My mother's brother, Art Popham, went to school at the University of Arizona in the 1930s. I suspect the hunting opportunities there had something to do with it—or perhaps a certain professor of Journalism named O'Connor. Anyway, my uncle heard about a border patrolman who knew something about Coues deer, so he looked him up and they hunted together. The next fall my uncle fetched along his Journalism teacher, thus introducing Jack O'Connor to George Parker. It was a smallish world then, and perhaps it still is; George Parker's lifelong buddy was Colonel Charles Askins, and they all hunted together in 1930s Arizona and Sonora.

George Parker took his first Coues deer in 1919. His first record-class buck fell in 1926; his last in 1969. Altogether he still has eight Coues bucks listed in the Boone & Crockett book—an incredible number of big bucks for one man to wrest from their rugged habitat. By his own admission, Parker hunted them under vastly different circumstances than they're hunted today. In his youth there was no hunting pressure, and he could successfully hunt deer by simply riding through likely areas until a buck jumped, then "bail and blaze." Parker told me that he didn't use a riflescope until the mid-1930's, and he used binoculars for the first time in 1941.

In his later years it was a different game. The deer were still there, but not nearly as many, and they had retreated deep into rougher country. Binoculars became the primary hunting tool, and the rifles needed to be more accurate and to shoot flatter. Parker's best bucks were taken in the 1960s, which makes his record even more outstanding; he took some fine deer in the early, easier days—but he made the transition to modern hunting, and made it well.

Marvin and Warner Glenn introduced me so effectively to Coues deer hunting that they got me hooked for life. They hunt the mountains of extreme southeastern Arizona on tough-riding mules. In truth, their hunting is a combination of George Parker's old-time jump-shooting and modern glassing. They use the mules to get deep into Coues deer country before first light, then

Ludo Wurfbain's trophy Coues buck came from the same canyon as Boddington's, one year later. Although the hunting is hard, Coues deer may be the easiest of the deer to get in the record book.

Boddington's best-ever Coues deer was taken high in the Catalina Mountains. After glassing him from long range while he chased does, he was stalked to about 225 yards.

they'll spend the peak morning hours glassing likely basins and saddles. Midday can be spent glassing, riding through likely areas, and even driving canyons with mounted drivers and a couple of shooters posted on likely escape routes. Evenings are generally spent stationary, glassing.

My first Coues buck was taken just like Parker and O'Connor's were in the old days: We rode into a little saddle, and two very nice bucks stood in a swale just over 100 yards away. I got one of them; my hunting partner got the other. In a dozen years, that remains the only the Coues buck I've taken by jump-shooting; all the rest have been spotted with binoculars first and then stalked.

It was around 1979 when I first met Duwane Adams of San Manuel, Arizona. In the years since then Duwane has put together an extremely successful guiding operation specializing in Coues deer, and his seminars on glassing techniques have earned him national recognition. In 1979, though, he was an Arizona hunter who was hooked on Coues deer—and had taken several good ones. Duwane had read a story I'd written on Coues deer hunting, and he invited me over to show me the way he hunts them. I thought I understood glassing, but not the way Duwane does it.

He hunts on foot in some of Arizona's roughest country—the canyons of the Catalina and Galiuro Mountains. But he uses his legs with intelligence, climbing high to known vantage points with the aid of a flashlight, long before first light. At that point most of the legwork is over. In the pre-dawn chill Duwane wraps up in a heavy canvas deer bag he carries, and rests. Then, in the first blush of dawn, with great ceremony, he sets up a full-sized camera tripod and sets atop it big, bulky, optically superb Zeiss 15x60 binoculars. For hours on end, for as long as it takes, he dismantles the hills until he finds the buck he's looking for.

Over the years a Coues deer hunt with Duwane has become an annual ritual—and the funny thing is that we almost always find the deer we're looking for. No, they aren't always monsters; all too often time is short, and we settle for what we can find. But the bucks are there. That's the real secret to Duwane's hunting; he believes the bucks are there, and he keeps looking until he finds them. In good Coues deer country, some distance off the roads where virtually all the hunting pressure is, there are surprising numbers of these little deer. They aren't hunted hard, and the buck/doe ratio has always struck me as very high. Just last December, in a single morning Duwane and I glassed some 30 deer from one vantage point, and I believe we must have seen 11 bucks.

It's a pleasant type of hunting. The early morning hike in with flashlights is generally a killer, but it's cool—and in the dark you can't look ahead to the heights you know you must scale. Once there, the cold seeps in and in spite of the dry clothes in my pack, I usually shake uncontrollably for an hour or so. Then the warming sun takes effect, and it becomes an idyllic way to hunt. We're glassing away into vast distance, so we can talk freely and endlessly while we glass,

Coues deer hunting means hard work, long climbs in some of America's toughest mountains. Fortunately a Coues buck makes a light load to pack out if you're successful.

solving all the world's problems until, eventually, Duwane will say, "Boddington, I've got a barn-burner for you!" Once in a great while I'll beat him at the game—but not often. Nobody is better with those big glasses than Adams.

When a suitable buck is spotted, and he's in a position where there's some chance of reaching him, it's time to pack up quickly, take careful landmarks, and head out. Sometimes, of course, the buck is long gone when you get to where he was, but these deer aren't overly spooky. Once you find a buck and determine a route to reach him, the odds are in your favor. On the December day I just mentioned, we spotted a monster chasing some does on a bare shale slide. Above him were several other deer, including a few lesser bucks.

It took an extremely tough hour to reach them, and the big buck was indeed gone, vanished. Had we had plenty of time, the best thing would have been to back off and try to relocate him—if not that day, then the next. Especially if he was as good as he looked from a mile and more away. But in this case it was my last morning, and I had to head to Los Angeles within a couple of hours. So we found one of the other bucks and took him with a very long shot. That's okay, too; they can't all be big, and next year we'll know a real good canyon to glass.

Another friend of mine, Jay Gates from Kingman, Arizona, has also been extremely successful hunting big Coues deer. Jay is a loner who likes to backpack into rough country and stay there. He also hunts by glassing, but he uses the more conventional means of standard-sized binoculars backed up by a spotting scope. Like Duwane, Jay relies on careful scouting to pick out a good area, then he backpacks in and lives with the deer until he finds what he's looking for. Unlike Duwane, Jay doesn't live in Coues deer country, so I find his track record on these tough little deer extremely impressive. His secrets to success are to stay in top physical condition, find a good area, and then go in and stay in long enough to hunt it thoroughly.

Shortly before he passed away, I asked George Parker if he had any advice for a hunter in search of a good Coues deer. He scratched his head for a while. "Scouting," he said, "is the real key today. If it isn't possible to do that personally, then find a good guide and pay him well!" I'd echo that. Coues deer can be hunted successfully if you choose your area well, if you are in good shape to handle the country, and if you give it enough time. Ace bowhunter Chuck Adams proved that in January 1989. The Coues deer was one of very few North American species Chuck hadn't hunted. He set aside virtually all of the January bow season, did his homework via local contacts and topo maps, and he drew two Arizona state tags and bought a third tag on the San Carlos Apache Reservation. In 14 days, hunting on his own, Chuck arrowed three Coues deer, the biggest of which will go near the top of the Pope and Young listings.

Yes, it can be done. But in spite of such success, Chuck admitted that these little deer were among the most difficult animals he'd ever hunted. Chuck had several things going for him, of course. The peak of the rut is normally early January, when he was hunting, so deer movement is very high. And Chuck is an extremely experienced hunter, is in tip-top physical condition, and he shoots a bow the way most of us wish we could shoot a rifle. He also hunted a full 14 days to launch his three arrows, and he was prepared to hunt 21 days if needed.

With rifle or bow, without that kind of time a guided hunt is the best course, especially for a first timer. The country is big, and while there are indeed more Coues deer than anyone realizes, and more bucks, they're thinly scattered and the very devil to glass. There aren't any real hotspots; once you get off the beaten track most of the mountain ranges in southeastern Arizona and southwestern New Mexico are good. Take your pick; the Catalinas, Santa Ritas, Galiuros, Peloncillos, Dragoons, Chiricahuas, Huachucas, and a dozen other small ranges are all good—if you get back into them and really look. The Gila Wilderness in New Mexico is a virtually untouched Coues deer hotspot that may be worth a shot, but it's probably no better than the traditional ranges in Arizona.

One of the problems with Coues deer hunting lies in knowing what you're looking at once you spot a buck. Remember that even the very best Coues buck is not impressive by eastern whitetail standards. Duwane Adams showed a fine buck to a top bowhunter a couple of years ago, and the hunter reckoned he'd pass that one and keep on looking. Duwane suggested that he take a better look; if he could get that buck, he'd be a new bowhunting world record. The hunter took Duwane's advice and made the stalk, but he missed the shot, so who knows if it was really that big. I'll bet it was, though!

An ear-wide eight-pointer will have a spread of about 13 inches, and that's actually a very fine Coues buck. My best head has a 17-inch spread with good mass—and that's a real monster, right at the Boone & Crockett minimum of 110 points. For the first-timer, unless he happens to be a deadly serious trophy hunter, visible antlers at about 150 yards means the buck is a keeper. Any eight-point Coues buck—a "3x3" excluding eyeguards according to western point count—is a buck to be proud of. To an eastern whitetail hunter, a small eight-pointer may appear very wimpy—but take it by a local sporting goods store in Arizona, and you'll hear exclamations of "nice buck!"

And yet, given good legs, good lungs, and plenty of time, the really great Coues bucks are there for the taking. In fact, the Coues deer just might be the easiest of the North American deer to get into Boone and Crockett today. But you won't find them driving the roads. Unlike blacktail, mule deer, and whitetail deer, I've never seen a Coues deer from any road—let alone a decent buck. You can find them, but you'll need to hike into their desert mountains and really look. And that's the fun part of hunting them!

CHAPTER XI

COUES DEER IN SONORA

Whenever I hunt deer in new country, there's a tingle of anticipation that always runs through my mind before the trip begins. The research has long ago been completed and studied, all the stories have been told, the decisions have been made, and now it's finally time to see exactly what the area really has to offer. If you're the kind of hunter who can't help but want to look over the next mountain just to see what's on the other side, you know the feeling. Maybe—just maybe—this is the honey hole you've been searching for all these years.

That feeling was overwhelming one December not too long ago as I boarded an Aeromexico 727 and headed south from Tucson, Arizona, to Hermosillo, capital city of the Mexican state of Sonora, to hunt Coues deer.

A hunt in old Mexico always holds more than its share of surprises for visitors from the United States. It's sort of like entering a mystery world, where you aren't at all sure what to expect. We've all heard the stories about banditos who prey on unsuspecting tourists, of corrupt policemen and government officials, difficulties with gun permits and hunting licenses, lost baggage, and misplaced airline reservations. For heaven's sake, don't drink the water—don't even let them put an ice cube in that rum and coke—and the savvy visitor won't eat vegetables washed in tap water, either. Mexican drivers make a New York cabby look like Mother Teresa, and if you can't speak fluent Spanish, you'll be lied to, panhandled, and looked down upon all while just asking directions to the hotel. Or so the stories go.

What's it honestly like to go deer hunting in Mexico? Is it as bad as all that? Is it safe? And are there any deer there to speak of?

First, let's talk about the Coues deer population. Coues deer are widely distributed in Sonora, but as in their range in Arizona and New Mexico, not all of the state holds deer. They are found in the foothills and mountains bordering the desert, and there are pockets where the population is higher than in other places. There are also some very big desert mule deer in Sonora, and in Chapter XVI, you'll see how you can combine a Coues deer and desert mule hunt in one package.

Generally speaking, the Coues deer population there is excellent, to say the least. In good country, you can look at many more deer in a day than on a typical public-land Arizona or New Mexico hunt, and the quality of the bucks is impressive as well.

Along with my friend Alex Ramoz, a taxidermist and booking agent from San Jose, California, I was invited into the homes of several prominent Hermosillo residents in December of 1988, men who also love to hunt big-game. Most had some awfully big desert mule deer bucks hanging, but the thing that caught my eye was the quality Coues deer heads on those walls. One gentleman we saw had a monster muley, about 38 inches wide, and a pair of others in the 30-inch class, prominently displayed. But this same gentleman had six Coues deer bucks mounted, each of which would have scored at or above the 110-point Boone & Crockett minimum score. He was proud of those bucks, to be sure, but he really didn't think it was all that big a deal. "They're nice bucks," he said, "but they aren't really great. I have friends who have some much bigger than those."

The local taxidermist that Alex uses to prepare his clients' deer for shipment into the U.S. (Alex books hunts for Sonora Outfitters, run by Hermosillo residents Alberto Noriega and Leon Hoffer) showed us his horn room. He had umpteen sets of Coues deer antlers that would score over 80 B & C points, several that would push 100 points, and a couple that would knock the snot out of the B & C minimum. If you know anything at all about Coues deer hunting, you can't help but be impressed with the quantity of quality heads around town.

And these aren't deer that were shot back when coffee was a nickel, bread a dime, and you had to crank-start the old Ford. These were all deer that had been taken in the past five years, an indication that the population is doing quite well, thank you. It's the opportunity to get a crack at a quality buck like these that makes hunting Sonora worth the effort.

Sonora Outfitters has the hunting rights to several large ranches leased in and around Hermosillo for both mule deer and Coues deer. That's the way that virtually all Mexican deer hunting is conducted—on leased private land. The bulk of that outfit's Coues deer hunting is done on a large ranch located about four hours north of the city, along the Sonora River.

Accommodations are very nice. The main ranch house is used for cooking, meals, and a cocktail around the fire after the hunt is through for the day. Hunters stay in separate brick and wood cabins, complete with beds, showers, a big fireplace, and lots of room to spread out. The food is excellent, with dinners centered around huge steaks of prime Sonoran beef, lobster tails, and fresh fish from the Sea of Cortez, as well as more traditional Mexican dishes. The bar's open, and there is a nonstop supply of soda pop, mineral water, and cold Mexican beer.

The weather in December is surprisingly chilly. One morning there was a skiff of ice on the small ponds near the houses, and you might be in for a rain shower or two. Be sure and bring clothing appropriate for this kind of weather, as well as for midday, when the temperatures warm up again.

You can hunt any of three ways here—on foot, on horseback, or out of a vehicle if hiking the rugged mountain country of the ranch isn't your thing, and you get along with horses about as well as you do the IRS. Naturally, those who

Robb shot this average eight-point buck after looking over 50 deer and 15 other bucks in a half day's looking in Sonora. Coues deer hunting doesn't get any better than that!

Sonoran desert mountain canyons hold perhaps the highest concentration of Coues deer in the world. Glassing and still-hunting are the best ways to hunt this open terrain.

hunt with horses or on foot have a better chance at taking a really good buck, but respectable bucks are taken from the vehicle, too, so don't be afraid to take a rest from hiking and saddles for a day and glass from a vehicle.

I hunted on foot the very first day right out of the main ranch house with two guides. We started out about a half an hour before first light, and by the time the sun was up we were on top of the first ridge, glassing for deer—sort of. You'll find that Mexican guides have pretty poor optical equipment, and they really don't know how to use what they have. What they do have are eyes that can spot deer like nobody's business, a real advantage in Coues deer hunting. These little whitetails are easily the most difficult big-game animals to spot that I've ever hunted, and trained eyes are always welcome.

The way these people like to hunt is to poke along, glassing a little bit but primarily peeking over canyon rims and jumping deer. It's the antithesis of the way I like to hunt Coues deer, which is get high, sit a long time, and glass. Before the day was over, I had my two compadres convinced, especially when I broke out the spotting scope and showed them how to use it.

The day was threatening rain, and it sprinkled on us a bit just before lunch. But by then we had covered about five miles of country, and had seen, honest-to-goodness, 47 different Coues deer. As a point of reference, if you spot a dozen Coues deer in a day on public land in Arizona or New Mexico, you've had a fairly good day, and 20 deer would be an excellent day. I couldn't believe all the deer.

For some reason the rut was yet to get into full swing, and the bigger bucks weren't chasing the does as they should have been the week before Christmas. But of the first 45 deer we saw, 15 were bucks, and six of those were eight-pointers. I haven't hunted with other Sonoran outfits yet, but every time an eight-pointer jumped up the guides would hop up and down and try to get me to shoot it, even though they weren't the kind of bucks I was looking for. You have to understand trophy judging and make the final decision for yourself. The fact that I speak mediocre Spanish and could converse a little with my guides helped settle them down a bit.

About 1:00 p.m. we were sitting on top of a ridge, glassing, when we spotted two bucks bedded on a canyon face a good mile away. Actually, one of the dogs spotted the deer, pointing the animals out before we finally got some optics on them. The two hounds were along because the ranch has a tremendous population of mountain lions, and if we had struck a fresh track with the dogs, the focus of my hunt would have changed quickly. Dogs are an exception in Coues deer hunting, but these were no bother. (However, if you do book a Coues deer hunt in Sonora, be sure and ask about the possibility of adding a mountain lion to the bag. It's a distinct possibility in the right country, and the price differential is not all that great.)

These two bucks were worth looking at more closely, so we got into a deep wash and headed down the mountain. It was an odd "stalk," passing hounds down the six- to 10-foot vertical drops in the wash, attempting to sneak along quietly, and trying to keep from giggling so loudly that we'd spook the deer. We had quite a time. Fortunately, the wind was right, and in about an hour we were as close as we were going to get.

Unfortunately, that was a good 400 yards (the guides later said 500 meters, but I doubt that!). The bucks were lying on a steep hillside across the canyon; getting closer would be impossible. I decided that the better of the two looked good to me, certainly a bigger Coues deer than I'd ever shot, so I decided to give it a try. Finding a rest wasn't the easiest thing in the world, but I finally got relatively comfortable by laying my day pack in the lower branches of a small thorny tree, kicking my legs out at a 90-degree angle, and scrunching in. The bucks were standing now, nibbling at the buds of small shrubs, and my buck was broadside. At the shot, he came tumbling down that slope like a mountain goat, stopping just 20 feet from the edge of a vertical drop of a good 200 feet.

We reached him a half hour later. He was a fine deer indeed, 15 inches wide with eight nice points and medium mass. He certainly wasn't one like the bucks I'd seen in town, but he was a dandy, and that stalk and shot capped off one incredible day of Coues-deer hunting. Besides, now I could go mountain lion hunting for the next four days. (We never got one, by the way.)

What I saw later that week convinced me that I had shot too soon. Bob Gomes, a client of Alex' from Waterford, California, shot a whale of a buck two days later, a massive eight-pointer whose main beams almost touched in front. It scored right at 109 Boone & Crockett points. Alex himself shot a fine buck the next day, a 9-pointer, after missing a solid 100-point deer at long range. The next week, while we were hunting mule deer closer to Hermosillo, Mitch Thorsen of Santa Rosa, California shot a 110-point 8-pointer in just one day of hunting.

That's how good the hunting can be. Now, what about all the negatives we've heard about hunting in Mexico over the years?

By law, you're required to hunt big game in Mexico with a licensed guide and outfitter. There's no do-it-yourself hunting here for Americans, so in planning and researching the hunt, your job is to find a quality outfitter who not only has the deer, but also will take care of you the minute you step off the airplane.

Finding that outfitter can be difficult. The hunting picture is constantly changing in Sonora as new outfitters pop up, old outfitters get out of the business, and governmental regulations are revised. Personally, I wouldn't hunt with an outfitter in Mexico, especially a new outfitter, without thoroughly checking him out, and that means calling references. And even with the established name outfits, ask questions. Make sure that they still have the ranches they claim to have, and ask a hundred and one questions.

Deer Hunting Coast to Coast

You are required to have a birth certificate, voter registration card, or valid passport to enter Mexico from the U.S. I've used all three over the years, and the passport is the one that will prevent the most hassles. You must also have the proper gun permits and hunting licenses, and that can be an interesting process.

Personally obtaining the necessary gun permits is much more trouble than you care to deal with, believe me. As it is, you need a letter from your local police station declaring that you're not a criminal, several passport-sized photos, and other documentation. Some outfitters will take care of this for you, but most will not. The easiest way to get all the paperwork is to employ a service that will handle it for you for a minor fee. It may be the smartest money you'll spend on the trip. Two services that handle the permit process quickly and efficiently are the Mexican Hunting Association, 3302 Josie Ave., Long Beach, CA 90808, phone (213) 421-1619, and Romero's Mexico Service, 1600 W. Coast Highway, Newport Beach, CA 92663, phone (714) 548-3481. Be sure to begin the process early. Every year, it seems, there's another reason why things go slowly, and the greater the margin of error you allow, the better off you'll be. Both these services can also obtain deer licenses for you, but your outfitter may prefer to take care of that himself. Check with him to be sure who will be responsible for this.

Once you arrive in Hermosillo or Guaymas, the two major hubs for Sonoran deer hunting, you'll be met by your outfitter's representatives. You'll also have to go through customs, where your gun permits will be checked to be sure that the serial number of the rifle you have brought matches the one listed on the permit. Then you're off to the hunting area.

Sonora is the wealthiest state in all of Mexico, and I really enjoy Hermosillo. It's relatively clean, the hotels are nice, and the food excellent and very reasonably priced. The Mexican people themselves are very helpful to those Americans who remember that they're in someone else's country and show a little respect and patience. A surprising number of Mexicans speak English, and in many cases the better hotels won't hire them unless they do. If you speak any Spanish at all, the Mexicans will like you all the more, but Spanish certainly isn't a prerequisite.

The problem comes with your guides, who will rarely speak any English. Be sure before you go out hunting with non-English-speaking guides that you have communicated to your outfitter exactly how you want to hunt, the kind of buck you're looking for, and how unhappy you'll be if he tells the guides all this and they tell you to shoot a deer that turns out to be appreciably smaller. The outfitter wants you to be happy and to shoot the buck you want; thus, good communication is essential.

On my next Sonoran Coues deer hunt, I'm going to have the guides take me high on the mountain before first light, set up my optics, and glass hard for the first couple of days. That will be a different style for them, but it's how I like to

Boone & Crockett-class bucks aren't out of the question in Sonora by any means. Bob Gomes shot this huge eight-pointer that scored 119 B&C points just north of Hermosillio.

Horseback hunts, just like those written about by the legendary Jack O'Connor, can still be enjoyed in Sonora. It's a terrific way to see lots of country—and Coues deer bucks!

hunt, and after all, the client should have a say in the matter. By the same token, if you've never hunted these little whitetails before, it's probably best to let the guides show you around their way, at least until you get a feel for the hunting. Remember, it's their job to get you a good buck, and they'll try hard to do just that.

I've never had any digestive tract problems from either the food or water in Mexico, and I've been hunting and fishing the country annually for nearly two decades. However, some people have weaker constitutions than others, so bringing a little anti-diarrhea medicine isn't a bad idea. Also bring any personal medicines you may need, a spare pair of eyeglasses or contact lenses, and toiletries. Little things that might be hard to come by, like chewing gum, always come with me, too, and be sure you have plenty of film and batteries for your camera.

Once you've shot your buck, the guides will cape it out for you. Hopefully you'll have time to have it salted and dried well at an in-town taxidermist, who will also dust it for those bugs the U.S. Department of Agriculture doesn't like to see. The best way to get both cape and antlers home is to carry them as excess baggage. One thing the Mexicans are a bit lax on is using enough tape on the packing box, so bring some of your own. At customs at your U.S. point of entry you'll have to have the cape and antlers inspected, and the officials will want to see your hunting license, deer permit, and passport. It sounds like a hassle, but the officials in Tucson, Arizona, do this often and are efficient and friendly.

One final note on hunting deer in Mexico—do not, under any circumstances, violate any game laws. Unfortunately, one of the down sides to deer hunting in this beautiful country is the hard truth that game laws are being violated left and right, and there are Mexican officials who are being "taken care of" by some outfitters to look the other way, and so on. I saw people hunting after the season legally closed in 1988, and I'm sure the clients themselves didn't know they were doing anything wrong. Find out the seasons, dates, and legalities involved, and follow them. The last thing you need in your life is to be rousted by the local authorities for a game violation. They can make your life miserable if they so choose, and when they're done the U.S. authorities will want to speak with you about Lacey Act violations. It's also apparent that in many places in Mexico the deer are being hunted by local ranchers 365 days a year, primarily for the pot. There's not much you can do about this, even on a ranch where your outfitter has leased the hunting rights. Accept it as a fact of life.

So what's the bottom line on Sonoran deer hunting? I enjoy myself thoroughly every time I go to Mexico, probably because I understand that Mexico is not the United States, a fact one must always remember. Things break down, things don't work, people are late, and phone connections can be bad. A thousand-and-one other little irritants will get to you if you let them. The secret is to hang loose, relax, and enjoy the adventure. Because believe me, there's no better Coues deer hunting anywhere on earth.

CHAPTER XII

TROPICAL WHITETAILS

A lmost any authoritative book on deer will tell you that there are 38 accepted whitetail subspecies scattered between South, Central, and North America. Those with a scientific slant will usually have an excellent map that delineates the subspecies boundaries, together with a matrix that gives the Latin names and common names. As indicated earlier, there are 17 whitetail subspecies found within the boundaries of the United States and Canada. Most of these comprise our well-known, commonly-hunted deer—but even in the United States there are a half-dozen virtually unknown whitetail deer.

To be specific, these would include the Bull Island, Hunting Island, Hilton Head Island, and Blackbeard Island whitetails off the coast of South Carolina and Georgia. To the untrained eye, all four are indistinguishable from their mainland counterparts. The tiny Florida Key whitetail would be part of this group as well, and this one may be the most distinctive of them.

Of the 17 races of whitetail found north of the Rio Grande, three extend their range deep into old Mexico. These are the Texas whitetail, the Coues whitetail, and another of the little known subspecies, the Carmen Mountains deer. The Carmen Mountains deer touches U.S. soil only in the Big Bend National Park of southwest Texas, and perhaps in isolated pockets as far west as Presidio and as far north as Marathon. The strain is pure in the Big Bend, but farther north it is probably tainted with the larger Texas whitetail.

The Carmen Mountains deer—small, scarce, and little known—is, so to speak, the tip of a whitetail iceberg that spreads south across Mexico, through Central America, and over the northern half of South America. Very little is known in the English-speaking world about either the current or the historic status of the whitetail deer throughout this vast region. It is likely there are some areas where deer remain abundant, but the general status of wildlife in Central and South America is not encouraging.

The Boone & Crockett Club record book lumps all North American whitetails into one category, excepting only the Coues deer. That's a simple and straightforward way of dealing with a massive problem, but it pretty much leaves all the southern subspecies out in the cold. Of all the whitetails from Mexico southward, only the Texas subspecies has a chance of attaining record proportions. When the Safari Club International created its record book, it was faced with a different problem. For one thing, it couldn't ignore the eight South American subspecies since it was a worldwide record book covering all the continents, not just North America. For another, it didn't seem fair to the many Mexican and Central American whitetails—and their hunters, if indeed there were any.

Part of a record book's function is to gather data, so the Safari Club opened up a category for "Tropical whitetail deer," including the Carmen Mountains whitetail and 13 other Mexican and Central American subspecies, plus the 8 South American whitetails. In a subsequent edition these deer were separated into two categories: Tropical whitetail, North America, including all the subspecies from the Carmen Mountains deer south to the Panama Canal; and Tropical whitetail, South America, covering the rest.

To date there have been no minimums established, meaning entries are accepted at the editor's discretion. And to date the results haven't been overwhelming. There have been a scattering of entries from Costa Rica, most likely subspecies *Odocoileus virginianus truei*, the Nicaraguan whitetail. The largest of these have been small 8-pointers. South of the Canal, a few adventurous hunters, including some Americans, have taken whitetails in Peru, Colombia, and Venezuela. Other than a big (comparatively) nontypical 12-pointer taken by a friend of mine, Ellen Enzler-Herring, the South American deer that we know about have been small-antlered deer.

South American deer are beyond the subject of this book, but the deer of Mexico's interior are interesting—and it's unfortunate that so little is known about them. The Safari Club is well represented in Mexico, and it was hoped that the Tropical whitetails catch-all category would bring in a number of entries. It hasn't happened; the only entry up to the 1986 edition is a small six-pointer picked up by George Johnson deep in Mexico in 1933. And yet it's likely that there are huntable deer in Mexico's hinterlands since virtually every Mexican state all the way to the Yucatan still lists a season for deer.

In general, at least as far as is known, the various whitetails of Mexico and Central America are collectively very small deer. At the extremes, some may be as small as the Florida Key deer, and I don't believe that any are larger than the Coues deer. According to the references, the Mexican deer with the largest antlers is *O. v. mexicanus*, the Mexican tableland deer of the interior plateau southwest of Veracruz.

The little deer south of the border have always fascinated me. True, they don't have impressive antlers compared with northern whitetails. But they're different. In particular, I had a hankering to hunt the Carmen Mountains whitetail of southwest Texas and Coahuila. A very few of these pretty little deer have been taken in Texas; although protected in the Big Bend National Park, they exist on a few private ranches just to the north and west. I guess what started it all was a Byron Dalrymple story that I read when I was a kid about the time he had hunted a west Texas ranch that held mule deer, whitetail deer, and what the locals called fantails— Carmen Mountains deer. I'd never heard of them before, but I did some research at the school library and discovered they existed.

In accordance with Bergmann's Law, the ears and tails of tropical deer are proportionately larger to allow heat dissipation. That's why these deer are locally called "fan-tails."

The Burro Mountains of northwestern Coahuila are lonely and desolate, a unique mixture of pine trees and tropical plants. This is the heartland of the Carmen Mountains whitetail.

Deer Hunting Coast to Coast

Not many years later I tried to put together such a hunt, only to discover that west Texas is locked up tighter than a drum. It can be tough to find a place to hunt anywhere in Texas, but in that big ranch country in the southwest it might be the most difficult of all. It's probably just as well I didn't put it together; the biologists reckon there's very little chance of the pure Carmen Mountains strain existing very far out of Big Bend park. Since two whitetail subspecies are highly unlikely to occupy the same ground without intermixing, any ranch that is supposed to have both Carmen Mountains and Texas deer would be suspect.

I quit trying to find a way to hunt the Carmen Mountains whitetail; it seemed altogether too difficult. Then, in January 1988, I had an opportunity to hunt Carmen Mountains whitetail on their home turf, deep in the mountains of northwestern Coahuila. La Serrania del Carmen—the Carmen Mountains—lie to the south of Big Bend park. The Carmens themselves, I understand, cannot be hunted. Just to the southeast lie the Burro Mountains, some of which are occupied by large private ranches where hunting is possible. This is all big, lonely country—little traveled and little known, with very few roads. The deer receive a bit of pressure from ranchers, but their limiting factor is probably predation by mountain lions—of which there are many—and black bears. This corner of Coahuila is virtually the last stronghold of the black bear in northern Mexico, which grows huge there.

According to the subspecies maps I consulted, the deer inhabiting the Burro Mountains are indeed Carmen Mountains whitetails, *Ocodoileus virginianus carminis*—but beyond that there was little I could find out about the area. When we finally got there, I could understand why. Together with outfitter Jess Rankin and fellow hunter Huck Spaulding, I traveled southwest from San Antonio, crossing the border at Eagle Pass. From there we drove into Sabinas Coahuila and spent the night—but that was just the beginning of the journey.

In the morning we teamed up with Mexican outfitter Olegario Gomez and New Zealander Malcolm North and his son James, and then began winding our way northwest, back towards the border but far off the beaten track. We'd been on unpaved roads for eight hours, and it was long after dark when we finally arrived at Roberto Spence's remote Rancho del Pino Solo, Ranch of the Lone Pine. Roberto, or simply Bob, turned out to be one of the most amazing men I've met—and certainly the most bilingual. His grandfather homesteaded northern Coahuila from New Zealand, and Bob was educated in the United States but raised speaking both languages, he switched forth from perfect English to flawless Spanish with no hitch and no accent—except a slight Texas twang to his English.

We talked long into the nights about his mountains and his deer. Spence wasn't a hunter himself. He had long recognized that his little mountain deer were indeed different from the "big deer" on other family property near Sabinas—but it had

Boddington's Carmen Mountains whitetail was a small typical 8-pointer—and it hangs in a place of honor amongst deer from the larger northern subspecies.

never been important. Far more pressing, over the years, had been the problems he had had with bears and mountain lions taking his colts. I hadn't yet seen a deer, nor did I have any idea what the country looked like—but now I was more excited than I had been since the trip had been proposed. Subspecies maps be damned—the man who had lived there all his life knew his deer were different from the "big whitetail" on the other side of the mountains!

Indeed they were. Not only different from big whitetail, but also different from any Coues deer I've ever seen. We saw one shortly after dawn the first morning, a little eight-pointer in a pine-covered saddle. Huck was unable to get a shot, but I saw the buck clearly. He was a lovely little thing, very small but with outsized ears—and when he lit out, he showed the most beautiful big flag of a snowy tail, much larger than I've ever seen on a Coues deer.

The country was different, too—broad, well-watered valleys between steep-sided, flat-topped buttes. The valleys had good grass and dense fields of a large, sharp-pointed yucca. The hillsides had oaks and tall pines similar to a Ponderosa—and amongst these stately pines and scrubby oaks were groves of massive palm trees. It was enchanting country, and the deer used it differently than any mountain deer in my experience. We looked for them high and low on the hillsides, as you would normally look for deer, but we never found them there. We found them in saddles, yes, between the valleys—but we found most of them on the valley floor, along yucca and palm-lined watercourses, and in the high grass that stood over their backs.

There weren't tremendous numbers of them but would see up to a half-dozen bucks a day, and a couple of them would look pretty good—or at least what we assumed was good for these unknown little deer. Malcolm North took first honors with a pretty 6-pointer with good mass to his antlers, and I eagerly measured the tail, ear width, and eye-to-nose distance. Of course I had no idea what these measurements were supposed to be for Carmen Mountains deer, but the ears were indeed wide, the tail was enormously long, and the deer field-dressed at about 60 to 65 pounds. After seeing Malcolm's, I wanted one desperately. Still, they were scarce enough that I wasn't willing to lay bets.

When my chance came, it was in the same saddle where we'd seen a buck on the first morning. Jess and I walked into it in mid-afternoon, hoping to see the same buck again. On through the saddle, alongside a grassy watercourse down below, the flash of sunlight on an antler caught my eye. It wasn't the same buck; this one had dark antlers and a wider spread, and looked very good. I cast around for a rest, and finally lay prone along a leaning oak. It was swaying slightly in the breeze, but it didn't matter much because I was shaking like a leaf. You'd have thought this little buck was a 35-inch mule deer or a Boone and Crockett whitetail, because he had me completely unglued.

I didn't hit him as well as I should have, and I knew it. He went down at the shot and we lost sight of him in the long grass. Jess went down to look for him, following my hand signals, yet he found nothing. Sick at heart and afraid, I went down to join him—and stumbled across the buck in the bottom of the creek bed. He was a wide seven-pointer with long points. I had him mounted, and he's one of my most prized trophies—although it does get tiresome explaining what that little bitty deer is doing among what seem to be much nicer trophies.

CHAPTER XIII

MULE DEER

I f the whitetail deer is truly the greatest game animal on the North American continent (and, perhaps, the world), then its close cousin, the mule deer, must also rank high on the list. Mule deer occupy a range only about half as large as the whitetail's, and that factor alone limits the number of sportsmen who have the opportunity to hunt them each fall. And yet interest in mule deer hunting has never been greater, both among residents of the region where the animals live, and among those who travel thousands of miles for no other reason than to match wits with them.

Though closely related, mule deer and whitetails are the antithesis of each other in many ways. While a whitetail may spend its entire life in a very small area, a mule deer may travel as much as 50 miles or more from summer to winter range. Whitetails love edge country and have adapted well to the edges man has left in his seemingly insatiable desire to develop virgin land. On the other hand, mule deer are less forgiving of the bulldozer and the plow, faring much better in rugged, undeveloped territory. Whitetail populations are so dense in some portions of their range that they're like rabbits, but in the vast expanse of mule deer country, the deer like their elbow room. Even if the population in a given area is good, it may be difficult to find even a single mule deer.

And yet, a mature, seasoned mule deer buck has much in common with a similar whitetail. Mule deer possess good eyes, excellent hearing, and an even better sense of smell, and a trophy-class buck has honed these senses to a fine edge. A careless hunter will blunder into mule deer country thinking he's invisible, and he'll never even know that a big buck that's seen, or smelled, or heard the intruder more than a mile off was ever in the neighborhood. Once they know you're prowling around, mule deer bucks may choose to leave the country entirely, or just melt into the cover and let you walk right past. And those stories of bucks running up to the ridgeline, then stopping to look back and giving the hunter plenty of time for an easy shot—well, that might have been the case in grandpa's day, and young bucks may do it now, but a mature buck rarely pulls that stunt any more.

There are few sights in all of big-game hunting more memorable than that of a large, heavy-antlered mule deer buck standing against a backdrop of steep, reach-for-the-sky Rocky Mountain peaks, a lush conifer forest, or an alpine bowl. One of the reasons mule-deer-hunting is so appealing to easterners who have whitetails running out of their ears back home is the breathtaking country that most mule deer call home. Once you've hunted muley bucks in this vista, it will be in your blood for life. And yet, mule-deer-hunting isn't all mountains and forests. Some of the best mule-deer-hunting today is found in high elevation sagebrush flats and hills, and the deserts of the Southwest, country that is spectacular in its own right and offers its own unique set of challenges.

What makes a trophy-class mule deer buck? The yardstick of past generations was a heavy-antlered buck with four points per side plus eyeguards, and an antler spread of 30 inches. Hunters are always talking about "thirty-inchers," and that figure represents the Holy Grail to a large portion of the serious mule-deer-hunting fraternity. But the truth of the matter is that finding a 30-inch buck today isn't an easy trick at all. They may have been fairly common back in the 1950s and early 1960s, but that certainly isn't the case today. There are some scattered pockets that hold a few big bucks like this, and we'll discuss them in subsequent chapters, but for any mule deer hunter to go out and expect to take a buck of this caliber is wishful thinking. They just don't grow on trees.

In talking about 30-inch class bucks, hunters are generally talking about the largest of the mule deer subspecies; with some of the smaller subspecies, 20-inch antlers are awfully large.

The Boone & Crockett Club has a minimum score of 185 points for typical mule deer, and it takes a real barn-burner to meet those standards. In the awards period from 1983-85, only 36 animals made the grade. The world record typical buck scored 225 6/8 points. In the nontypical category it's the same story. Only 25 bucks scored more than the 225-point minimum. The world record nontypical buck is a massive deer that scored 355 2/8 points.

As is the case with any big-game animal, record book scores are nice and give us all a point of reference, but in no way are they the final measurement of a buck's worth as a trophy that has rightfully earned a place of honor in your den. There are many areas in which the mule deer range that simply don't produce antlers large enough even to come close to meeting record book minimums. An old buck, one that's weathered the storms of many seasons, is tough to come by no matter where you hunt. Jack Atcheson, Jr., the Butte, Montana, hunting consultant, sends hundreds of clients mule-deer-hunting each year. It's his opinion today that a heavy-antlered 25-inch buck is a good one, and one in the 27- or 28-inch class a real whopper. A 30-incher? "A guy might get one today, but we hear of very, very few," Jack told me. "They're like finding a four-leaf clover."

Instead, today's hunter looking for a representative buck would do well to study the area that had been chosen to hunt and see exactly what kind of bucks it has produced in recent years. Use those deer as your basis of comparison. Some areas have a knack of growing nontypical racks, and many hunters like that. Some, however, prefer the symmetry of the classic set of antlers, and that's what they go looking for. The vast majority of mule deer hunters today are looking for a representative member of the species, a buck with antlers that have some height, a little mass, and are at least ear wide (which is 22 to 24 inches, on the average).

Rocky Mountain mule deer are the largest of the subspecies, often weighing 300-plus pounds on the hoof. A monstrous nontypical buck is one of hunting's most prized trophies. (Photo by D. Robert Franz)

Any buck like these, earned with hard work on an enjoyable hunt, is one to be proud of.

We'll be talking about how and where to hunt mule deer under a wide variety of conditions in subsequent chapters. But first, let's talk a little about the animal itself and its history.

Eight subspecies of mule deer *(Odocoileus hemionus)* are widely recognized, yet in terms of record keeping, Boone & Crockett recognizes but three—Rocky Mountain mule deer *(O. h. hemionus)*, Columbian blacktail *(O. h. columbianus)* and Sitka blacktail *(O. h. sitkensis)*. Others include California mule deer *(O. h. californicus)*, Southern mule deer *(O. h. fuliginatus)*, Peninsula mule deer *(O. h. peninsulae)*, Desert mule deer *(O. h. crooki)*, and Burro deer *(O. h. eremicus)*. Some authorities question the existence of burro deer, believing this animal to be identical to *O. h. crooki*. Safari Club International also has a separate desert mule deer category that includes both *O. h. crooki* and *O. h. eremicus*. These individual mule deer subspecies are not habitat specific, meaning that any of the various subspecies could thrive in the habitat of any other subspecies, if conditions were right. Living where they do, they've taken on certain characteristics that have permitted them to thrive.

It is interesting to note that the range of the Rocky Mountain mule deer is larger than that of all the other subspecies combined. It occupies all of the Rocky Mountain and intermountain regions, and there are scattered populations as far north as northern Alberta and British Columbia, and as far east as Minnesota, Manitoba, and Iowa.

The Rocky Mountain mule deer is an adaptive animal, though certainly not to the extent that whitetails are. For example, it is believed that the mule deer of the plains country (where they were plentiful prior to the 1930's before a combination of drought, tough winters, overgrazing by livestock, and hunting pressure thinned them severely) are once again expanding their range eastward towards the Mississippi River. Some biologists believe that they will complete this expansion in the next century or two.

The other subspecies are defined as much by habitat as by physiology, except the blacktails, which have obviously different physical characteristics than other mule deer subspecies, most notably the tail and metatarsal glands. Each subspecies will be discussed further in subsequent chapters.

As is true with whitetails, mule deer subscribe to Bergman's rule, which states that the further away from the equator a species gets, the larger its body size. This doesn't necessarily apply to antler growth, which is affected more by heredity and nutrition. With mule deer, that's more apparent within each subspecies than within the genus itself. Two examples come readily to mind. The Rocky Mountain mule deer bucks of southern Colorado, northern Arizona, and northern New Mexico have the potential to grow some tremendous antlers, yet they rarely

Finding a mule deer buck with wide antler spread and good mass is without question one of the toughest challenges in modern North American hunting. Are you up to the challenge?

Robb shot this 24-inch 3x4 buck in Nevada on a weekend trip after first looking at over 100 deer. Though not a record-class animal, the hunt was fun, and the freezer was filled for the winter.

weigh more than 250 pounds on the hoof (though there are some exceptions). In the mountains of southern British Columbia bucks are huge in the body, with older specimens weighing over 300 pounds fairly common. Their antlers, however, will never match the best produced by deer of the same subspecies far to the south. The same is true with blacktails. The Columbia blacktail has a small body in comparison to the Sitka blacktail, yet usually grows a larger set on antlers.

Estimates place the total population of mule deer at the time of white settlement of North America at 10 million animals, a number which dropped to an estimated half a million by 1908. By 1930, the U.S. Forest Service estimated that there were 750,000 total deer (including whitetails) occupying western national forest lands, a number that increased to three million by 1965. The overall mule deer population peaked in the late 1950's and early 1960's, when a general decline began to take place. Today the total mule deer population is estimated at right around one million animals.

Mule deer have a tenuous relationship with habitat, and it is habitat loss more than anything today which affects specific herd populations. More and more, housing tracts and recreational developments are eating away at critical winter range and/or migration routes that lead from summer to winter range. This is having a disastrous effect on the deer in many areas. More so than hunting regulations and pressure, the problem of habitat loss is the one that will define the future of the mule deer in North America, and it is not a simple one.

Mule deer need diversified habitat, with several choices of forage and cover, to reach their maximum potential. When one type of habitat (sagebrush flats, for example) is developed exclusively, leaving only one type of open space (midlife conifers, for example), the deer may be left lacking in food, cover, or both. When a housing tract is built on the only available migration route from high country summer range to low country winter range, rather than adapt, the deer often will abandon the area entirely, their numbers dwindling severely. These are questions modern land-use planners are faced with every day in the West, and as is often the case, wildlife takes a backseat to monied special interests.

With shrinking habitat and an increased interest from sport hunters, many states are continually fine-tuning their hunting regulations to try to maximize hunter satisfaction. In some areas, antler restrictions allow harvest only of bucks sporting three- or four-point racks or better, a move designed to rebuild populations of mature, trophy-class bucks. Limited permit and restricted access areas are also intended to give hunters quality hunting with a chance at mature animals. At the same time, many areas permit the harvest of spike bucks, a regulation aimed at helping those interested only in meat for the pot to put some venison in the freezer. The quality vs. quantity argument will continue to be a factor in mule-deer-hunting in coming years.

Doe hunting is another major issue in many areas throughout the mule deer range. The harvest of a biologically determined number of does from a mule deer herd on a regular basis is healthy for the population in general, yet time and again doe hunts are opposed for emotional reasons by the nonhunting public and, at times, uninformed sportsmen. More work needs to be done to educate all interested parties on this touchy political topic.

But habitat battles, political struggles, and other management problems are not what's on a sportsman's mind when the hunting season rolls around. Then it's time to put all the pre-season planning to the test, pack your gear, and head for the wide-open spaces of the West. A fall just wouldn't be the same if at least part of it weren't spent high among the peaks somewhere, matching wits with one of North America's truly great game animals. From Canada to Mexico and the Pacific Ocean to the Mississippi River, mule deer populations are strong and hunting opportunities plentiful.

When you take on a mule deer hunt, you also take on the big country that he calls home. Together they'll test you, and before it's all over, you'll have plenty of time to reflect upon much in life beside the question of just where a buck might be hiding. You can bet it will be one of the most memorable times of your life.

CHAPTER XIV

HIGH COUNTRY MULE DEER

As the false dawn illuminated the panorama below, the temperature seemed to drop another 10 degrees. Still, the rainbow of red and orange and violet and blue that highlighted the wispy clouds brought a surreal appearance to the vista, the sort of scene Alfred Hitchcock might have painted into one of his thrillers. I nestled into my coat collar and began glassing, and soon had spotted several small bands of mule deer feeding along the opposite slope. As the sun began to crawl over the eastern peaks, its golden rays glinted off the tines of a small band of bucks. Three of the seven were four-pointers.

I fingered my bow and smiled contentedly. The sight caused me to reflect on lots of things for a moment. One of those thoughts was the feeling that I get deep down inside every fall, when I sit on top of one of the continent's tallest mountains and look for mule deer.

I've been more than fortunate in my lifetime, having had the opportunity to hunt all over the world for all sorts of game. There have been expensive safaris in Africa, pageantry-filled European hunts, Alaskan adventures, and other hunts of every type and description. But despite all these exotic trips—good ones all—there isn't anyplace I'd rather be on a crisp fall morning than in the high country of the West's mountains, hunting mule deer bucks.

Hunting alpine country for a good muley buck is a cornucopia of delights to anyone who truly loves the outdoors. The scenery, whether you are in the San Juans of Colorado, the Tetons of Wyoming, the Pintlars of Montana, the Purcells of British Columbia, the Wasatch Front in Utah, or untold other high country hideaways, is breathtaking. The air is so clear it's almost frightening, and the clouds chase each other across the sky like puppies scampering after their tails. There are so many stars at night you could never hope to count them all. The mountains are humbling, too, so big that as you sit on a craggy old rock pile and look them over you begin to realize just how insignificant one man is in the good Lord's scheme of things. The smells are the odors of freshness and life.

It's terrain that can turn on you, too, leaving the unprepared cold and wet and miserable with an unannounced rainstorm or snowfall. There are plenty of loose rocks to slip and crack a kneecap on, branches to poke you in the eye, and other assorted "gotchas" that will certainly make the careless wish they'd never left the backyard.

The high country is a place to be respected, above all else. But for those who know how to unlock its secrets, how to cope with its rough and unforgiving nature, it offers unparalleled pleasure and reward. It's also home to the best mule-deer-hunting in the world.

Deer Hunting Coast to Coast

But hunting good bucks in the alpine country isn't a piece of cake by any means. Here's an example of what I mean.

In August of 1988, Dwight Schuh and I attacked the San Juan Mountains in southern Colorado in hopes of finding a couple of truly big mule deer bucks to shoot an arrow at. We had two of Dwight's llamas as pack animals, and while they carried camp for us, we still backpacked 25 pounds apiece up the trail to the hunting area.

We were hunting steep terrain between 11,000 and 12,000 feet high, and for 10 days we hiked up, down, and around that steep terrain, covering an average of 10 to 12 miles per day. We endured frost on the pumpkin, daily rain squalls, lightning and thunder storms, blistered feet, and the usual assortment of broken parts and little miseries that go with the territory. There weren't any hot tubs bubbling in camp when we arrived back after dark each day, nor were there thick steaks or hot bread to eat. We made do with a warm sponge bath once every few days and lots of pancakes and macaroni and cheese. We did look at nearly 50 different bucks and perhaps 100 head of elk, but we never shot an arrow. All the same, in my book it was one of the most enjoyable and rewarding deer hunts I've ever been on. When we finally came down and touched base with civilization, a scale at the motel showed that I'd lost 12 pounds off my already lean 165-pound frame.

The point of that story is a simple one. It takes preparation to hunt alpine bowls and basins for mule deer, but it also takes heart. If you're the kind of hunter who turns back at the first sign of physical discomfort, there are other places you should be hunting. If you aren't in reasonable physical condition and ready to go to war with the mountain, you're probably better off hunting lower down. If you don't have the equipment and the mental toughness to stick it out, no matter the weather, you'll have a more enjoyable, and probably more successful, hunt in easier places.

But if you're the kind of hunter who enjoys wet socks and cold feet, numb fingers and dirty shirts, not enough food and too much hiking, then you're the kind of person who will relish the challenge of the alpine country. And believe me, once you've tasted what it has to offer, you'll be hooked for life.

The key to hunting alpine country, of course, is locating deer. And finding mule deer in this bigger-than-life world boils down to what we call the "pocket principle."

The pocket principle simply states that in any given territory, 90 percent of the bucks occupy only 10 percent of the available habitat. They congregate in these "pockets," and only those hunters with the persistence and patience to find them will do so without passing them by.

That was certainly true on the trip mentioned earlier. Though Dwight and I saw lots of bucks, they were in fact concentrated in small pockets, the deer themselves

Topographic maps are as important as your weapon in wilderness area hunting. Maps will show you potential feeding, bedding, and watering areas for deer, and how to get to them.

High country hunting will reward you will breath-taking vistas and a feeling of being at the very top of the world. In the backcountry you'll see few others, and plenty of good bucks.

in groups of anywhere from 3 to 11. These pockets were miles from each other; we had to move camp two or three times to really scour the area the way we wanted to. To an easterner accustomed to beginning his whitetail hunt as soon as he hops off the back porch, it's a whole new world of deer hunting. The whitetail hunter may be in good deer country right in his back yard. In alpine mule deer habitat, you first have to locate the good country before you can begin hunting.

To understand the pocket principle, you need to understand a bit about a mule deer's habits. Most important is the fact that bucks generally live either alone or in small bachelor groups. Except during the rut, when all bets are off, they shun the company of fawns and does the way old uncle Bartholomew avoids the company of women and little children at a family gathering. Old Bart doesn't want to be bothered with the nagging and chattering of the young folks and ladies, and neither, it seems, does a big, mature buck.

Also, it is important to realize that does and fawns occupy the most hospitable sections of good deer habitat, forcing the bucks into the fringe areas. Biologically this makes sense, giving the does and young deer access to plenty of high-quality feed and water, and adequate cover from predators and the elements. Individual bucks, in the meantime, can get by quite nicely on the fringe areas. These are most often related vertically, not horizontally, to the does and fawns. This is one reason why you can often find the better bucks at the top of the mountain, in the alpine country, as well as in the sage brush flats along the mountain's base, while the mid-levels hold mom, the kids, and the adolescent bucks.

One reason I like to hunt the alpine regions during the early rifle season is that most of the deer you see will be bucks. In the August and early September bow seasons, you see lots of bucks up high but a few does, too. A bit later the does, who seem to migrate down the mountain first, have for the most part already left, leaving the rugged high country to the bucks. It may take some looking to locate a pocket of deer, but once I've found the animals, I can be pretty sure that they'll have antlers. And where there are one or two, there will often be more.

I also believe that the bigger bucks that prefer the alpine country will stay there until the snow is chest deep. If a sudden warm front comes in and melts the snowpack down, bucks will migrate back up to their favorite haunts and stay there, as long as they can find food. If the snows come again, down they'll go, but with any melt they'll go back up again, too. If the winds are strong and a slope is shaped just right, it can remain relatively snow-free all winter. That's the kind of pocket that just might produce a real whopper, if you can reach it.

The key to hunting alpine bucks most of the time is to spot them before they see you, then plan a stalk. If the wind permits it, always hunt from above, glassing down into canyons and basins, off rocky fingers, and the like. You have to be extremely cautious in hunting the high country. The air is thin, and sounds travel forever. A mule-deer expert once told me that he felt a mule deer buck, with those

Late-season conditions can be brutal; you have to be prepared physically, mentally, and have proper clothing. Robb shot this funny-forked buck at -20 degrees in Montana in November.

big radar-dish ears, could hear at 100 yards sounds we have trouble hearing at 10 yards. I don't doubt it. Bucks are usually in places where they can see just about everything in their domain, and while their eyesight isn't the greatest, they can spot movement and a skylined hunter miles off. When they do spot an approaching hunter, they'll often bail off an easy slope and down into dark timber, where it takes more luck than I've got to find them again. They spend most of their time looking for trouble from below, but not all of it. You can't be too sneaky.

When planning your alpine hunt, use topographic maps meticulously to find areas that need to be glassed before you even enter the country. Early in the season that might be the north- and east-facing slopes near the ridge tops, places where food grows best thanks to sunlight and the accumulation of snow during the winter. Later in winter it might be slopes that face the prevailing winds. It pays to have a plan, and the maps will give you just that. It saves lots of time, and keeps you from wandering willy-nilly, wondering where the deer might be. I like to hunt steep, rocky, rough terrain above timberline, especially if the rough stuff is adjacent to an avalanche chute where a buck can feed, with a thick patch of young aspens or rimrock for bedding, and several escape routes close by.

In trying to determine a buck's behavioral patterns during the course of the year, keep in mind the acronym "FESS." It stands for food, escape, sex, and solitude, and describes a muley's movements all through the year.

In early season, when many archery hunts are opening up, food is a buck's primary concern. Antler growth is occurring now, and he needs lots of energy to sustain that growth. Deer often feed right out in the open now, and spotting them will never be easier than in late summer.

Once the antlers have matured and the velvet has come off, bucks have another priority—escape. Most rifle seasons occur during late September and October, and with energy demands not as great as they were just weeks ago, a buck is looking to save his hide from the horde of blaze-orange shirts invading his territory. That's why alpine hunting can be so good. The hunter who can get into some tough-to-reach country, rugged terrain that excludes other less enthusiastic sportsmen, will often find that the bucks have moved right in with him to escape the army below.

Smart bucks will stay in the heavy cover more, and spotting them with your optics is tough except at first and last light. On the Colorado hunt mentioned earlier, Dwight and I found a couple of well-worn trails in among the heavy timber where horses, and therefore outfitters, couldn't go. I'd like to set up a tree stand in October over one of them and see what passes by in the course of a week.

When November rolls around, the deer go into the rut, and the reproductive urge becomes the driving force in their lives. Hunting the rut can pose its own special set of problems, which we've detailed more closely in Chapter XXV. The sex drive makes even the smartest buck as giddy as a high school freshman on his first date, and if you can draw a permit for a rut hunt in good country, by all means take advantage of it.

The pocket principle still applies to rut hunting, by the way. In each group of does there will be one mature, dominant buck, and while he may not be out in the open with the does all the time, you can be sure he's there. There will also be lesser bucks trying to get in on the action, so it often pays to stick with a group of hot does a while to see exactly what kind of buck they draw.

Once the rut is over and the sex drive has lost its hold on their sanity, the bucks will again seek the peace and quiet of solitude. Often they'll move to the fringes of the winter habitat, and that means back up the mountain as far as they can. In some late-season special hunts, hunters make the mistake of seeing lesser bucks mixed in with does during a false rut, and believing those are the only bucks around. In reality, the bigger bucks may be done with the rut and have headed back up toward their alpine homes. It takes a special kind of hunter to challenge the high country now, but again, the rewards may be worth the price.

Alpine hunting for mule deer is a special time. We're very fortunate in this country to have literally thousands of square miles of high mountain public land that hold solid mule deer populations. If you travel there this fall, maybe I'll see you on a lonely pass to the other side. You can be sure that's where I'll be.

CHAPTER XV

BADLANDS BUCKS

I t doesn't look like mule deer country, that huge expanse stretching from the east front of the Rocky Mountains eastward into the Great Plains. Nor does much of the broken land lying between the Rockies and Sierra Nevadas. Some of it is hilly country, like the Black Hills of the South Dakota, but much of it is high sagebrush plains broken by deeply eroded watercourses. Where it's well-watered, the ridges may be covered with cedars and the watercourses lined with cottonwood or aspen. But more often than not a tree of any kind is a rarity. It isn't sort of terrain that we imagine mule deer to favor—and where we dream of hunting them. But it is mule deer country—and some of it is very good indeed.

I was introduced to mule deer in just such an area, along the wandering streams and on the sagebrush ridges of eastern Wyoming. This foothill-and-plain country actually encompasses as much of the mule deer's total habitat as do the more mountains. From the Texas Panhandle north through Oklahoma, Kansas, Nebraska, and the Dakotas, and well into Saskatchewan and even western Manitoba, mule deer range all across the east front of the Rockies. Farther west, some of the finest mule deer can be found in the broken lands of western Colorado, Utah, and Nevada. This is all Rocky Mountain mule deer habitat; the smaller desert subspecies do indeed inhabit similar terrain, but they're found farther south and west. These states have alpine hunting—but they also have vast areas of low juniper ridges and steep-sided canyons, which are mule deer habitat, too.

Historically, the very best muleys have not come from these lower areas. Prairie mule deer are what we often call "willow-horned" or "pencil-horned"—good conformation, and often a wide spread and decent point length, but little mass to the antlers. There are exceptions. The famed Arizona Strip is badlands mule-deer-hunting at its best—and it can still produce the monsters it was famous for a half-century ago. Southeastern Nevada, too—broken, juniper-ridge country, not terribly high—has been producing some of the best muleys ever to come out of Nevada.

Typically the badlands are very difficult to hunt. Although physically easier than true high country, the terrain is marked by a uniform sameness—mile after mile after mile of eroded gullies and low ridges. The deer may well feel a particular affinity for one specific ridge over another—but it's hard for people to pick the right spot. It's also terrain that, generally, will not hold huge numbers of deer. And the few deer that are present have unlimited places to be when you're looking for them—thousands upon thousands of little folds and gullies, too many for any one hunter to look into.

121

Deer Hunting Coast to Coast

And yet the deer do at times make terrible mistakes. Perhaps it's because, while the country may look much the same to you and me, it doesn't to the deer. In my experience, badlands mule deer are much more habitual than alpine muleys. If you find a particular canyon system that holds bucks, don't push it extremely hard—but hunt it often. Unlike in much mule-deer-hunting, if a buck eludes you one day, your chances of finding him nearby on another day are very good indeed.

The converse, however is that, just because a particular area looks like deer country to you, don't assume it looks that way to the local deer. Several years ago, in the sagebrush hills of eastern Wyoming, I was fortunate enough to draw both a deer and an antelope tag. It had been some time since I'd been able to put together such a combination, and while I wasn't worried about the antelope, I desperately wanted to fill the deer tag. With what little scouting time I had before the season, I looked the ranch over, and I picked out a complex canyon system that fell off of a prominent knoll like the spokes of a wheel. To me, it looked like the best deer country on the ranch. I was convinced that there must be a good buck somewhere in those canyons.

I combed them on foot for days, and I sneaked up on, spooked, got the drop on, and messed up on a whole bunch of does. I never saw a buck, not even a spike or forky. Had I been smart, I would have moved on. But I kept looking at this canyon system, and I was convinced it was the deer hangout in that neighborhood. It sure looked it, anyway. And the does apparently agreed...but not the bucks. The last day, while I combed canyon after canyon, a couple of guys in our party found several excellent badlands mule deer. They were just a couple of miles to the south of where I was hunting, and they weren't in country that looked like a muley haunt. At least not to me. It was a stretch of sagebrush ridges with shallow draws, not the deep-cut erosion gullies with trees along the bottoms that I'd been hunting. Who knows? The bucks liked it, and if I hadn't been so stubborn I might have found them first.

On another occasion I did find the bucks, four of them. I blundered into a grassy little header and bumped them out of their beds. They were all mixed up together and were gone before I could sort them out and get a shot. But I was pretty certain one of them was a reasonable sort of 4x4. I honestly didn't know where those deer went; there was no significant cover for miles, but they had just gone to ground. Rather than comb the draws for them, I let them be—and found them back in the same place the next morning.

When I was a kid, the huge expanse from western Kansas to the Rockies—and on north into Canada—was all mule deer country. We hunted along the watercourses, and the mule deer were there. Today the whitetail has probed deeply into this territory—and in the main has followed the waterways. Many of the willow-lined streams in this region today have become top producers of big

The badlands are glassing country. Once deer are located it may be possible to drive them out, but the country is generally too vast—and deer too scattered—to still hunt effectively.

Photographed in eastern Colorado, this buck is clearly a whitetail/mule deer cross. Look at the muley tail, whitetail antlers, muley face, in-between ears. (Photo by D. Robert Franz)

whitetails. It's possible that mule deer don't compete very well with whitetails; certainly when the whitetails move in in any number mule deer tend to be hard to find. In much of this country today, especially some drainages in eastern Colorado and Wyoming, the whitetail has seemingly evicted the mule deer. In such country today you no longer look for muleys along the creek bottoms. Instead you look for them along the highest ridges and in sagebrush swales and coulees.

A byproduct of the whitetail's incursion into historic mule deer territory is that once in a while you may find a whitetail/mule deer cross. This phenomenon seems to be getting more commonplace as the two species meet across an ever increasing range. When I was a youngster—certainly not that long ago—we believed it was impossible for whitetails and muleys to cross. The first documented cross that received publicity was found in Alberta. My friend Russell Thornberry wrote one of the first magazine stories about crossbreeds, back in the early 1980s. Since then documented crosses have been found from Texas to Canada. An outfitter friend of mine in west Texas took a Texas whitetail/desert mule deer cross for one of his clients, and had it verified by the local biologist.

Recently I met an Arizona hunter who swears crosses between desert mule deer and Coues whitetails aren't uncommon. I'm not prepared to accept that, but I had to accept the pictures wildlife photographer Robert Franz took in the fall of '88. Taken in eastern Colorado, these were the first completely identifiable, unquestionably authentic photos of a live whitetail/mule deer cross, on the hoof, in the wild, that I've ever seen. The coloration seems more mule deer, the ears more whitetail, the tail an obvious hybrid, and the antlers just plain weird.

The actual physical traits of such a hybrid could be anything, but it seems that they are almost always the result of the more aggressive whitetail buck mating with a mule deer doe. At this writing crosses are still extremely uncommon—but just how uncommon that is nobody seems to know. For certain they are more common now than they were 20 years ago—when such a thing was unheard of and believed impossible. Are the crosses fertile? That's a question I haven't been able to get a straight answer. If they are, then you have to question what this means to the mule deer as we know it. If the whitetail continues to expand his habitat at today's rate, and mule deer continue to suffer erosion of habitat due to human development, the mule deer could be in serious trouble a century or so from now—or much less.

Fortunately nature has a way of taking care of such things—although her methods are often unpleasant. Up until a couple of years ago the whitetail population explosion in eastern Montana was a matter of some concern—especially regarding its effect on mule deer numbers. For a while it was possible to purchase up to five whitetail doe tags in addition to a buck

Getting a buck from the bottom of a canyon usually means just one thing: packframe. Sometimes, though, luck, ingenuity, and a good winch can save a lot of work.

This 29-inch mule deer was taken in the Missouri Breaks of eastern Montana—classic badlands hunting. This buck is no record, but on today's market he's a great buck anywhere.

tag—but hunter interest wasn't high enough to check the deer numbers. In 1987 a bluetongue epidemic decimated the whitetail herds in this region—but, strangely enough, didn't seem to touch the mule deer.

The proximity of whitetail and mule deer throughout this region would seem to offer a unique opportunity for a combination hunt for both species, and certainly such a hunt would be quite possible. However, almost no areas where both species occur currently offer multiple buck tags. The only exceptions would be southern Alberta and southeastern British Columbia. However, the hunter planning to travel some distance to hunt could, by really doing some homework and applying for the proper licenses, plan to hunt adjoining states. The area where Colorado, Wyoming, and Nebraska join offers interesting opportunities. Likewise, southeastern Montana, adjoining not only Wyoming but also both Dakotas, creates interesting possibilities.

However, unless a hunter has lots of time on his hands, the wisest course these days is to figure out what you want to hunt most—and then concentrate. Most combination hunts turn out to be mediocre for everything—or very good for one animal and poor for the other. It is, for instance, very difficult to find good mule deer in most elk country today, and vice versa.

One exception to this rule is that the "badland" country east of the Rockies is a very good region to plan a mule deer/pronghorn combination hunt, especially in eastern Montana or eastern Wyoming. With some exceptions, neither area is necessarily the best trophy country for either species—but good, representative heads of both are certainly available, and they live close enough together to be hunted successfully on a relatively short hunt. In fact, as long as one isn't insistent on a head of record book quality, a pronghorn/mule deer combination remains one of America's most pleasing and enjoyable hunts.

To plan such a combination hunt it's obviously necessary to pick an area where the seasons overlap. In most cases today both licenses will be on a drawing, so there's always the chance of getting both. In extreme eastern Wyoming most of the hunting country is tied up in private land. That's a double-edged sword since access is limited the licenses are relatively easy to draw, but it's absolutely essential that you locate a place to hunt before you go tooling up the day before the season. An outfitted hunt is always an option, but the local chambers of commerce in area towns will generally help you find ranchers that welcome hunters (although, today, that welcome usually requires an access fee). Do that kind of planning before you ever apply for licenses!

There are also vast areas of BLM land and other public lands, and maps are readily available. But be warned: Areas that are primarily occupied by public lands are often very hard to draw permits in.

At this writing, eastern Montana is actually a better bet for this type of hunting than Wyoming (or anyplace else). The Missouri Breaks region of eastern

Montana, and southeastern Montana around Broadus, have been producing a surprising number of superb mule deer in recent years. The bluetongue greatly thinned whitetail numbers throughout much of this country, which is probably good news for the mule deer in coming seasons. Eastern Montana also produces very fine pronghorns. There aren't as many as in Wyoming, and they aren't hunted as hard—but trophy quality averages a bit better.

As in Wyoming, much of the country is tied up in private land, but there are also vast public holdings. Montana's pronghorn licenses are on a drawing by area, but generally aren't difficult to obtain. In the past an expensive combination license (including an elk tag) was required for a nonresident to hunt Montana's deer. Today there's a limited quota first-come, first-served deer license, plus a "set aside" quota of outfitter tags and landowner tags. Whether you wish to engage an outfitter, hunt on your own, or hunt on private land, these days the odds of obtaining a Montana deer license are better than ever.

This country also offers some truly outstanding bird hunting, whether for the pot or to round out an enjoyable hunt. Depending on where you are, you might find sage grouse, sharptailed grouse, Hungarian partridge, or even ringnecked pheasant—and often some combination of two or three of these species.

One of the most enjoyable deer hunts I've been on in years took place in the Missouri Breaks of eastern Montana, not terribly far from Fort Peck Reservoir. The mule deer are found primarily in the broken lands of the Breaks themselves, along juniper ridges and in the steep-sided erosion canyons. On the sagebrush flats some distance away I shot a very nice pronghorn, but the kind of mule deer I was looking for gave me the slip. I saw him, though—not once but twice.

The first time was very early in the hunt. I picked him up in the spotting scope far away on a ridge at first light, and watched him work his way down into a maze of draws and canyons. Getting him out of there wasn't a one-man job, so we gathered up the rest of the party and spent the midday hours pushing draws on foot. He traveled farther than we thought he would—which is typical for badlands mule deer. We found him in one last draw, this one much farther away than we thought he could possibly be, but a draw that looked so good we just had to give it a try. I got one quick running shot at him, but put the bullet behind him. A Pennsylvania hunter on the opposite ridge—who didn't yet have a deer and had to leave within the hour—dropped him with a magnificent running shot. He wasn't a "book" buck—but he was a heavy-horned, absolutely perfect 4x4 with an outside spread of exactly 29 inches.

On the last morning I could hunt we glassed a buck of similar size far off, just going over a distant ridge with three does. We ran across the broken land for more than a mile, and there was absolutely no reason why we couldn't find that buck. It was early, cold and frosty—and he was rutting heavily. He should have been on the far side of that ridge with his does, but he was long gone, and we never saw him again. I got a nice buck that afternoon, but nothing like those two giants.

Timing is important in badlands country. If there's any possible way to plan a hunt so that it coincides with the rut, it's more important there than in much mule deer habitat. The problem is that the country is vast, and often doesn't have enough relief for really advantageous glassing. The rut is needed to bring the bigger bucks up onto the exposed ridges where you can see them, and without it you can count on tough hunting. I left the day after that big four-point gave us the slip. That was the day that the rut really arrived. I was hunting with Jack Atcheson, Jr. and I was the last of his hunters for the season. Once I was on the road back to Billings, Jack and his guides went to work hunting big bucks for themselves. And that afternoon those bucks were chasing does on every ridge. They took two fine deer that evening and two more the next morning—and then packed up the camp for the season.

During the rut, glassing will be the most effective technique. As with all mule-deer-hunting, glassing is also important during the tough pre-rut hunting—but covering lots of ground is more important yet. Two or three hunters, working in concert, can effectively push likely-looking draws. You may need to push a lot of draws in such country—but the deer will be there. You have to believe that, and you have to stay ready even if you haven't seen a deer for hours, even days.

On our very first mule deer hunt, in broken land north of Gillette, Wyoming, my dad and I were combing draw after draw in the face of a coming storm. There was plenty of fresh sign, but we were inexperienced and had come to believe we weren't going to see a deer. Dad stepped around a little corner in a draw and came face to face with a fine buck—but he wasn't ready, and in that moment's hesitation the deer turned tail and was gone. I've never forgotten that, and I've always tried to stay ready (but occasionally I haven't been ready enough!).

Badlands bucks. They're there, they see relatively little hunting pressure, and they can grow large. A friend of mine took a wonderful 32-inch-spread 4x4 in broken land in northwestern Kansas last year. That isn't all that far from where I saw one of the prettiest muleys I've ever laid eyes on. He was in the Chalk Bluffs of northeastern Colorado—and Lord, how I wish the deer season had been open. But it wasn't, so I could do nothing but just watch him in his bed on the far rimrock. The really big bucks aren't particularly common in that vast region—but they're there, and they're every bit as much fun to hunt as their high country brothers. Perhaps, if you throw in some sage grouse and Huns, and perhaps a pronghorn, they're even more fun!

CHAPTER XVI

DESERT MULE DEER

I t was a warm, sunny afternoon the day before New Year's, 1988. The temperature was in the mid-60s, and the bright sun shone off the desert floor and its prickly flora created a kind of brownish glare that made it hard to see into shadowed hollows and gullies.

Suddenly, a hundred yards or so ahead a mule deer buck jumped up running, spooked from his bed by our approach. Neither of us could react quickly enough to get off a shot before the buck bounded over a small hill, gone forever. The whole scene lasted less than two seconds.

I'll never forget the sight of that big-bodied buck as he topped the rise, sunlight glinting off his enormous rack. Both my partner and I guessed the buck to have a spread in the 34- to 35-inch class. The antlers were massive, too, with deep forks, long beams and several cheater points jutting out in all directions. He was the largest buck I have ever seen on the hoof.

I saw three other bucks worth noting on this five-day trip. One was a 28-incher I saw the first half-hour of the hunt and passed up after getting within 50 yards. The second was a solid 30-inch class animal with high, heavy antlers and deep forks; he spooked when I stumbled into some unseen range cattle and spoiled my shot. The third was a fine, heavy-antlered 32-inch 5x6 that Californian Ron Pemberton shot the first afternoon of the hunt.

This was my introduction to hunting the desert mule deer of Sonora, Mexico. I was hunting with Sonora Outfitters on one their leased ranches near Hermosillo, the state's capital city. Given what I saw in a week's time, and after talking with several other sportsmen familiar with what's available there, I have come to believe that that is truly the best place in the world right now for a deer hunter to take a buck that he can honestly call record book class.

The desert mule deer, *Odocoileus hemionous crooki*, has the second largest distribution of the various mule deer subspecies behind the Rocky Mountain mule deer. Its range includes southeastern Arizona, southern New Mexico, western Texas, and extends for hundreds of miles down into old Mexico. These deer are surprisingly large, with big bones and body weights that approach 250 pounds on the hoof, sometimes they are even heavier. If more and better food were available to them, they might possibly be the heaviest of all the mule deer. That and Bergman's rule limits this deer's size. If it were any larger, it might have trouble dissipating heat in the brutal summer desert sun.

At first glance, the desert country these deer call home appears so harsh that one wonders how anything could live here, much less a big-bodied deer. Many parts of the range are so arid that forage is relatively meager compared to the lush meadows of an alpine bowl, and water is worse than scarce during much of the year. The desert is open country, and as such harbors intense heat—and intense cold as well. There is little cover from both the weather and potential enemies. And yet the desert mule deer thrives in such habitat, sustaining itself on meager rations and hiding in small clumps of vegetation, gullies and washes, and cactus patches.

Physically, desert mule deer are the palest of the mule deer in terms of body color, with light tannish-gray hides, small rump patches, and a dark stripe running down the center of the tail. Their ears are also a bit larger than in other mule deer subspecies, probably to help cool the animal in summer. The average width of the ears, tip to tip, is 24 inches.

In the southwestern United States, there are literally thousands of square miles of public land on which one can hunt desert mule deer. In much of this range, the deer are very much underhunted. Our good friend Duwane Adams, the well-known Arizona Coues deer guide, told both of us once that almost no one hunts the desert mule deer around his home in San Manuel, Arizona, and yet he believes that a skilled hunter could probably get a crack at a buck there in the 25- to 28-inch class in a week's time. Where else in mule deer range have you heard a claim like that made?

The key to hunting them in this arid country is water. Find waterholes in otherwise arid country, and you're bound to have bucks nearby. Biologists believe that these deer must water every other day, and will water every day if they can. They do get some water from the various plants they eat, most notably cholla, ocatillo, tesora, and prickly pear. Nibbled cactus is a good indicator of whether or not there are any deer in the area. In some wide open desert country, large cholla patches are like magnets to these deer, and should always be investigated.

The best way to hunt these deer is the spot-and-stalk method, particularly if you can get up on a relatively high vantage point and see lots of country. The first thing you'll notice is that deer densities are not all that great in comparison with some other mule deer habitat, and it takes lots of looking to find what deer there are. It's the kind of country in which not seeing lots of deer should not be discouraging, because, as the saying goes, "even when there's lots of them, there aren't many of them!"

Sometimes mini-drives will work well, especially if a skilled shooter is placed on a high vantage point and two or three others work the desert floor below him in a sort of semi-still hunt. Taking a stand near a waterhole is another good method if the hunter has lots of patience and is sure that this is the only good water source for a few miles.

But while there are some good bucks roaming the deserts in the United States, the best desert mule-deer-hunting by far right now is in the state of Sonora, Mexico. Chapter XI covers in-depth what it's like to set up a deer hunt in Mexico,

Here's what you're hoping for. This heavy-beamed, 32-inch 6x7 buck taken by Californian Ron Pemberton in 1988 is the kind of mule deer we all dream about, but most of us never see.

Sonoran deserts are big and open, dotted with a few small hills, cuts, and washes. Deer densities are not great, but the chances of finding a huge buck are as good as anywhere on earth. (Photo by Jon Sundra)

and should be studied by any reader seriously contemplating such a trip. It is sufficient to say here that you must hunt with a licensed Mexican outfitter, that there is a fair amount of mindboggling paperwork involving rifle permits and licenses, and that Murphy's Law certainly applies to Mexico in general, and hunting in particular. The key is to hang loose, enjoy yourself, and make sure that you've taken care of all the details well before the trip. Then you can concentrate on the task at hand, which is finding one of these monster bucks to shoot at.

Nearly all the outfitted hunting in Sonora is done with either Hermosillo or Guadalajara as its hub. Hunters can drive into either city, but most take a commercial flight. Your outfitter or his representative should be at the airport to greet you and help you get through customs with your baggage and rifle. You may have a meal in town and pick up a few supplies before heading to the hunting area, which can be right next to town, or several hours down the road.

The hunting country is flat, with a few small hills and buttes scattered here and there, all covered with thorny vegetation. Water is scarce.

Hunting is done in basically two ways. In some areas you spend most of the time in a hunting vehicle, cruising dirt tracks and looking down into the thick cover from the back of the truck. In others you spend the entire hunt on foot, walking with a guide. The Mexicans like to call this method tracking, and while they do look for fresh tracks and follow any they find, mostly you are walking through the desert trying to jump a deer. You have to be quick to take advantage of the situation, and since most guides don't speak any English and there isn't a lot of time for discussion anyway, in the final analysis you are the one who makes a trophy judgment. You must know in your own mind what kind of buck you're after before the hunt begins.

You may get lucky and actually spot a buck before he sees you as he's moving through the cover, feeding, or courting a doe during the rut, which is in late December. (The season runs from early November through December 31.) If you do, then you may have an opportunity to look the deer over, get a solid rest, and make a controlled shot. But it's best to be prepared for lots of walking and a quick shot.

Shooting can be short or long, and again you may be carrying your rifle 5 or 10 miles a day. Flat-shooting cartridges are definitely best here, with rounds like the .270, .280, 7mm magnum, .30-06, .308, and .300 magnums best. An ideal rig might be a lightweight, 22-inch barreled rifle in any of the above calibers topped with a straight 4X or 2-7X variable scope. Whatever your rifle, be sure you can shoot it well offhand and can get into a comfortable, rested long-range shooting position quickly if need be. Chances are during a week's hunt you'll only get a couple of opportunities, and you don't want to miss.

When tracking or walking, be sure you stay right up tight against your guide. Don't straggle 5 or 10 yards behind. Why? Because if a buck jumps, he's going

In some areas, hunters spend much of their time in 4x4 vehicles. In others, you spend most of the day walking through the desert, hoping to jump a big buck from its bed. (Photo by Jon Sundra)

This buck is representative of many taken in Sonora today. You must decide if he's what you want before entering the desert; when a buck jumps and runs, there's little time for analysis. (Photo by Ludo Wurfbain)

to jump because the first man in the line—the guide—spooked him, not the last. Time is of the essence, and that second or two it takes you to get to where the guide is standing when the deer breaks may be all the edge that buck needs to get clean away.

In terms of clothing, be prepared for chilly mornings and warm days. A good coat is a must. I like to wear jeans, lightweight hiking boots and thick, padded socks, a light flannel shirt topping a T-shirt, and baseball cap. Light gloves are a good idea, too. Be sure and bring a day pack, water bottle, and binoculars. If you have a spare pair of binoculars bring them, because chances are better than good that your guide won't have any and will want to borrow yours. Hunting knife, whetstone, lightweight rain suit (you never know) and camera are all items you'll need.

Sonoran mule deer hunts aren't inexpensive, as these hunts go. In 1988 Sonora Outfitters charged hunters $2750 for a week's hunt, with a $1000 trophy fee if a deer was taken. That's about what most other outfitters charge for this hunt, although some run as high as $6000. Success rates vary, of course. Many outfitters boast of "near 100 percent success" or "85 percent success last year," and so on. In truth, this doesn't mean that 85 percent of the hunters shot magnificent, 30-inch-plus, heavy-antlered bucks. Many of the deer taken are in the 25- to 28-inch class, still an excellent buck by today's standards.

But, as one man who has hunted Sonora several times told me in a small cantina in Hermosillo, "Today in Sonora the chances are probably fifty-fifty that a hard hunter will at least see a buck very close to, if not larger than, thirty-inches wide with lots of mass. That's terrific, but the thing that gets my blood boiling is the fact that there's not a totally unrealistic chance of taking a buck here over forty-inches. Where else in the world can you even think about such a possibility?" For Wyoming taxidermist Toby Johnson, that dream came true in 1986. Hunting with Sonora Outfitters, he shot a buck with an outside spread of 42 inches, the largest antler spread of any buck ever to make it into the Boone & Crockett record book. That's the stuff that a deer hunter's dreams are made of.

CHAPTER XVII

BIG BUCKS ARE WHERE YOU FIND THEM

T
alk with anyone who seriously hunts big game in North America and ask him what he thinks the most difficult species to place in the record book today is. The truly serious, impartial hunter who knows his business and hunting will tell you that, hands down, it's a mule deer buck.

Think about it. Though they don't qualify for record book entry because they live and are hunted in fenced enclosures, you can pay the money and shoot an elk that meets minimum book standards. You can even do the same with a whitetail deer, and besides, there are really quite a few whitetails taken each year by fair-chase hunters that meet minimum book standards. Mountain sheep? The tough part is drawing a tag. The same is true for more obscure animals like Shiras moose and mountain goats.

Today, the most difficult animal to take in record book size is a mule deer, pure and simple. There are no fenced ranches that we know of that can guarantee a 195-point typical mule deer, no matter how much money a person has. Guides in the western states are more concerned with their overall success rates than with taking one or two trophy-class animals a year, and so they take representative heads for their clients whenever they can, as a rule. Even those hunters who draw a special tag for a late-season or rut hunt may find several awfully nice bucks, but a book-class deer? Very few are taken even then. In fact, one very reputable booking agent we know quite well told us that he tells his clients that any heavy-antlered mule deer buck with some height to the rack with four points per side and a width of 25 inches is a keeper today. "The dream buck with heavy antlers and a thirty-inch rack is a fantasy anymore for all but a small handful of people today," he said.

And yet, it is possible to find real trophy-quality muleys throughout the animal's range. Some places are better than others, of course, and we'll talk about them shortly. Some places used to be good for big bucks, but have cooled off today for any number of reasons. They may have received too much hunting pressure in recent years, or there may have been a severe winter die-off. Man may have encroached upon the habitat to the degree that most of the deer have flat up and left for greener pastures, places that might offer a safer life but not the nutrients needed to grow huge sets of antlers.

And there are very few sportsmen who are willing to bite the bullet and put in the time and effort required in hunting for trophy bucks. The true trophy hunter might go an entire season without ever firing a shot, holding out for a monster. More than likely that person hunts more than one state a year, if he can swing the time. And time is something that separates the vast majority of would-be trophy hunters from the very few who take the time necessary to get the job done.

True trophy hunting is a year-round process consisting of much more than just going deer hunting. There's research on new areas to be done, and pre-season scouting, and time spent at the range sharpening skills with rifle and bow. The real trophy hunter is always looking over the next ridgeline for that magic pocket of whopper bucks. He'll never find it, of course, but he might find a real monster every now and again and besides, it's the hunting that's the point, anyway. There's constant fiddling with gear, to make sure nothing breaks down during the precious few days the hunting seasons are actually open. A year-round fitness program keeps the serious hunter in shape to tackle the steep, mountainous, wide-open country big bucks call home. He studies game department regulations from the animal's entire range, looking for special hunts that may offer him a little extra edge. He applies for all the tags he can.

Of course, the key to all this is hunting in areas where there actually might be a trophy-class buck or two. As one writer of some repute who takes some awfully nice elk and deer each year, once said when asked how he became such a terrific hunter: "Heck, I'm really nothing more than a mediocre hunter who happens to be hunting some good places. It's research and finding these pockets of good hunting that allow me to kill some pretty big animals every year, not the fact that I'm some sort of super hunter. I'm really more of a klutz."

Where, then, can you go out and, if you're lucky, find that monstrous mule deer buck of your dreams? Here's an around-the-map look at some areas that are producing some fine heads today.

It's very possible that the best place to find a real monster mule deer these days isn't even in the United States, but rather in Sonora, Mexico. There are some truly huge desert mule deer bucks coming from Sonora every year, something that will likely continue in coming years. We spoke more about the possibilities—and pitfalls—of hunting deer in Sonora in Chapters XI and XVI. Suffice it to say that, all things considered, this is probably the single best trophy mule deer area going today, bar none.

One of the lesser-known areas for good bucks is southeastern British Columbia, specifically in the Kootenay and Purcell mountain ranges. Long-time booking agent Jack Atcheson, Jr. calls this "the best place I know of today for a real trophy-class buck." The reason is that the deer aren't hunted all that hard, and have a chance to reach their full potential. The bigger bucks range as far north as the Williams Lake area. Best hunting occurs early, between September 1-15, while the bucks are above timberline. The catch is that nonresident aliens have to be guided here, and hunts are getting on the expensive side.

Montana kicks out some really good deer every year, too, with the northwestern portion of the state a good bet. The areas around Troy, Libby, and Eureka have some big deer, but it's rugged and tough to hunt. Along the Idaho border, near

Special-draw hunts during the late season are outstanding bets if you can draw a tag. Be sure and apply before deadlines have passed and that applications are correctly filled out.

This gray-faced buck was so old that his antler growth was actually in remission. But with a spread of 29-inches and six-inch bases, he's still much better than average today.

Darby, is another good choice. The Bitterroot and Cabinet mountain ranges still have some good bucks living in them. One of the biggest bucks I've heard of in recent years is a massive 273 6/8-point nontypical killed in the Powder River Breaks in 1988. There are very few truly great bucks east of the Continental Divide.

Idaho is a top choice right now for huge mule deer bucks. The southeastern corner of the state is a real "hot spot," and if you hunt with a bow the special draw late-season archery hunt is brutal, but you may see the biggest buck of your life. Ditto the November muzzleloader season. Adams County is where I killed my largest buck ever, a 29 1/2-incher, back in 1979, and it still is a good place to find an oversized animal. Bonneville County is also a winner, with a 286-point nontypical taken in 1985, and 198 2/8 typical and 237 3/8 nontypical bucks, both killed in 1988, as examples of what the area can produce.

Utah, once known as a prolific producer of big bucks, has fallen way off in the 1980s. However, the past few seasons have seen some true monsters come out, and wildlife managers think that trend will continue. One biologist told us that he caught a poacher this past year with an honest-to-God 50-incher in his possession! That deer was poached down near the Paunsegaunt special draw unit in southern Utah, an area that has kicked out several 30-inch-plus bucks in recent seasons. Uinta County has also produced some very good bucks recently, as evidenced by a 191 1/8-point typical shot there in 1988. Carbon County has been another good bet, with a non-typical 249 1/8-pointer coming from there in 1988. In addition, there are several special draw units in Utah and three high country special hunts, all of which are candidates as big-buck producers. The late-season muzzleloader hunt is a good one in this state.

Nevada is still a big secret to many deer hunters, though why this is so is amazing. Nevada offers some of the best overall mule-deer-hunting found anywhere (statewide success rates of over 50 percent, on the average), and the state is also known for some tremendous bucks. Even residents have to draw for a tag here, and the proportion of four-point bucks taken each fall is the best in the West. The northeastern part of the state around Elko is a prime spot for a big buck, with the Ruby Mountains also excellent. Careful research can help you find monster bucks in many other parts of this state.

Arizona is another comeback state for the trophy hunter. The Kaibab Plateau is once again producing some real big bucks, with units 12A and 12B the best bet. The catch is drawing a tag.

Colorado and record-book-class bucks have been synonymous for years, and more Boone & Crockett book entries have been taken there by far than anywhere else, including both the current No. 1 typical and nontypical heads. Today the book bucks are much harder to come by, but the genetics and habitat are there, and the deer are, too. It just may take some long, hard looking to find them.

Monsters like this in California? A special draw produced this monster non-typical in the Sierra Nevada range. Big bucks are definitely where you find them! (Photo by John Higley)

This muley weighed well over 300 pounds on the hoof, was 10 years old, and had six-inch antler bases. The area? Southeastern British Columbia, an excellent bet for a big buck today.

Historically, the largest number of monster bucks have come from the southwest region of the state, with the areas around Durango, Cortez, the Dolores River drainage, the Uncompahgre Plateau, the Grand and Battlement mesas still an excellent bet. The country is rugged as the day is long, and you'll have to work awfully hard for bucks there. The Flattops Wilderness Area is another excellent choice for a big buck, and the San Juan Mountains are steep and tough, but very promising. The northwest quarter of the state is likewise outstanding, but much of the better land is privately held and leased to outfitters or smaller hunting clubs. A plus in Colorado today is that there are several special draw hunts, and several three and four point antler restriction units that are allowing at least some of the bucks to mature before harvest.

Likewise, New Mexico has traditionally produced some very large muleys, and the chances of connecting there are still reasonable. The best areas for big bucks still lie in the northern portion of the state near Chama, although much of the better habitat is on private land. The Carson and Santa Fe national forests are worth looking into, but again the country is steep, rugged, and difficult to hunt.

Wyoming is another state that produced a few really big bucks in years past, but the news from there in recent seasons has been relatively quiet. That's not to say that there aren't any monster bucks left in Wyoming, because there certainly are. The back country areas of the Salt Range have produced a few 190-point-plus bucks in recent seasons, for example. A huge nontypical buck scoring 246 5/8 points was killed in 1988 in Lincoln County. Generally speaking, the largest bucks come from mountains along the western border. The No. 2 all-time typical buck came from the Hoback Canyon near Jackson, an area that's still a good one to hunt. And traditional areas like the Shoshone, Medicine Bow, and Bighorn national forests are well worth researching.

Oregon is overlooked by most as a potential producer of good mule deer bucks, but in the southeastern area actually holds some awfully big animals. The Steens Mountain and Trout Creek Mountains limited entry units are the places to investigate. It's flat, open sagebrush country.

In Washington, very few record book mule deer have ever been taken, but the Okanagan region, bordering British Columbia in the state's north-central area, is a sleeper. Look to the rugged slopes of the Cascade Mountains for trophy-class bucks, as valley deer are managed for numbers, not quality.

California is another state most people forget when it comes to big mule deer bucks, and rightfully so. Very few big bucks have been killed in this state in recent years, though a tremendous 307 7/8 nontypical buck was taken in 1988 in Shasta County. For trophy-class bucks, the Colorado River area holds some very large, and underhunted, burro deer (or desert mule deer, if you prefer to call them that), though the largest of this subspecies will probably never approach record book size. The northeast corner of the state, in special draw X-zones, are also reasonable bets for bigger-than-average bucks.

There are other areas that hold mule deer populations and some promise, but not when we're talking about really big bucks. Kansas, for example, has lots of potential, but it isn't currently open to nonresident hunting and the deer haven' yet fully reached their growth potential. Alberta holds some fairly nice bucks, bu they're few and far between, and traveling hunters are rightly concentrating on whitetails here. The same is true for Texas. In the Dakotas, deer are managed for quantity instead of quality, and big bucks are as rare as a two-headed nicke Nebraska's mule deer herd isn't really worth considering if big antlers are you dream. Ditto the Baja, California, peninsula.

The big bucks are not a product of yesterday. They are still available, though certainly not in the quantities found in the 1950s and 1960s. Today trophy buck are taken by those willing to work for them, and by those who enjoy the smiles of Lady Luck. When it's all said and done, it's wise to remember that, when i comes to hunting a true monster-class mule deer buck, it's much better to be lucky than good.

CHAPTER XVIII

AUGUST BUCKS

T he sweat dripped from my brow and into my eyes in a slow rhythm, each drop stingingly hot and as bothersome as the hum of the black flies and the buzz of the mosquitoes. My back was resting up against an ancient white oak, and though I was in the shade, the tiny thermometer on my pack frame registered 105 degrees. I took a sip from the water bottle and settled in. It was a bit after noon on the second Saturday of August, opening day of California's A-zone deer season, and I had lots of time to kill.

I was set up on a steep sidehill in the oak-grassland foothills of central California, four up-and-down miles from the road and a million miles from any other hunters. Across the canyon and slightly below me at a distance of about 300 yards was a little flat, three oaks guarding a tiny seep that was the only water for miles. I hadn't seen any deer at first light, but poking around the water source I had seen fresh sign, and I knew there would be deer here sometime today. I hoped they would arrive before dark.

Napping off-and-on throughout the afternoon, I woke occasionally and glassed the thick brushy country with about as much hope as I have of winning the lottery. Even in this scorching weather, deer move during the day, often to drink, but if they came this afternoon, they had done so while I was dreaming of ice cream and a cool ocean breeze.

At five o'clock I pulled at the canteen again and got comfortable, adjusting my position to keep totally in the comfort of the shade. My pack frame was in front, ready for use as a rifle rest, and the glasses began to work.

The first deer just appeared, a doe and fawn that materialized out of the head-high brush as if by magic a half-hour before sundown. They strolled along, eating acorns and nibbling at the chemise, their tails wagging as happily as a puppy dog having his ears scratched.

Fifteen minutes later a buck came into view. He had tall antlers, not quite as wide as his ears, with deep forks and no eyeguards. A classic Pacific buck, as my dad used to call them. These bucks often get no better than forked horns, but in country where *any* legal buck is a good one, this one was awfully good.

I laid the rifle across my pack frame and got comfortable. The wispy breeze was in my face, and I had at least 20 minutes before shooting light was gone. When the buck moved away from the heavy brush a bit and turned his shoulder towards me I squeezed the trigger. The 150-grain bullet from my battered old .30-06 took him through the heart, and after a quick kick of his heels and a hundred-yard dash, he fell.

The truck didn't come into view until a bit after 11:00 that night. Loaded with the boned-out carcass and antlers, my pack weighed a ton by then. I was hot and sweaty, and every pore in my body felt impregnated with dirt and grit. But the full moon was shining brightly, the stars were radiant, and the air had cooled to a comfortable 75 degrees. Better yet, the ice chest contained a chilled six-pack. I placed the meat on the ice, pulled a folding lawn chair out of the truck, and collapsed. The sleeping bag, foam pad, and hard ground could have been grandpa's feather bed. I slept with a slight smugness and awoke refreshed, if a bit sore.

The satisfaction of taking a buck during California's A-zone hunt is hard to describe to anyone who hasn't participated in this insanity. I've hunted it for over 20 straight years now, and though I've traveled and hunted all over the world, I still look forward to it as much, if not more, than any other hunting trip I make each year.

The challenge of the hunt is what makes it so interesting, especially if you're hunting on public land. The weather is awfully hot, often over 100 degrees at midday and rarely cooling to below 70 degrees at night, even in the area's most northern reaches. Deer spend very little time moving except at night, though you can often ambush them between 10:30 a.m. and 2:00 p.m. at a water hole. The insects can drive you mad, and the country is some of the most difficult you'll ever hunt. The cover is a mixture of oaks, scattered conifers, and several varieties of brush that merge into often impenetrable thickets that can stretch for miles. The ground cover is full of foxtails that get into your socks and poison oak that gets into everything.

Because of the temperatures and habits of the deer, I've often spent two or three hours before daylight climbing through the thick brush to reach a promising area that really will only be productive hunting for the first hour of the morning, then turned around and hiked the three hours back out. Even in the best areas you may go two or three weekends without even seeing a deer, let alone a legal buck. Heck, when I was in high school and college I can remember hunting entire seasons without seeing a legal buck (in California, a buck must have a fork on at least one antler to be legal). Memories like that are what help make harvesting an A-zone buck so satisfying.

The A-zone is massive. It stretches all the way from Mendocino County in the north to Ventura County in the south, a distance of well over 600 miles. At its widest point east to west, it covers over 200 miles. It is also California's most productive deer area in terms of bucks killed, with annual harvests usually a bit over 6000 animals. That number is deceiving, however. In 1987, for example, 59,259 hunters took 6077 bucks for a success rate of 10.3 percent.

Private ranches cover the majority of the A-zone, and it is private property that produces the best hunting by far. On many ranches the success rate can approach 100 percent. Factor that into the overall hunter success rate, and you begin to see the challenge of a do-it-yourself public land hunt in this area. The best public land hunting occurs in Lake, Mendocino, Monterey, Napa, San Luis Obispo, and Santa Barbara counties.

The season is a long one, too. If you're really adventurous, you may want to try hunting during the archery-only season, which usually runs from the second weekend in July until the end of the month. Try stalking a bedded buck in 100-degree heat over crackling-dry ground cover sometime! The rifle season runs from the second weekend in August through the next-to-last weekend in September. I've found the best hunting during the rifle season to occur during opening weekend, and again the last week of the season. These bucks often go into rut in late September, and if you help little old ladies across the street, eat your vegetables, and don't litter, you may be lucky enough to have the deer begin their rut during the last week of the season. I shot a very nice 19 1/2-inch forked-horn the last Saturday of the 1988 season in Monterey County—a buck that was seriously chasing a pair of does in and around a big patch of oaks at about 10:00 A.M.

Just what are these interesting deer we hunt in the A-zone? Technically they are called California mule deer. In the zone's northern reaches they interbreed with the Columbia blacktail. They are distinguished from both blacktails and other subspecies of mule deer by the black stripe that runs down the center of the tail, from top to bottom. Also, the metatarsal gland (located on the lower half of the deer's hind leg) is between three and five inches in length, but always over three inches (the maximum found on blacktails) and usually closer to four inches. North of the Monterey-Santa Cruz county lines, the deer are officially classified as Columbia blacktail.

In California mule deer, the antlers resemble those of other mule deer except that many never grow anything other than forked horns. In addition to the Pacific buck characteristics mentioned earlier, California mule deer may also grow to the more common 4x4 configuration with small eyeguards, though a 3x3 is seen more often. Nontypical antlers are very rare. The antlers are likewise small in relation to other mule deer. A buck with a 20-inch outside spread is a real gorilla. I've seen a few that reached a spread of 24 inches, but those bucks I can count on the fingers of one hand, and I've seen close to 500 different A-zone bucks in my lifetime.

Most hunting is spot-and-stalk hunting, with hunters working ridgelines and glassing openings at first and last light. The past few seasons I've been taking a pair of 15x60 Zeiss binoculars and setting them on a tripod, getting on top of the highest point I can find before daylight, and glassing for bedded bucks. It's a time-consuming and often frustrating process, but it works.

Taking a stand at a water hole is also a good hunting method, especially in a dry year. I've shot several bucks this way, and the more I hunt the A-zone, the more I believe in watching water holes at midday. If the area hasn't been disturbed by other hunters much, this tactic can be deadly.

In areas of thick brush, or hilly areas with a combination of oak trees and brush, small drives can also be productive. At my favorite A-zone spot, there's a small area we always drive. Two drivers are plenty, with a stander set on a cliff overlooking the deer's escape route. In a recent season my best hunting buddy and I were in the area with a friend we really wanted to see tag a buck, so we drove the area for him. At just the right moment he started shooting, and when we reached him we were fully ready to help with the field-dressing and carrying process. We found the poor fellow speechless. He'd missed a solid 23-incher four times at 80 yards. I'd seen the buck the previous year, and saw him again right after this season closed, but that was our only shot at him. Two days later we tried the same drill, and this time our buddy took a very nice 14-inch forked-horn.

Durwood Hollis is as good an A-zone hunter as I've ever met, and we hunt together often. His favorite method is what I call the "Hollis troll." He likes to move slowly along through the oaks and chest-high brush, poking in and around small pockets and bedding areas early and late in the day. Durwood sees lots of deer this way, and before the season is over, he always tags a nice buck.

Meat care is critical. In the intense heat, meat can spoil, in a matter of hours. No matter where you kill your deer, field-dress it immediately. If I'm in the back country, miles from my ice chest, I'll do one of two things. If there's a running stream nearby, I'll field dress the animal, then get the entire carcass down to the stream. There, I'll peel the hide off and put the entire carcass into the cooling stream, leaving it there overnight if it's an evening kill, or all day if I shot the deer in the morning. Only after the water has cooled the animal will I get it back to camp. At camp or at my vehicle, I always have an ice chest large enough to hold a boned-out deer and plenty of ice.

In terms of gear necessary for hunting this early season, one must be prepared for hot weather. That means carrying lots of water. One friend of mine, a very experienced A-zone hunter, got carried away and hiked further than he should have from the road one morning. As fate would have it, he killed not one but two bucks in the same spot that morning, but by the time he'd field-dressed them, the vigorous hiking, 100-degree heat, and lack of any water—he'd forgotten his canteen—had left him virtually dehydrated. He returned to camp without any meat in the throes of heat exhaustion, and at one point I thought we were going to have to rush him out to a hospital for treatment. By the time he revived and we reached the animals, both carcasses had spoiled.

It was a lesson learned the hard way. Now we rarely hunt alone, and always carry lots of water, pack frames, and the tools needed to bone meat out on the spot.

Rifles can be about anything you like, but the flatter shooting the cartridge, the

This is Robb's best "A" zone buck ever in over 20 years of hunting them. Unlike most mule deer subspecies, these "Pacific" bucks rarely grow more than forked antlers with no eyeguards.

The best habitat in California's "A" zone is rolling oak grassland country ideally suited for glassing. Deer densities are low, except on private lands, where hunting can be outstanding.

better off you'll be, and lightweight rifles will feel much better at the end of the day. I prefer a bolt action rifle in cartridges like .243, 6mm, .25-06, 7x57, .270, .280, .308, and .30-06.

One of the nice things about hunting the A-zone is that a guided hunt on private land is very, very inexpensive when compared to guided deer hunts in neighboring states. A fully guided hunt will usually run over a weekend, and the tab will be somewhere between $500 and $750 in most cases. Add to that the fact that many ranches hold good populations of wild boar, and for a few dollars more you can also take a hog. If you're an out-of-stater who doesn't know the ropes and would like to give it a try, a guided hunt is a good way to get started.

I've brought in some of my friends from out of state a time or two for the hunt. You know the type. They're the kind of guys who have hunted the Rockies all their lives, and when you tell them that this might be a bit tougher deal, they just sort of look down their noses and grin. After the first few days, when they've sweated buckets, swatted mosquitoes, and spent the evenings picking foxtails and burrs out of their socks for hours, that smug expression changes to one with a little more humility.

Most of these experienced deer hunters agree, once it's all said and done: Pound for pound, California's A-zone is the toughest deer hunt in the country, bar none. When I go hunting mule deer anywhere else in the West, I look for the biggest antlers I can find, and turn down lots of bucks before settling on one that I like. In the A-zone, if he's legal, he's good enough. And I'm awfully grateful for the opportunity.

CHAPTER XIX

THE "OTHER" MULE DEER

T he magazine that I work for, Petersen's Hunting, has always kept its offices in Los Angeles—which is a heck of a cross to bear for a guy who loves to hunt. But, as in most places, if you work at it hard enough, you find that there are all kinds of opportunities—and a megalopolis like Los Angeles is no different. The local hunting is out there, if you take the time to find it.

Over the years, we've found excellent quail hunting in the foothills and valleys surprisingly close to town, and we regularly take advantage of the year-round wild hog hunting in the coast range about three hours' drive from my house. (Three hours isn't exactly close, but after all, it is closer than any big-game hunting where I grew up, and it's also available at any time of the year.)

Now, the fact that California holds superb hunting opportunities remains a surprise to me; I'm a midwesterner, and after 15 years on the coast, I'm still a little awed by California's massive human population. It comes as no surprise to my coauthor, Bob Robb, who grew up out here—and so hasn't had to search nearly as hard for good hunting. But one of my favorite boasts is that I've taken good mule deer an hour north of Los Angeles—and an hour south as well. That's interesting enough, especially if big cities terrify you as much as they do me. But it's more interesting when you realize that those two bucks are of totally different subspecies—they're just two of the "other" mule deer that are ignored by most hunters—unless those hunters happen to live where those deer are found.

The taxonomic "splitters"—the biological train of thought that sees different subspecies in every slight regional antler or color variation—went wild with the whitetail, creating, as we have seen, fully 38 subspecies. The opposite camp, called the "lumpers," were more successful in combining all of our various mule deer into just a handful of recognized subspecies. The major subspecies is, of course, the Rocky Mountain mule deer, the largest and most widespread of our muleys. The much smaller Columbia blacktail of the Pacific coast has always been considered separate, and more recently the Sitka blacktail of Alaska and northern British Columbia has received the distinction it deserves. The desert mule deer, *Odocoileus hemionus crooki*, another very widespread and numerous mule deer, has not yet received separate recognition in the Boone & Crockett record book, but is recognized as a different deer by most knowledgeable hunters.

That takes care of four of our mule deer subspecies, but the "other" muleys—fully seven subspecies—are ignored and/or unknown. And some of them may not even exist. When the splitters held sway, the mule deer of extreme northeastern California and northwestern Nevada were called Inyo mule deer, said to be lighter in the horn and a bit smaller than typical Rocky Mountain muleys. Even though their high Sierras habitat is typical high country mule deer range, northern California has produced very few deer that can compete with deer from the Rocky Mountain states—but that's hardly sufficient reason to classify a deer as different. Today most biologists lump the Inyo deer in with Rocky Mountain mule deer, and that's probably where they should be.

Similarly, the Tiburon Island and Cedros Island muleys of Mexico have been "lumped" with their mainland subspecies—which also seems proper. But there's another mysterious mule deer that remains in some doubt, plus there are three definite and distinct southwestern muleys. The odd one is the burro deer, *O. h. eremicus*, a subspecies said to inhabit the desert mountains of southeastern California and perhaps southwestern Arizona. Deer were never common in this region; it's some of America's most inhospitable terrain. Deer do exist out there, in certain isolated hills and mountain ranges, and they're still hunted.

The very occasional huge buck is taken—and controversy remains over just what these deer are. On the east, the so-called burro deer's range butts up against Arizona's desert mule deer. It's quite possible that the burro deer is just that—a *crooki*. However, the long-gone biologists who identified him felt that he was larger, shorter in the leg, and blockier in the body than the *crooki*. So they named him the burro deer (not, as one otherwise-excellent reference would have it, the burrow deer!). And he remains an enigma. I have always meant to travel to the dry mountains west of Yuma to hunt this deer, and perhaps one day I'll get around to it. It isn't really that far from where I live. If I shoot one, I'll call him a burro deer—but I don't know any more than anyone else whether or not they really exist as a different type of muley.

The California mule deer, *O. h. californicus*, is in no question at all. This pale-colored mule deer, smaller than Rocky Mountain deer but much larger than the blacktail, occupies a large expanse of country throughout most of central California. To the northwest he eventually runs into the blacktail deer, and a very large intergrade area exists between the two deer. The deer in this area are the "Pacific bucks" discussed in the previous chapter. To the northeast he butts up against the Rocky Mountain deer, and to the east of California's San Bernardino Mountains he runs into deserts so parched that no deer exist at all. To the south his range runs into that of the southern mule deer, a subspecies even less well-known.

The California mule deer is the deer I have hunted just to the north of Los Angeles. There, and in the ranges to the northwest and to the east, the California muley exists as a pure mule deer subspecies. Much farther up the coast, to the northwest, you get into that broad intergrade area between California muleys and blacktails. Up there we just call them "coastal deer"—and indeed they're a grab bag of different tail configurations, variable body size, and antlers that are rarely impressive no matter what you choose to call them. But in the little back country

Boddington took this southern mule deer in Orange County, south of Los Angeles. The southern muley is a small, very dark subspecies ranging from southern California to northern Baja.

The deer of California's central coast are generally a mixture of California mule deer and blacktail. This is a great coastal buck—but he's not a pure blacktail.

that remains, the California mule deer can grow to impressive size. No, he won't compete with Colorado's giant bucks, and no California mule deer has or ever will make the minimum score for entry in the Boone & Crockett book. But he can develop nontypical antler formations, and as a typical he will occasionally develop a spread approaching 30 inches.

I can well remember, just a few years ago, the splash in the local papers when a hunter brought a 28-inch 4x4 out of Big Tujunga Canyon—literally in sight of greater Los Angeles. And I've seen some of the heads that knowledgeable, persistent, hard-headed hunters take out of wilderness areas in Ventura County, just to the north of Malibu. They're there, and it's unfortunate that these deer receive recognition in no one's record book.

My hunting for them has been mostly on the vast Tejon Ranch, a cattle ranch covering nearly a half-million acres, lying an hour's drive due north from Los Angeles. Ranging from the valley floor to over 7,000 feet, the Tejon is one of those areas you refer to as a "deer factory." It is huntable, both on a season-lease basis by long-term lessees and on a day-lease basis.

We hunted a foothill region of deep-cut canyons with sagebrush hillsides and brushy bottoms, deer country that could have been Montana, Wyoming, or Nevada. And indeed the deer were there, and they still are. They're present, too, in the San Bernardino Mountains just east of Los Angeles. My taxidermist, Tom Radoumis, went up there "somewhere" for just a day last year, and they brought out three nice bucks—including a dandy 4x4. Nope, they won't tell me where they went.

South of Los Angeles, in the foothills of extremely congested Orange County, I have been fortunate on a couple of occasions to hunt the little southern mule deer, *O. h. fuliginatus*. This deer, smaller and significantly darker in color than the California muley, range from Orange County down through San Diego County and halfway down Mexico's Baja Peninsula. As is the case with much of America's best deer hunting, a cherished "in" on private land is the best way to hunt a southern mule deer—but not the only way. The rugged mountains just east of southern California's overdeveloped beaches hold good numbers of deer, and there is some public land. The vast Camp Pendleton Marine Corps base, just south of San Clemente, is a paradise for deer. I used to hunt it regularly when I was stationed there—and civilians have a goodly number of permits available to them by drawing.

It's possible that the very best southern mule-deer-hunting remaining is in the remote mountains of Mexico's Baja Peninsula, where the *O. h. fuliginatus* range halfway down. Uncontrolled meat hunting has unquestionably hammered the deer in Baja's settled coastal areas, but the interior mountains are vast, forbidding, and untouched. Some Mexican friends have sent me photographs of big nontypicals they take regularly in the northern Baja. That's the good news; the

The burro deer may be a separate subspecies, or may be desert mule deer—but they can get big. Gilbert Clemens took this state bow record on the California side of the Colorado River. (Photo by Jim Matthews)

bad news is that there's almost no way for an outsider to hunt deer in the Baja. There are numerous bird-shooting outfitters, but unlike in Sonora, no organization for big game at all. In the past it might theoretically have been possible to hunt on your own, but at this writing it seems certain that, from now on, nonresident, non-Mexican hunters will be required to hire a licensed guide/outfitter for all Mexican hunting.

I have a pretty good southern mule deer mounted on the wall to my immediate left. He's a 4x3 with good eyeguards, ear-wide at 19 inches. He's next to my best blacktail, and the antlers are quite similar in size. The capes are totally different; the southern deer has bigger ears and a shorter face, and he isn't gray at all; his coat runs from dark tan under the ears to very dark chocolate on chest and shoulders. I shot him early one morning as he crossed a chaparral ridge, and as I field-dressed him I could see the beginnings of rush hour traffic far away towards the coast.

The last of the "other" mule deer, the Peninsula muley, is a great unknown to American hunters—except that it's certain he exists, and is different. *O. h. peninsulae* ranges from between a third and halfway down the Baja Peninsula all the way to the southern tip. There must be a wide intergrade area between the peninsula deer and the southern deer, but very little information is available on Baja's deer. It is believed that *peninsulae* is fairly scarce, no doubt due to uncontrolled hunting—but I'll bet there are big bucks who have never seen a man in the remote mountains of the southern Baja.

The peninsula muley is supposed to have a significantly different appearance from the southern mule deer. About the same size, and thus yet another smallish subspecies, he is pale where the southern deer is dark. Antler size, well, who knows? He's for darn sure not going to produce B & C-quality antlers, but should produce typical 4x4 antlers. And if he's like the southern deer, nontypicals won't be uncommon. I suppose it doesn't matter too much; the peninsula deer is the only mule deer subspecies that cannot be readily hunted today.

As is the case with whitetail deer, it would be a real mess if any record book recognized and separated all our different mule deer, so I don't have a problem with all of our "other" muleys being ignored. But it does seem a shame that only the large Rocky Mountain subspecies can make the book, especially when the others offer equally interesting hunting for a deer that's just as pretty, if not quite so big.

CHAPTER XX

MULE DEER HUNTING LIKE THE GOOD OLD DAYS

A s hunters, we should be proud of this century's conservation efforts. After all, we did it: We ended the market hunting, imposed strict limits on ourselves, and even created the concept of ethical hunting—the "fair chase" so important to our sport. And we put our money where our mouth was, in license fees, in Pittman-Robertson Act taxes on our firearms and ammunition, and in the voluntary contributions that sportsmen have always given so willingly. And it all worked. Coast to coast, species after species was brought back, in many cases from the very brink of extinction, to relative plenty.

The extinction of the pronghorn was predicted at the turn of the century, and now he dots the prairies. Elk, too, were almost lost—but the nucleus herd in Yellowstone Park provided transplants that have proliferated throughout the Rockies and much of their historic range. Whitetail deer are far more common now than at any time in this continent's history. The truth is that, in the case of whitetail deer, the good old days are right now. Proof of this is in the hallowed top ten in Boone & Crockett—which has been almost completely turned over with new heads in the last couple of decades. In fact, one of the last truly old heads that still places high is the Jordan head, the wonderful typical that has stood as the world record since 1916.

The mule deer, too, benefits immensely from modern game conservation. Like the whitetail, the mule deer sank from a historic population in the millions to something like 500,000 in the early years of this century, and the road back was slow. In the mid-1930s my father spent his summers wrangling stock on a dude ranch near Frazier Park, Colorado—fine mule deer country. In those days, he never remembers laying eyes on a deer. But the mule deer did come back, slowly at first and then very quickly. The years during and just following World War II saw a tremendous mule deer population explosion, and the ensuing years were indeed the golden age of mule-deer-hunting.

With the whitetail, the good old days are now. But with the mule deer, they're over. Yes, we may now have about as many deer now, in raw numbers, as there were in the 1940s. But the great days of mule-deer-hunting lasted from the postwar years until, at the very latest, about 20 years ago. The differences are obvious to anyone who traveled the Rocky Mountain states in the 1960s. Today there are many more people hunting mule deer; and these deer aren't as adaptable as whitetails. The ski resorts and condominiums that dot the slopes aren't good news to the mule deer, nor is the mineral exploration the last few decades has brought.

A quick look at the records gives a clue to mule-deer-hunting's halcyon days.

Deer Hunting Coast to Coast

While the top spots for whitetails have been rapidly turning over, not so with mule deer. Almost all of the finest heads were taken between the 1940s and 1972, the year the reigning world record typical was taken. Since then the great mule deer have come slowly, if at all.

Harvest figures, too, are revealing. Every year across whitetail-dom, state after state posts record harvests. Not so the mule deer states. Colorado's record harvest was 1963. Idaho's was 1968. New Mexico's was 1970. Utah's was 1972. Literally dozens of whitetail states have gone to multiple-deer limits, necessary to increase the harvests and maintain a balanced herd. When I first hunted Montana in 1972 it was among the last of the Rocky Mountain states to have a general two-deer limit, and that ended a long time ago. Instead, the wave of the future is across-the-board permit drawings, not only for nonresidents, as is the case in Wyoming, but for everybody. Arizona led that parade in 1971, and Nevada followed in 1975.

Today there remain few mule deer states in which you can, without a lot of prior planning, just buy a license and go hunting. Colorado is one, of course—the trade-off for unlimited licenses is very short seasons. But it isn't like it was 30 years ago, nor will it probably ever be that way again.

I missed that era. Oh, I suppose you could say that I caught the tail end of it. In the mid 1960s we drove to Wyoming and simply bought deer licenses, and in the early 1970s I bought right over the counter Montana combo licenses that had two deer tags as well as an elk tag. But we were too unsophisticated during that time to take advantage of a bounty whose days were numbered. I have friends who not only lived it, but played it to the limit—and I marvel at their tales of the mule-deer-hunting that was.

My good friend Bob Tatsch, now in his sixties, started hunting Utah in the postwar years. In those days the 30-inch mule deer wasn't a grand quest—it was the kind of buck you expected to see on a normal hunt. And once you shot him, you could simply go to town and buy another tag. It wasn't so much, I suspect, that the hills held a great many more deer than they hold today. But there were much fewer hunters in search of them. The buck/doe ratios were higher, and more bucks lived to an older age. Bob has told me the numbers of bucks he saw taken in a single day, and I won't relate the figures because they seem too preposterous. It's been said, with some justification, that Utah sold her deer herd through the 1960s and into the 1970s—and that state isn't alone.

In those days was born the legend of the dumb mule deer, the deer that always stopped to look back, the deer that carried a magnificent rack but was almost laughably easy to hunt. Older mule deer hunters still remember that deer, but the current generation knows better. Today's muley hunter knows that an older, mature mule deer has become a will o' the wisp. He won't look back, and he'll be found in some of the nastiest real estate in his territory.

Hunters like Bob Tatsch can well remember the golden years, when good bucks were readily hunted not only in the Rockies but in now-crowded areas like the Malibu Mountains out of Los Angeles. It's a different world today. (Photo by Bob Tatsch)

Deer Hunting Coast to Coast

It's unlikely that the mule deer was ever dumb. He was just unsophisticated, and he was at the height of a population cycle that may never be repeated. Some back-to-back hard winters, increased human population in mule deer country, added to a steady increase in hunting pressure, and suddenly mule-deer-hunting was a different game. Hunters had to work harder and hunt smarter. But the numbers of big, mature bucks as percentages of the total herd will never be the same. Part of the problem, of course, is management goals. In many states, the public has demanded hunter success, "a deer for every hunter." Management for quantity rather than quality can indeed work, and has produced a lot of deer—but it will rarely produce big bucks.

Nevada is one of the few states that has managed to sell quality game management—but of course, it had one of America's smallest human populations to sell it to. In that state, hunters have come to accept that they can't have a deer tag each and every year. But if they get one, the odds swing in their favor; success rates are extremely high. More importantly, across the board, the buck/doe ratio is second to none—and in some units 4x4 muleys make up more than half of the harvest. And this in an era where an "average" mule deer buck harvested is under 2 1/2 years old. Arizona, too, is producing the kind of bucks she was famous for 40 years ago. Not as many, it's true, but as big. So, in isolated spots, there's still hope—if you can draw a tag.

A big mule deer is one of America's most magnificent animals, and a really great buck just might be this continent's most difficult trophy today. I've taken a few decent bucks—never one as good as I would really like—and I've worked my tail off for every one of them. Whenever I'm in mule deer country, I dream about the way it must have been back in the good old days, when the young bucks I was seeing so readily might have been dandies, and the average decent bucks I sweated for might have been record-class mossyhorns. And just a couple of times, in odd little pockets of country, I've gotten a glimmer of what the good old days must have been like.

To recapture that feeling, you must find an area that offers good, classic mule deer habitat, country that can support good numbers of deer and keep them in good shape—yet is lightly hunted. Lightly enough hunted that the deer aren't pressured. And the bucks live long enough—in a relatively unpressured state—to grow to full maturity and full antler potential. Such places are rare. In Colorado and northern New Mexico's classic big buck country, such places are gone. The big bucks are there, a few of them—but they're the survivors, and you can't hunt them the way mule deer used to be hunted. A few seasons ago, the remote mountains of Sonora, old Mexico, were such a pocket—but the pocket was discovered, and the deer learned quickly. I'm told that the canyons of southern Idaho are very promising. Certainly that area has been producing huge bucks—but I have a feeling they come hard there.

Mule Deer Hunting Like The Good Old Days

Without question, pockets of relatively untouched mule deer exist here and there throughout the West. They're there because few people know about them, and I'm not one of them. The Ute Indian Reservation is said to be such a place. So are some very large, very well-managed ranches in Utah. The Arizona Strip country remains largely untouched, big country holding very few deer—but still producing some monsters. The Kaibab Plateau is back, and the monsters are certainly there—if you can draw a tag.

There are two such pockets that I've been fortunate to find and which have given me the same hunting experience with mule deer as I suspect old-timers had. These two areas are widely separated. Neither has the habitat or herd genetics required to produce the very largest racks—but both areas, at least when I was there, were producing the best racks the deer were capable of, and the deer behaved the way I've always heard mule deer are supposed to. And that is a great thrill in itself!

One of these little hotspots was a pocket of country in the Kootenays of southeastern British Columbia, in a guide area controlled by Lloyd Harvey. B.C. isn't known for big mule deer, nor should it be. But the province does have the odd piece of perfect muley country, and this is one of them—a series of basins and bowls, some of it deep timber and some of it an old burn. It's remote enough that the resident hunters don't bother it too much, and it's stayed good because Lloyd takes care of it; annually he won't harvest much more than a half-dozen deer. By doing that, his average buck is 7 1/2 years old! Once in a great while he'll take a "Booner," but British Columbia deer generally lack the antler genetics to readily make the book. Instead, he takes old, gnarly, heavy-horned, trophy deer.

I had been moose hunting and had just a day left after we got our moose. We went up to take a look at the deer country, knowing time was too short. From a high ridge Lloyd showed me several bucks; we picked out a nice 4x4 and made our move. Partway there, on a ridge that had been burned over years before, I glanced to my right. Little more than a hundred yards away, just walking away at a slight angle, were two different mule deer bucks. Both of them were among the nicest deer I've ever seen. Lloyd was two steps ahead of me and he hadn't seen them. I should have knelt down and shot either deer; it wouldn't have much mattered which one.

Buck fever may well have set in. For some reason it seemed important that I catch Lloyd's attention before I shot—and in a situation like that nobody need be that courteous. By the time I got his attention the deer were a bit farther out, and were just about to go over a ridge. They didn't exactly look back—but they did hesitate slightly. And I shot the one that seemed to be the largest. The problem was that I didn't shoot him very well. The shot had felt good, but there was little blood. And then no blood at all. The bottom line is that we just plain lost that deer, and he was a dandy.

Deer Hunting Coast to Coast

A year later Lloyd called me on his radio phone. He'd been chasing an elk in the same basin, and he'd found our deer. He wasn't 50 yards from where we had lost the track—but he'd done what hurt deer never do—turned uphill. The antlers were in unusually good shape; just one tine had been chewed on by a porcupine. I haven't seen them yet; they're up at Atcheson's Taxidermy in Montana—but that's a mounted head that will have both memories and lessons behind it. Next fall I'm going back to that little pocket of country. The deer will act right, and perhaps I can, too!

The other spot I've been to where mature mule deer act the way the old timers claim they did—is even more oddball: California's Santa Rosa Island. The deer aren't native there; they were introduced by the island's former owner in the 1920s. In the decades since they've spread out over most of the 55,000-acre island, and to some extent they've unquestionably become inbred and slightly stunted as well. However, genetically these deer aren't our small California bucks; the original transplants came out of Arizona's Kaibab Plateau—before the Kaibab's well-known population crash.

The island also has a wonderful herd of Roosevelt elk, and that was what took me there the first time. On that trip I discovered the deer, and it's the deer that have taken me back—and will again. It isn't a place where there's a chance for a book-quality buck; these island deer tend to have excellent mass but just reasonable spreads into the high 20s. Some of the points are also often short, and the Kaibab influence shows itself with odd "cheater" points on many racks. It really doesn't matter if they book out or not; B & C wouldn't accept them in any case, since no hunting license is required.

But in Santa Rosa's bottomless canyons and rimrocked ridges, they're a great game animal. And in spite of a decade of very modest hunting pressure, they don't act like any mule deer I've ever seen. My hunting partner, Darroll Smith, stalked and shot a lovely typical 4x4 bedded high up on the rimrock one day—and it was an absolute classic of the way mule-deer-hunting is supposed to be.

On that same hunt, I missed a beautiful, wide-antlered buck, and we watched him vanish into a deep canyon system choked with oak brush. Under most circumstances today, that buck would be gone—there just aren't second chances with modern muleys. But we decided to give it a try. Darroll and outfitter Wayne Long went around to the far side while I hiked across a side canyon and up the far ridge, hoping to see into the canyon where the deer had vanished. I found him surprisingly quickly; he had gone up a narrow side canyon and bedded in the lee of a big boulder. It was a logical place, it's true—but how often do you really find big bucks where you expect to?

On a subsequent trip, hunting alone, I located a magnificent island buck out on a sand dune peninsula. He was lacking a point on one side, making him a very

To find the big bucks today you have to look for hidden pockets of country off the beaten track. They're often high and incredibly rough—but they're there if you work at it.

A backpack camp in the high country is one of the best ways to seek big mulies today. Such a hunt takes lots of planning and physical conditioning, and is not for the inexperienced—but can yield muleys like the good old days.

heavy, very wide 4x3 with good eyeguards, but I was undecided until I got close. When I did get in close and had decided this was a buck I wanted on the wall, a fog bank rolled in and I lost him. Heck, I darn near got lost myself. Visibility went down to inches, and there was no choice but to back off and try later. The amazing thing was that I found him later that afternoon, and his mounted head is a classic Santa Rosa Island buck.

The future isn't good for that particular place. The Vail family sold the island to the Nature Conservancy, and it's becoming part of the Channel Islands National Park. The Vails have retained a cattle lease—and in turn sublet hunting rights to Wayne Long's Multiple Use Managers, the firm that started the hunting on the island in the 1970s. For now, it remains a place where the buck/doe ratio is high, the bucks grow old, and once in a great while a mature buck will even pause for that last backward glance muleys used to be famous for. But it won't last; long-term plans call for returning the island to its state before European settlement, which means removal (read that "eradication") of the deer, elk, and wild hogs which presently abound.

There are undoubtedly many hidden little hotspots where mule deer exist as they did in the good old days—whether 20 years or 200 years or 2,000 years ago. The problem is that they're fragile. Man will end Santa Rosa's hunting, but a hard winter could radically change Lloyd Harvey's deer situation. And across the board, in all the little pockets I don't know about, things could change overnight. Too many people find such the deer, a hard winter reduces them, they become overpopulated and suffer a die-off—or any combination of calamities. Fortunately mule deer still inhabit a very broad range, and that range contains much rugged, untraveled country. Secret big buck hideouts may be lost to hunters every year, but somewhere out there others are building up, waiting to be discovered. If you find such a hotspot, cherish it—and keep your mouth shut!

CHAPTER XXI

COLUMBIA BLACKTAILS

I remember the day as if it were my first kiss. It was a typical November morning in Humboldt County, California, cold and so foggy that you couldn't see across the street. The weatherman had predicted clear, sunny skies for the day, and that meant be patient, sit by the fire, and wait.

We knew where we wanted to hunt, and how. The big, open meadow surrounded by old-growth fir, oak, and redwood and known as cow prairie was only a hour's easy hike from the main road, and that's where Charles Barnum and I would set up shop for the day. "We want to wait and let the thermals start working up anyway," Charles said over the first cup of hot chocolate. "No use getting anxious."

That was easy for him to say. The hunt had already started out badly for me, the airlines having sent both my duffel and rifle case to the middle of next week. I was lounging in borrowed clothes and a pair of boots a half-size too large, trying to get familiar with Charles' old European .243. I had visions of not being able to get out at all.

But soon the sun began to burn through the mist, and we were off. I was hunting on the Barnum's 17,000-acre Redwood Creek Ranch, and Charles knew it intimately. The hike to cow prairie was like a stroll in the park, and by 8:30 we were in position to begin glassing. Cow prairie consisted of low-growth grass and small hills and bumps, all set on a 20-degree slope. In that terrain, it was easy for an animal to be hidden from us, even though it was really standing right out in the open.

We were looking over a small group of cattle feeding placidly in the meadow when Charles spotted the first does. A few minutes later he spotted a buck, and one glance at him through my 10x40s was all it took to say, "We need to get closer and have a better look." A half-mile circular hike and a 100-yard belly crawl later, I was within 80 yards of the buck and four does.

The buck's head was down behind a small hump as he fed with not a care in the world. I put the glasses on him, and when he lifted his head I was afraid the pounding of my heart would spook him all by itself. He was a heavy-antlered 3x4, with a spread that later measured 21 inches. I didn't move again until he put his head down for another bite, and then only to drop the binoculars and bring the rifle to bear. When the head came up again I shot, the 100-grain bullet taking him right through the sternum and literally knocking the deer head over heels.

That buck, taken in 1986, was by far the best blacktail buck I had ever taken, and I have hunted them pretty seriously for over 20 years in three states. In all those years, taking small bucks has always been my fate. That never dampened my enthusiasm for hunting blacktails, but instead seemed to fuel my interest. If there's a tougher trophy-class buck for the average deer hunter to take than the Columbia blacktail, I've yet to hunt him.

Columbia blacktail inhabit a relatively narrow band that hugs the Pacific coast from northern British Columbia down through Washington, Oregon, and northern California. It is a very adaptive deer, living in the densest, wettest rain forests on the continent, but also in mountainous forests and even dry, open chaparral. They are a small deer when compared to the other subspecies of mule deer, with which they freely interbreed. Mature bucks will weigh in the neighborhood of 140 pounds on the hoof, stand 36 to 38 inches high at the shoulder, and measure perhaps five feet in overall length. The coat is very similar to that of other mule deer, except that the summer and early fall coat will tend to be a bit more on the reddish side. The winter coat turns a mild gray color.

A true blacktail can be discerned from other mule deer subspecies in two ways. The first is the tail, which averages 9 to 10 inches in length from the rump to the hair tips. The top of the tail is a deep brownish-black color, a hue that extends all the way to the tip. The underside of the tail is an off-white. Together with the Sitka blacktail, it is the only mule deer subspecies with this all-black tail. As far as biologists can tell, blacktails do not use their tails for signaling, as do the various whitetail subspecies.

The other way to tell a true blacktail is by measuring the metatarsal gland, located about midway between the hock and hoof on the hind leg. A blacktail has a metatarsal gland that measures 2 1/2 to 3 inches in length, and it is found midway down the foot. A mule deer has a metatarsal gland measuring closer to 5 inches long, and it is located well above and extends down to the middle of the foot. Cross-breeds have metatarsal glands that fall somewhere in between these two measurements.

Blacktail bucks carry the trademark bifurcated antler configuration of the other mule deer subspecies, but on a smaller scale. In my years of hunting, I've noticed two distinct types of antlers. The first are the aforementioned mule-deer-type racks, which sport 3 or 4 points per side and a small eyeguard. The other is what my father used to call a "Pacific buck." These deer never carry anything other than a forked-horn, or 2-points-per-side, rack, with no eyeguards at all. I've seen Pacific bucks with antlers over 20 inches wide, 18 inches tall, and bases of near 5 inches. The uneducated hunter might turn down a buck like this, but to those who live in blacktail country, this is a deer to be proud of.

If you're a true trophy hunter, you'll be looking for a buck that has 4 points per side, an outside spread of 20 inches, and antlers at least 16 inches in height. The individual points should measure between 3 and 6 inches in length, and a good way to judge a buck through your optics is to look at the back points. If they are three to four inches long, and the buck has everything else, he's a real keeper. The

Blacktails can be distinguished from other mule deer subspecies by an all-black upper tail, as well as a difference in the length of their metatarsal glands.

A true Boone & Crockett-class blacktail buck, like this 128-point deer Robb shot in northern California in 1988, is one of the most difficult trophies to find in all of North America.

other key to a record book-class blacktail is the eyeguards; they need to be over one inch in length, and finding them over two inches long is rare.

If you've never hunted blacktails before, don't expect to see a buck like this. They just don't grow on trees. More than likely you'll find small forked-horns and three-pointers, if you find any bucks at all, and more often than not they'll be moving through thick cover and give you no time to judge them. In blacktail hunting, most three-point and any four-point buck is a taker, a buck to be proud of. When I'm hunting general seasons on public land, I personally find it very difficult to turn down any reasonable forked-horn buck.

The boundaries dividing Columbia blacktail from other mule deer subspecies differ slightly, depending upon whether you follow the dictates of the Boone & Crockett Club or Safari Club International. If that sort of distinction is important to you, be sure and check out where you'll be hunting before you go. Generally speaking, the differences occur in California. Boone & Crockett draws the east-west line along Interstate 5 from its junction with state highway 299 in the north, south to the town of Anderson where I-5 crosses the Sacramento River, following the river to its confluence with the San Joaquin River, which is then followed to the southern border of Stansilaus County. From there the line runs west to the eastern border of Santa Clara County. The east and south borders of Santa Clara County are then followed to the southern border of Santa Cruz County, which runs to the edge of Monterey Bay on the Pacific Ocean. Safari Club International is a bit more liberal with its boundaries in some areas.

One of the reasons trophy hunting for blacktails is so difficult is that there are very, very few guides who offer a true Columbia blacktail hunt. That's because most guides don't see a large client demand for blacktail hunting and because the success of such hunts can't be guaranteed. The only two guides that I'm aware of at this writing offering quality Columbia blacktail hunts are Californians Charles Barnum of Eureka, and George Flournoy of Standish. There are a few other California ranches and guides that advertise blacktail hunts, when in fact they are hunting outside the recognized boundary areas for the species. Before you book a hunt with any outfitter advertising Columbia blacktail, be sure to check on exactly where you'll be doing the actual hunting.

I know of no outfitters in either Washington or Oregon offering blacktail, though rumblings that may change are heard every year. And while there is some blacktail hunting available in British Columbia, in much of the better areas (Vancouver Island, for example) wolf predation has knocked the deer populations down so badly that it isn't really a good enough bet to travel there and make a blacktail your primary quarry.

Hunting blacktails on your own is a tremendous challenge. Unfortunately in California, where I do most of my hunting, most of the better blacktail country is found on private property. For an outsider to walk in and get permission to hunt

The only thing keeping this superb buck from making the Boone & Crockett book is a lack of eyeguards. Ludo Wurfbain took the deer on northern California's Redwood Creek Ranch. (Photo by Ludo Wurfbain)

Blacktail are very cautious and secretive animals. Care must be taken when setting up stands and blinds overlooking open meadows and forest trails to ensure maximum concealment.

this land is next to impossible, and that's a shame. I have several friends who routinely take book-class blacktail bucks from private land in northwestern California, but none of the rest of us will ever see that opportunity.

For the adventurous and hardy hunter who has a pack animal or doesn't mind a backpack hunt, two areas in California produce some top-notch blacktail hunting. They are the Trinity Alps Primitive Area and the Marble Mountains Wilderness Area. Both hold excellent blacktail populations, but the country is as rugged and tough as any in North America, the cover in places virtually impenetrable, and concentrations of deer are not easy to find. However, the chances of harvesting a very nice buck here are about as good as on any public lands in the deer's entire range.

I've hunted the Trinity Alps three times on backpack hunts over the years, killing two nice bucks. The only time I didn't take a deer was during an archery hunt, and it wasn't because I didn't see anything, either. I just couldn't seem to get any closer than 75 yards.

In California, Oregon, and Washington, the best blacktail hunting occurs over the opening weekend of the general rifle seasons (usually in October), the final week of that season, and again during some special late-season hunts.

California designates its special late-season hunt as XS-1, with 25 permits issued by lottery for the Shasta-Trinity region. Hunter success runs right at 75 percent, and some very good bucks are taken each year. In Oregon, a special muzzleloader hunt runs from late November into mid-December, and it is a winner. Bucks are rutting, and often they can be seen chasing does out in open agricultural fields and away from the heavy timber where they spend the rest of the year. An archery season also runs from mid-November through early December, and that's a hunt I hope to try this year. Two hunting buddies, Dwight Schuh and Bill Krenz, hunted it in 1987, and they both rattled in and killed very nice bucks. Washington state also offers late November start dates for special muzzleloader and archery hunts in the blacktail areas, and both are good bets.

How you hunt blacktails depends largely on where you're at. In the mountainous forest country, spot-and-stalk hunting is my favorite tactic. I like to get high before sunup, set my optics up, and glass any open meadows and pockets I can see right at first light, and again right at dusk.

In the rainforests of Oregon and Washington, still hunting is popular but awfully tough. Still hunters in eastern whitetail country have several advantages over blacktail hunters in that their seasons are usually late; most of the leaves have dropped off the trees and the ground cover is minimal. In the rainforests the trees are conifers that never drop a needle, and the ground cover is made up of ferns, berry tangles, and other miserable stuff that makes one wonder how to get through it without a machete. You can jump a buck at under 40 yards and literally never see it. A successful still hunter is slow motion personified.

Stand hunting is a good bet in the thick cover. The problem is determining just where the stand should be placed. A mature blacktail buck has a very small home range, and travels little during the day for the simple reason that all the food, water, and cover he needs is right at hand. I've seen some major trails in the forests of Oregon and Washington, and took a big Washington state Pacific buck some years back by sitting on the same trail for three weekends in a row (this was after one weekend of learning the hard way that still hunting was definitely not my thing!). I have some friends who like to place a stand at the junction of two or more major trails in the deep woods, especially when the woods are full of other would-be still hunters.

In the late season, rattling has proven to be a fairly effective and very much under-utilized way to bring a good buck to you. Dwight Schuh and Bill Krenz discovered that they had to climb a tree before rattling, though, because the country was so thick that if they rattled a buck up from the ground they just plain never saw the deer before it saw them and spooked. Charles Barnum and I experimented with a deer decoy in November, 1988 on his ranch, using a medium-sized three-point decoy placed in an open meadow. Bucks that came within sight of the decoy came in for a closer look, too. We didn't give the decoy enough time to really get a feel for what it can do, but I saw enough in one week to convince me that it has lots of potential, especially in areas where the buck/doe ratio is high.

And in most of the Columbia blacktail's range, that is the case. Biologists I spoke to in northwestern California told me that they felt, if anything, that blacktail deer were actually underhunted in much of their range. That's because the deer's range includes thousands of acres of thick forest with little road access, and much of that is controlled by private interests. Such country gets very little hunting pressure, and the bucks have a chance to reach their full potential.

During 1988 I again had the opportunity to hunt the Redwood Creek Ranch with Charles and my friend Lyle Dorey, an outfitter from Canada. Lyle took a quality 4X4 buck, and I shot an awfully good 4X4 that gross-scored 135 Boone & Crockett points, a broken tine knocking him down to 128 net points, two shy of B & C's 130-point minimum standard. I've been fortunate enough over the years to hunt a lot of different places around the world for a lot of different animals, but none occupies a more honored spot on my wall than my two big blacktail bucks. I've paid over 20 years' worth of dues to get them.

A big blacktail is the kind of trophy that John Houseman would have liked to have hunted, had he been so inclined. None come cheaply. You have to earn them. And that's what makes hunting these little forest ghosts so special.

CHAPTER XXII

SITKA BLACKTAILS

The Sitka blacktail of southeast Alaska has become one of that state's most popular big-game animals in recent years. This is true for residents and nonresidents alike, though the two groups look at the deer a bit differently. The vast majority of local hunters shoot Sitka deer for the pot, and there are few chunks of venison taken anywhere that are tastier. Nonresidents, however, come looking for trophy-class bucks, an adventure that can make for quite a hunt.

Odocoileus hemionus sitkensis is a mule deer subspecies, but a recent one by geological standards. Sitka deer were not present in Alaska until after the Pleistocene Epoch ice fields receded, and then their northernmost distribution was limited to the Alexander Archipelago. The Pacific Ocean on the west, the tall mainland mountains to the east, and the northern icefields and glaciers restricted their natural expansion. Beginning in 1917, transplants extended the stocky little deer's range north along the Alaskan coast, throughout Prince William Sound, and into the Kodiak Archipelago.

Sitka deer differ in appearance more than you might imagine from their close cousin, the Columbia blacktail. They are much stockier in the body, and average in the neighborhood of 150 pounds on the hoof. They have shorter faces, too, and though their antlers are also smaller in width and height, they are often heavier than those of the Columbia blacktail.

The earliest records of Sitka deer harvests in southeastern Alaska indicate that Alaskan natives sold 2774 deer to the Russian settlement of Sitka in 1861. Market hunting for both meat and hides was widespread in the early 1900s, and the sweet venison of the blacktail was a primary food source of local miners and traders. During the 1940s and 1950s, the harvest fluctuated between 5000 and 15,000 animals per year. Game department estimates now indicate that the state's population has stabilized at near 100,000 animals. The annual harvest averages around 14,000 deer.

Sitka populations can and do experience drastic fluctuations, with most declines caused by severe winters and subsequent starvation. As this is written, the population cycle is high, and hunting prospects are excellent throughout the deer's range. At present, the limit of Sitka deer in many areas is five or six animals per hunter per season, the most liberal deer limit found anywhere in a northern environment and a real attraction for hunters. The lengthy season, stretching from August all the way through January in some cases, is another plus.

Even if you're traveling to Alaska to hunt another species in another region, it makes sense to consider spending the money to go Sitka deer hunting for a few days while you're already in the state. One note on bag limits—Alaska law requires that all edible meat be brought out of the back country and utilized, and Sitka buck makes for a very full backpack. Also, most guides will limit their customers to no more than two bucks per trip. That allows the hunter a chance to take the first representative buck he sees, and then hunt on for a much larger, record-book-class buck.

These little deer inhabit widely varying country within their range, and the hunting conditions encountered will depend upon the time of year almost as much as where you choose to go hunting. At any given time, you can find Sitka deer on coastal beaches, in dense conifer rainforests, and up in high alpine tundra regions. I've seen Sitka deer browsing placidly on seaweed along the beach, and on the same hunt I've seen them grazing happily in a mountain bowl side by side with mountain goats.

As the popularity of Sitka blacktail hunting increases, so do your options in terms of how, and where, you hunt them. Because the deer's habitat—and therefore, its habits—vary greatly in the various regions of Alaska, so to do the techniques that will prove successful for you. Here, then, is a rundown by region and how to hunt each successfully.

Southeast Alaska

Outdoor writer Chris Batin has hunted Sitka deer throughout Alaska, and his comments on southeast Alaska are especially pertinent to the traveling hunter. "Populations in this part of Alaska are spotty, and hunters need to study game department winter-mortality reports before planning a hunt here," Batin says. "If mild winters have occurred, the hunting can be fairly good in this region, though you'll have trouble finding antler growth as large as on Kodiak Island." The exception to that statement is Prince of Wales Island. A handful of local hunters have taken some tremendous Sitka bucks from that island in the past couple of seasons. However, there are no outfitters currently offering Sitka hunting on Prince of Wales Island, making it totally a do-it-yourself adventure.

Better hunting occurs on the ABC islands—Admiralty, Baranof, and Chicagof. Deer are scattered throughout these islands, and success can be found wherever there is sufficient feed. Early in the season, meaning August, most deer are above timberline in high alpine tundra country. They'll stay there until late September and October, when they move into the heavy forest terrain. Hunting them there is reminiscent of hunting the rainforests of Washington and Oregon for Columbia blacktails, but some locals have used tree stands successfully. When the snows come late in the season and the rut's on in November, the deer migrate further down toward the beaches. In fact, studies show that in very bad winters 90 percent of the entire deer population will spend its time within a quarter of a mile

This is a typical Sitka buck, featuring relatively heavy antlers with a narrow spread and forked tines. Body size will surprise you; these deer often weigh over 150 pounds on the hoof.

Most nonresident Sitka hunting occurs on Kodiak Island. Before snows fall, the better bucks are located on the top of the island in open tundra-like pockets, bowls, and alder thickets.

of the beach. It takes at least a foot and a half of snow to get the bigger bucks moving down from the high country.

"Your choice of a specific hunting area late in the season in this region is critical," says Batin. "Study weather patterns and snowfall in the areas you intend to hunt. Generally speaking, areas that receive heavier snowfall have lower deer densities. That is usually the southeast mainland and nearby islands."

Hunters can reach the offshore islands and secluded mainland areas by small boat or charter aircraft. As you can expect, though, once you're in hunting country, there are no roads or vehicles. It's you, your legs, and your gear from then on.

Prince William Sound

Sitka deer were not introduced into this region until 1917, and ever since, the overall population has been one that fluctuates like a yo-yo. Major die-offs have been recorded at least once each decade since the 1940s, and, generally speaking, hunting in this region is marginal.

The best hunting here occurs on the larger islands, including Hawkins, Hichinbrook, and Montague islands, which support the vast majority of the region's total deer population. Other islands that offer reasonable hunting include Latouche, Green, Knight, and the Naked Island group, and they are less heavily hunted than the other islands. The mainland is very marginal for deer, except between Gravina Point and the Rude River, and even this area is fair deer country at best.

The deer in Prince William Sound are strongly affected by weather patterns. For example, a 3 1/2-year old doe ear-tagged in 1967 was killed in November, 1977 on the same beach where she had been originally tagged. As a deer hunter, that tells us that this old doe had probably migrated up and down the same drainage all her life, a habit that is indicative of Sitka movement patterns in general. Find concentrations of deer, and you can usually locate them again by looking up or down only a few miles.

As with southeastern Alaska deer, in August you hunt these bucks above timberline in lush alpine bowls loaded with high-quality feed. From mid-September until the first significant snowfall, they move down into the timber, and hunting is awfully tough. The winter period in November is when most hunting occurs, and this is when the snows have moved the deer down near the beaches. Probably 70 to 80 percent of the annual harvest in this region occurs at this time, when hunters work out of boats.

The winter harvest can be so easy, when snows are up past a buck's shoulders and he can't really move, that ethical questions have been raised by concerned local sportsmen and Alaska game department personnel. Personally, I can't see what satisfaction a true trophy hunter would get from a set of antlers hanging on his wall that came from a buck shot under such circumstances. However, it is a legal hunt and one excellent way to fill the freezer with prime venison. And when the winters are mild, the deer stay off the beaches, and the hunting gets tough again. Mother Nature has a way of evening things up over time.

Kodiak Island

Most nonresident Sitka blacktail hunting takes place on massive, 3670-square mile Kodiak Island, for several reasons. The island has less severe weather than other deer areas in the state as a rule. It has a wider dispersal of deer, and much more quality winter range, than other areas, too. The spectacular scenery is like nowhere else. And there are several guided options available to the Kodiak hunter as well.

Deer movements here are like they are in other regions. However, early in the season you will see bucks scattered from the beaches all the way up to alpine tundra, though the better bucks will be high. As the season progresses, the deer drop down into thick—at times impenetrable—alder cover. This is usually in October, lasting until snows move them lower, and is by far the toughest time to hunt these deer. The alders are bad enough, but rain squalls can come in and sit for days, too, making it doubly miserable. When Chris Batin, Larry Suiter, and I hunted Kodiak in October of 1988 that's exactly what happened. We got deer, but it was wet, slippery, and downright miserable, more like work than fun. Late in the season, when the snows come, the deer drop down with the snowline. A good rule of thumb in hunting Kodiak bucks late in the season is to climb to the snowline and hunt right along its edge, because that's where you'll find most of the better bucks. They don't want to drop any lower, but they have to stay where they can find adequate food.

Accessibility determines hunting pressure on Kodiak Island, as well as neighboring Afognak and Raspberry islands, which also hold decent deer populations. Most hunters travel to their hunting areas by boat or chartered aircraft. The aircraft often have trouble landing in many of the more windswept areas, however, and boat access is becoming more and more popular. It's important to remember that you can't hunt on Kodiak in the fall on a tight time schedule, either. Your pickup aircraft or boat can get weathered in back at the base for several days at a time. Be prepared at all times to be stuck here, and you'll avoid most problems.

Northern British Columbia

Although rarely hunted there except by residents, Sitka deer also occur along the northern coast of British Columbia and in the Queen Charlotte Islands. Deer hunting there is generally characterized by rain, rain, and still more rain—and the dense vegetation that rainfall creates. Hunting conditions are akin to hunting the northern equivalent of a tropical rainforest. The deer are certainly there and, like Alaska, seasons are long and bag limits generous. But the odds are with the deer, especially for the nonresident on a typically short hunt.

Unlike Alaska, nonresidents must be guided, and there are indeed a few outfitters in the Queen Charlottes, most of them fishing operators who also take out a few hunters in the fall. This is a unique hunt in a most unusual area visited by few sportsmen, and the deer are plentiful. However, the terrain makes hunting so difficult that success is not high, and the deer come nowhere near the quality available in Alaska's better areas.

Hunting Sitka Blacktails

As in all deer hunting, it's best to hunt Sitkas from above whenever possible. This is especially true early in the season, when most good bucks are in the alpine bowls. On Kodiak, a climb of 1000 to 2000 vertical feet each day to reach hunting country isn't unusual. If you find a concentration of deer in an area a good distance from base camp, don't be afraid to spike out for a night or two.

You'll find Sitka deer less spooky than many deer you've hunted in the past, but that is changing rapidly as hunting pressure is educating the better bucks in a hurry. Move slowly, use your binoculars, and watch the wind. Peek over edges and into small bowls and gullies. There you'll often find pockets of concentrated deer. When storms are moving in and the wind's howling, most bucks head for shelter—either timber or alder thickets. Then you poke along slowly, glassing, but staying alert as you'll jump deer right out from under your feet.

A do-it-yourself Sitka hunt is terrific fun, and can be extremely successful. However, you have to plan ahead, do lots of legwork arranging charter flights, have the proper gear, and be willing to backpack up some steep mountains. It's by far my favorite way to go.

A fully guided hunt is also possible, and many brown bear guides have supplemented their business the past few years by offering hunts for deer only. The cost is around $2500 for a five-day hunt, plus tags, a hunting license, and air charter fees, which can get expensive. A fully guided hunt is the way to go if you have the money, have limited time, and don't want to research the hunting yourself.

Another very popular way to hunt is by boat. In years past, commercial fishing boats would bring hunting clients to Sitka deer areas, dropping them off at first light on a beach and picking them up again at dark. Hunters can shower on the boats, and hot meals, often centered around superb seafood, are the norm. Today there are some very plush charter boats that specialize in this Sitka hunting, offering the hunt, meals, a bunk, and all the trimmings for about half the cost of a fully guided hunt. You can find charter boats in coastal cities like Cordova, Homer, Valdez, and Kodiak, among others. A list of licensed guides is available

A superb Sitka buck looks something like Chuck Adams' 95-pointer. With light pressure, liberal limits, and high deer populations, it's as much fun as you'll ever have hunting deer. (Photo by Chuck Adams)

Careful planning is needed to set up an unguided hunt. Flights must be coordinated, and care is needed to keep baggage weight below allowable limits. Over-baggage charges are high.

from the Alaska Professional Hunter's Association, P.O. Box 91932, Anchorage, Alaska 99509.

A discussion of hunting Sitka blacktails wouldn't be complete without a note or two on brown bears. Throughout the deer's range, but especially on Kodiak Island, deer and bears share the same territory, and if you hunt for very long you're apt to see a bear or two. Protocol is important.

In 1988, I shot a very nice three-point buck at the top of a Kodiak mountain with Chris Batin. We checked the deer to make sure it was dead, and seeing that it was, decided to keep hunting for a half an hour or so. The light was too dark for photographs with rain clouds forming overhead, and besides, we were in a pocket of bucks and wanted to peek over the ridgetop to see if there were any other good ones around. Returning in an hour, we found that deer flat gone, carried off by a brown bear who couldn't believe his good fortune. I looked for that buck for five hours that day, and parts of two other days, but never did see it again. That same day we spotted a very good buck feeding on the edge of a cliff, with a smaller buck next to him. Unfortunately, a brown bear was picking berries a hundred yards away from them. It wasn't a good time to shoot a deer, and we had to watch him disappear over the edge.

Later in the same season, a resident hunter tried using a fawn bleat call near an alder thicket. A brown bear came to his call, and it was two days before the authorities found the hunter's body. The bear was still with him, and had to be dispatched.

The point is, the bears are there, and they can be a problem. Avoid them whenever possible, and they'll leave you alone, too. Don't ever leave a deer carcass overnight and expect to go back for it the next day, because the chances are good that a bear will have beaten you to the spoils. Calls can be effective on Sitka deer, both the mouth type and rattling, but be careful where you use them. Hunt with a friend. Cache your food a good distance away from your tents. Above all, use common sense.

Alaska Master Guide Dick Rohrer, who specializes in brown bear hunting but also runs very successful guided Sitka hunts, recommends that his guided hunters carry their favorite deer rifles with them. That's because the guides are carrying a backup bear rifle. For nonguided hunters, Dick recommends using something with a bit more pop, like a .30-06 with heavy bullets, .338, .35 Whelen, or another rifle that could act as a bear stopper in a pinch. I hunted Kodiak with my .280 Remington, but next time you can bet I'll be packing my .338.

I hope I won't need it, but it will certainly help me sleep at night.

CHAPTER XXIII

EXOTIC DEER

A merica's native deer cover so huge an expanse—and variety—of terrain and habitat, and are themselves so diverse, that it's almost impossible for a book of this type to be truly complete. On the other hand, no book on modern American deer hunting could be complete without at least mentioning our non-native deer, the so-called exotics.

According to the dictionary, exotic is actually the correct word to describe these deer species introduced from foreign lands. Unfortunately, "exotic" has become somewhat of a buzzword denoting fish-in-a-barrel hunts behind game fences. That's not an altogether unjustified accusation, either—some of the "hunting" on certain game ranches and hunting preserves is just plain shameful. But that isn't the case everywhere. There's hunting for exotics that offers the same kind of challenge our native deer do, and there are free-ranging herds of non-native deer that have been present for much longer than, say, whitetail deer have been in Colorado.

Some years ago I had hoped that the taint of the word "exotic" might be removed by stressing the alternate—and equally correct—titles of non-native game or non-indigenous species. Now I don't think it much matters. Hunters are a traditional, hide-bound, and usually narrow-minded, bunch (I should know—ask my wife!). A great many of us decided a long, long time ago that these funny-looking foreign deer didn't have any business here, and that's that. Nothing, it seems, can change that attitude—but fortunately not everybody agrees.

The three most popular, and most common, exotic deer in America are the fallow deer from Europe, axis deer from India, and sika deer from Japan, Formosa, and Manchuria. All three can readily be hunted in several parts of the country, on preserves and/or in a free-ranging state. Much less common, and found only on a few Texas ranches, is the Asian barasingha, or swamp deer. European red deer, a close relative of our elk and just slightly smaller, are becoming somewhat popular as an exotic. They have not developed any free-ranging populations that I know of, and hopefully they won't—red deer and elk will interbreed freely, and red deer in present or future elk range would be a disaster.

Without a doubt there are other exotic species, very unusual and limited in number, that I don't know about. I understand a few sambar deer from India were once released onto a Florida island, but I don't know their current status. Certainly there are many worldwide species of deer that perhaps could have been introduced, but for whatever reason the fallow, sika, and axis deer are far and away the most common—and the only ones that offer true hunting possibilities, rather than just a chance for shooting or collecting.

Fallow deer have been here the longest by far; it's said that George Washington had some on his lawn at Mount Vernon. Originally a deer of Europe and perhaps Asia Minor, the fallow's historic range is actually unknown; it has been semi-domesticated and certainly raised and transported by man for thousands of years. The Romans, for instance, are credited with having introduced fallow deer into Spain some 2,000 years ago.

They're an attractive deer with distinctively palmated antlers, and they come in a wild variation of colors—brown, spotted, white, and nearly black. They're generally either a placid deer by nature, or their long association with man has made them so. Under most circumstances the fallow deer isn't much of a game animal—but the odd thing is that he can be, and its unwise to write him off as a pushover.

Fallow deer are available on shooting preserves and game ranches literally across the United States; they handle cold weather well, and breeding stock is readily available. There are definitely free-ranging populations in the Texas Hill Country, and similar yet lesser-known herds have been established in several parts of the country. Southwest Kentucky's Land Between the Lakes has a herd of several hundred fallow deer, with hunting possible. In Wilcox County, central Alabama, there has been a free-ranging herd of as many as 1,000 fallow deer. Several of Georgia's offshore islands have fallow deer, and so does James Island off the coast of British Columbia. There are even a few in northern California. Under most circumstances, game departments have addressed the hunting of these exotics by simply calling them "deer" and allowing their harvest under normal state deer seasons with a normal deer license—but that isn't true across the board, so check with local authorities.

In a true free-ranging situation, and on some game ranches, for reasons I've never been able to figure out, fallow deer can be as wild as March hares and just as hard to hunt as any deer. White fallows do stand out like a sore thumb, but the brown, black, and spotted animals—which seem to be the survivors on free range—are well camouflaged and become very alert.

Generally, though, the fallow deer is an edge-habitat creature, and isn't as sneaky in nature as the sika deer. The sika (pronounced syka) deer is a round-antlered deer, genus *Cervus*, and thus a relative of our elk. During the mating season he roars not unlike an elk's bugle, and the males fight like wild Irishmen. After the October-November rut, it gets difficult to find males without broken tines. The sika is a cover-loving deer, and given adequate heavy brush in his range, he will just flat disappear. I've seen sika deer on Texas ranches, and had the owner tell me that he had no idea how they got there or how many were present.

European fallow deer occur in a wide variety of colors ranging from very dark to pure white. Domesticated for centuries, they're often the least wary of the exotic deer—but under the right conditions can offer excellent hunting.

The sika deer from Japan, Formosa, and Manchuria is a mid-sized deer closely related to the elk. During the rut they roar like stags and fight fiercely, often breaking tines.

Sika deer in three subspecies of varying sizes are found on Texas ranches. The Manchurian sika is said to be the largest, and herds that have remained pure are prized. Most Texas sika deer are of an unknown mixture, however, and other than in potential trophy size, the three varieties are very similar. Sika deer grow an elk-like antler that normally has three points coming forward off the main beam for a typical 4x4 configuration. Very dark in color and elk-like in appearance, they're a pretty deer and can readily be hunted on numerous game ranches in Texas and elsewhere. They have become established as a widespread free-ranging population of unknown size in the Texas Hill Country, but perhaps the most interesting sika deer hunting is in Virginia and Maryland.

Introduced onto Maryland's James Island around 1916, sika deer spread not only to nearby islands but also to the southern portion of Maryland's Eastern Shore. In fact, they manage so well there that Maryland has several thousand free-ranging sikas, and Dorchester County has special regulations that, in recent seasons, have allowed the taking of as many as nine sika deer annually. In Virginia, sika deer were released in what is now the Chincoteague Island National Wildlife Refuge. In raw numbers Virginia doesn't have nearly as many as Maryland, but they have enough for public hunting to be available on the refuge, with a multiple bag limit.

The axis deer is often described as the most beautiful deer in the world, and I wouldn't dream of disputing that. With a coat that remains spotted throughout the deer's life and short, rounded ears, the axis has a pleasing appearance—and his antlers are beautiful. Typically they consist of long, heavy main beams that rise up, out, and back in for a "beer barrel" shape. Normally there is a forward-pointing brow tine, and a second tine that points back or in, about two-thirds up the main beam. A herd animal of forest glades, the axis deer is not a heavycover deer, nor, being tropical, is he well-suited to cold climates. The axis deer has done extremely well in Texas and, together with the blackbuck antelope, also from India, is probably the most popular and sought-after exotic.

First introduced in Texas in 1932, axis deer have spread out over much of the Hill Country. A number of years ago it was estimated that there were 10,000 free-ranging axis deer in Texas, and certainly that number has grown substantially by now. Axis deer are also common on the Hawaiian islands of Lanai and Molokai, where some outstanding hunting for them is available. Unlike the fallow deer and sika deer, which have established token populations in little pockets all across the U.S., the only other place where axis deer are known to be established is a private herd in Marin County, California, north of San Francisco, and possibly on Brahma Island, Florida.

Over the years I've come to have mixed feelings about the exotics. They're interesting as trophies, quite beautiful, and their venison—particularly that of axis deer—is magnificent. Breeding herds, whether free-ranging or on large enough

The most popular exotic deer is the lovely axis deer from India. A large-bodied deer that keeps its spots throughout its lifetime, it's one of the most prized non-native trophies—and also offers some of the world's best venison.

acreage that the animals can use natural abilities to evade hunters, do offer excellent hunting opportunities. And often that hunting is available at a time of year when other seasons are closed. Axis deer, for instance, aren't on a set antler cycle; as a tropical deer an axis buck can be in hard antler anytime, although most bucks have hard antlers from May through October. On the other hand, all too often the exotics are not hunted at all, but simply shot on a put-and-take basis, sometimes on shamefully small acreage. It isn't much fun, and it's an outrageous parody of the hunting experience—and the anti-hunting groups, with justification, have a field day with this kind of thing.

I don't have any problem with a well-managed game ranch. Thanks to them, Texas has the world's best and biggest herd of axis deer, plus a selection of otherwise rare game species such as blackbuck, barasingha deer, addax, and scimitar-horned oryx. Not all of us who would like to hunt these beautiful exotics can gain access to free-ranging herds, whether in the U.S. or on the animals' home range. A good game ranch with large acreage and appropriate natural habitat is certainly a sound option. And without the patronage of sportsmen, the animals wouldn't be there at all. The best part of any hunt, though, is the total experience. With exotics, it pays to make absolutely certain you know what you're getting yourself into: If you pay attention and check things out, you can find excellent hunting and a quality experience for any of our exotic deer.

CHAPTER XXIV

DEER HUNTING TACTICS

There's an old saying that's applicable to the way many people approach their deer hunting each fall: "Even a blind squirrel finds an acorn every now and then." Some folks stumble blindly around the woods without no game plan, hoping that just by being there they'll luck into a buck and shoot it.

Surprisingly enough, many deer are taken just this way, though it seems unfair to those of us who work hard at our hunting. But everyone has to learn sometime, and there's no substitute for experience in the deer woods when it comes to filling your tags. When the young or novice hunter heads into the woods long on enthusiasm and short on knowledge, he or she is bound to make some very basic mistakes and, consequently, miss some opportunities. Those who learn from their mistakes are destined to become consistently successful deer hunters. Those who continue to hunt willy-nilly are the ones who complain that there aren't any deer left in the woods.

The key to filling deer tags consistently is to use the knowledge gleaned from each and every deer hunting trip you have ever taken, as well as information learned from others, and formulate a game plan for the hunt. This two-pronged approach will help you enter the woods with a real advantage over the blind squirrels. Instead of aimlessly wandering around, hoping the gods will smile on you because you helped a senior citizen across the street last weekend, and haven't littered for a month, you'll be hunting a certain way, at a specific time, based on the knowledge that this way the odds are skewed a little in your favor. And if your goal is to find a mature, large-antlered buck, the hunt is a lot like a trip to the casinos in Las Vegas or Atlantic City: While the odds are always with the house, the gambler who understands the game inside and out, and plays it smart, is usually the one who winds up smiling at the end of the day.

There are just about as many ways to hunt deer as there are stars in the sky. The following pages of describe only the basic techniques of the most popular—and successful—deer hunting tactics used throughout the country. Keep in mind that there are many variations of each technique, and often by doing something just a little bit different than the rest of the crowd, you'll see deer that aren't used to what you're doing.

That's one reason several huge bucks are killed each year by pure novice hunters. The veterans continue to hunt the same ground in the same manner year after year, and the deer have learned their tactics and go into the same escape mode every fall. The rookie hunter who doesn't know any better, may be fumbling along, working to no particular plan—and before you know it runs into a monster buck that's lived five or six or seven years by zigging when the veteran hunters zagged. While it pays to have a plan, it also pays to hang loose.

That happened to me one fall in northern California, back in the days when my enthusiasm far outweighed my finesse. Several friends had hunted a particular ridge for years by driving it to some standers down below, and as a newcomer I was elected to help drive. We entered the thick pine woods and headed down a steep slope, making noise and generally raising Cain. I came to a small ridge bordering a creekbed, and for some reason slowed down so much that I actually stopped for a few minutes.

I was trying to get my bearings, using my binoculars to study the heavy cover not 35 yards ahead. I caught a small movement out of the corner of my eye just as I was about to continue walking, and when I slowly turned my head, a nice three-point mule deer was sneaking back through the drive up that creek bottom. I shot him when he got to 25 yards, but I'm sure he would have come much closer because he never looked my way. Instead he was concentrating on the ruckus that the others were making. He was the only buck we got that weekend. Even a so-called "expert" may be a blind squirrel every now and then.

Pre-Season Scouting

"All right," you may be asking yourself about now. "I thought this chapter was going to tell me how to go about hunting deer, not some simple stuff like scouting?"

First things first. Before you can go out and shoot a deer, you have to find one to shoot at. The novice hunter is the one who charges head-first into the woods, sets up a his stand at random, and hopes a buck will walk by. After a few seasons of haphazard success, questions arise concerning why the deer are in certain places, and why they aren't in others. That novice begins to learn about hunting country, and in so doing begins to hunt smart. Soon, he begins seeing more deer and larger bucks. It's all beginning to fall into place.

Just think how many wasted hunted days, and seasons, could have been saved by hunting smart right from the start. And smart hunters are scouters.

Pre-season scouting is something we all do. If we have the time and live in the area we're hunting most, we can scout all year on foot, learning the terrain and maybe a little bit about the deer. We can ask questions of other hunters, state fish and game officials, farmers, local taxidermists, forestry personnel, loggers, and anyone else we may meet in the woods. We look for trails, fence crossings, beds, tracks, droppings, rubs, food sources, and other indicators of deer presence.

If we don't live in our hunting area, we scout by telephone and by using maps, asking intelligent questions and trying to get a feel of the country we think might hold the kind of deer we're after. We ask about access to public land. We may even call private landowners well before the season opens to ask for permission to hunt.

Deer hunting styles are limited only by your imagination. Study the country, adapt your hunting methods to current parameters, and perhaps a buck like this will be yours this fall. (Photo by Nick Sisley)

Deer calling, using both mouth-blown calls and rattling antlers, is becoming more and more popular each year. It's effective no matter the species of deer you're hunting.

In truth, learning to scout well is one of the most important deer-hunting tactics you can master. As one well-known deer hunter told me, "I'm really a pretty mediocre hunter who hunts good places. That's why I kill so many good bucks." Hunting deer where they are is the key to this whole puzzle. And that begins with pre-season scouting.

Penetrating Deer Defenses

Before one even begins thinking about hunting deer successfully, a quick review of a deer's basic defense mechanisms is in order.

Deer are finely-tuned survival machines. They can't afford to make a mistake, because the results are grim and permanent. Bucks that have made it through several hunting seasons with their hides intact know all about man, and what his presence in the woods means. The deer's defenses are up, and as hunters our job is to penetrate those defenses.

Deer have good eyesight, very good hearing, and excellent noses. We must keep from being seen, and that means staying off the skyline, not moving too quickly, and not letting sunlight glint off shiny metal objects or skin. To keep from being heard, we must learn to move as silently as possible in the woods, choosing routes that minimize contact with brush, loose rocks, trees, and other natural noise-makers. It means leaving jangling keys and coins at home, and wearing appropriate clothing for the type of hunting we're doing.

The deer's sense of smell is his first line of defense. It's the one sense that needs no confirmation from any of the other senses to tell him what the problem is before he gets out of the country right now. Hunt into the wind, or with a cross-wind, at all times. Tree stands help get you and your smell up off the ground and away from a deer's nose, but beware of scent trails left going to and from the stand.

The point is, never underestimate a deer's ability to detect you in the woods. We're playing the game on their turf, and they know all the tricks. Carelessness breeds an unsuccessful hunt, especially when we're talking about trophy-quality bucks.

It's important to keep in mind the things all deer have in common. Like people, they are comfort-oriented. They bed with luxury in mind, making beds near to lush feed and water. They like sunny slopes in extremely cold weather, and shaded areas in hot temperatures. In very strong winds they bed on the lee side of a slope. In dense cover they tuck their beds deep into the foliage, refusing to move unless a hunter almost steps right on them. Bedding areas are always near familiar escape routes. And in many instances, deer will follow the path of least resistance. In heavily-hunted locations, bucks will aim to move into areas where the hunters are not. Usually these areas are tough and miserable to the hunter, the main reason the majority of sportsmen don't go there.

Tree stands keep scent up off the ground, and the hunter out of a buck's line of sight. Stands must be placed meticulously, and care to keep human scent pollution to a minimum is critical.

Drives are popular in the thick, dense country that comprises much of our whitetail range. Good drives are not easy to do, but they can be deadly on even the largest bucks. (Photo by Nick Sisley)

Deer Hunting Coast to Coast

Stand Hunting

Stand hunting may be the most successful overall deer hunting strategies of all. The reason is simple. By letting the deer do the moving, you let them make the mistakes. A clumsy hunter, tramping through the woods, telegraphs danger by sound, sight, and smell. But by remaining motionless, that hunter ensures that the deer has a tougher time detecting him, and by moving, the deer makes himself easier to see. All things considered, I take a stand whenever possible.

In many parts of the country—upper Midwest, Southeast, and Northeast—the terrain dictates stand hunting because it is thick and noisy. Some regions of the Southwest, like Texas, are also ideal for standers. In the West's open country, stand hunting is not used as much except in thick river bottoms, along winter migration routes, and in the rainforests of the Pacific Northwest.

Picking a stand location is crucial to the success of this method. Scouting will usually help determine your stand location. Stand site selection is dictated by three basic principles. First, make sure the stand offers a clear view of trails, water holes, or feeding areas. Second, make sure the tree stand or ground blind adequately conceals the hunter yet offers clear shooting lanes. And third, set the stand on the downwind side of where the deer are expected to appear. Also, make sure the stand conforms naturally in shape, size, and coloration to the terrain and foliage you're hunting.

Approach the stand from the downwind side, moving quietly and cautiously well before sunrise and sundown. Mask your foot trail by wearing rubber-soled boots and/or using a commercial masking scent. Don't be quick to leave the stand during the day, especially during rutting seasons when deer might wander by at any time. Take a lunch and drinks, and a plastic bottle to urinate in when te nature calls.

Patience is the key to successful stand hunting. Don't fidget around, but stay quiet and alert. Wear quiet clothing, and enough of it to make sure you're plenty warm. In tree stands, wear a safety belt. In ground blinds, move any sticks, loose rocks, or other noise-making objects out of the way well before daylight. Once in the blind, take a few "practice swings" by mounting the gun or bow toward likely shooting lanes to become familiar with the feel of the actual shooting position.

Hunting on Foot

Hunting deer on foot is the most versatile technique, and it is the toughest to master. Learning to move like the proverbial cat through the woods, seeing deer before they see you, is incredibly difficult. By becoming an active aggressor, the hunter risks detection with each step. But it can, and is, done successfully by hundreds of sportsmen each year. There are several variations to hunting on foot, and we'll discuss each briefly.

Still hunting is another term for moving steadily and silently through the woods. This is a technique best employed in thick cover, with little chance for long-distance shooting. The best still hunting occurs when deer are up and moving, meaning early and late in the day, or when stormy or unusual weather has them on the move. It's very, very difficult to still hunt unseen bedded deer in thick cover.

The key is to move slowly, pausing frequently, and studying the woods intently. Keep to the shadows, against tree trunks and brush piles to break your outline, and keep the wind in your face. The old adage, "walk one step, then wait two" is excellent advice in still hunting.

Stalking is the art of spotting game at long range, then moving in for a shot. We've covered spot-and-stalk hunting more extensively in Chapter XXVI, but basically, any deer habitat that affords a view of lots of country offers promising stalking. Deer can be stalked when up and moving or when bedded. Keep in mind that deer have excellent peripheral vision, so approach from above and behind whenever possible. Better yet, keep out of sight altogether.

Many hunters like to go jumpshooting, one of the most exciting techniques a foot hunter may employ. In hard-hunted areas of the country, deer often like to hole up in thick patches of cover and let the hunter walk right on by. Throwing rocks and sticks into these patches of cover will sometimes get nervous deer up and running, forcing the hunter to not only make a quick decision on the quality of the trophy but also shoot quickly. Because some deer refuse to move even if rocks land right next to them, hunters with partners might take turns, alternately playing shooter and dog. The dog goes right in among the cover, hoping to move the deer by his physical presence.

One of the most popular foot hunting methods in America combines taking a stand and still hunting—driving. Deer drives are done in all parts of the country, but work best in thick terrain too difficult to hunt by other methods. It takes several hunters to make a drive work.

The most successful drives are planned like a military campaign, the drive general being someone who knows the country and can anticipate the movements of pushed deer. He will set the standers and position the drivers, giving everyone explicit instructions. The key is to have standers who will stay where they're supposed to be, and drivers who move slowly and methodically through the woods. Standers should be placed on the downwind side whenever possible, and may be in ground blinds or tree stands. I prefer the drivers to move quietly, but in the South, traditional deer drives use hounds, and the racket is something. Both types have their proponents, and both produce deer.

One note: If you're a driver, stay alert. Many a big-racked buck has been taken by a driver as it tried to circle back and sneak through the drive.

A smart solo hunter can participate in a "poor man's drive" by allowing other hunters to move deer around. By climbing to a good vantage point in relatively open terrain well before daylight, the lone hunter can watch as less ambitious sportsmen work the lower country. It's amazing how many deer these people will push past your stand, if you're patient and have picked the right place to wait.

Some very successful hunters are trackers, and tracking deer can be an excellent method for the persistent. Deer tracking is best done in fresh snow, and it takes lots of skill and time to track a buck. Deer tracking is most popular in large areas where deer densities are low and there's usually snow on the ground—Maine, for example. Following a deer track can lead to who knows where in dense woods, so the tracker must be a skilled woodsman and should carry both compass and maps at all times.

Deer Calling

One of the exciting new techniques available is deer calling. While deer callers have been around forever, the technique is just now gaining wide acceptance over much of the country. There's a good reason for this—it works! And all species of deer will respond to vocal deer calls.

Perhaps the most popular vocal call is the fawn bleat, imitating the sounds of a hurt or frightened fawn. There are several commercially made bleating calls on the market today, complete with instructions. No one is sure why deer respond to this type of call, but most feel it is out of curiosity or a general concern for the safety of one of their own. Vocal calls seem to work best in thick, heavy cover with limited visibility.

Other vocalized deer calls, often used by tree-stand hunters perched near primary scrapes, include the grunt and snort. These are the challenge calls of a rutting whitetail buck, and the hunter hopes that a nearby dominant buck will hear the sounds and come in, ready to whip the intruder. I've seen blacktail bucks respond to grunt and snort calls, but have yet to meet anyone who has used them with regular effectiveness on mule deer.

Horn-rattling is covered in detail in Chapter XXV. Rattling will work on whitetails and blacktails, but its effectiveness on mule deer is still suspect. Trying to rattle in a whitetail buck in Alberta one frosty November morning, I did rattle up a small forked-horn mule deer, so it can work at times. The jury is still out on how consistently effective it really is.

The building of mock scrapes is also covered in Chapter XXV. Generally speaking, a mock scrape is built by the hunter in an attempt to trick a whitetail buck into thinking it's the real McCoy. A stand is set downwind within shooting range. The mock-scrape builder needs lots of tools, including a plastic tarp to lay supplies on; a short stick with a short-forked end in order to knock tips off overhanging limbs and to scrape and to leave grooves in the ground; rubber gloves; small screw-top jars containing estrus products, cotton swabs; and various buck-lure products. The importance of not leaving human scent or an

Still-hunting is one of the most difficult of all hunting methods, requiring cat-like stealth and the patience of Job. Yet the satisfaction of talking a buck on his own terms is unequaled. (Photo by Judd Cooney)

overabundance of boot tracks in snow cannot be overemphasized when building a mock scrape.

Float Hunting

Float hunting is another popular method in areas where waterways are the best paths through dense deer habitat. Canoes, flat-bottom John boats, and more conventional craft can all be used when floating. It is important to conform to standard safe boating procedures when float hunting, and especially to wear a Coast Guard-approved flotation vest. Keep from banging against the sides of the boat, especially if it's made from aluminum; even the slightest sounds travel great distances over water.

As you can see, there are several ways to fill a deer tag. Hunting methods should be selected with two things in mind. First, tailor your tactics to the terrain, weather, relative hunting pressure, and species you're hunting. And second, hunt in a manner that's comfortable for you. Often that means combining two or more of these "standard" techniques, adapting them to a specific situation.

One friend likes to hunt mule deer by the spot-and-stalk method, period, in country where he can watch deer bed down before moving in on them. He refuses to hunt country that isn't conducive to this method, and he's awfully good at it. While he may be missing out on some excellent hunting in areas that aren't geared toward his specialty, he's always comfortable, and confident that he can punch his tags each and every time out.

That's the real key: It isn't so important which technique you use. It is important that the technique chosen be suited to the area you're hunting—and that you be totally familiar and comfortable with your hunting method!

CHAPTER XXV

HUNTING THE RUT

For most of us, the best time to go deer hunting is whenever we can get out and spend some time in the field. That's just the way it goes for a family man with a regular-hours job who'd probably like to be out hunting a lot more than he can. And while the early seasons give us beautiful weather and often uncrowded conditions, there's nothing like the October woods. If you're a trophy hunter you want to be hunting during the rut, if at all possible.

Why? Because during the rutting period, the urge to reproduce has made a mature buck deer about as crazy as a sophomore on his first date. His entire being revolves around the mating call, and often he throws caution to the winds. During the rut, a mature, heavy-antlered buck will be much more active at all hours of day and night, and therefore much more likely to show himself away from heavy cover and regular escape trails during legal shooting hours. If ever a trophy-class buck is going to do something really dumb, it's then

In his classic book, *Hunting Trophy Deer*, John Wooters sums it up best: "And the brutal truth is that no matter how skilled the hunter, the majority of all really big bucks are taken because they made a mistake, and not because they couldn't cope with the hunter's cunning. In fact, the highest art of the whitetail hunter is to place himself in a position to take advantage of a big buck's mistake if and when it occurs." Amen, John. When it comes to taking trophy bucks of all species, we need all the help we can get.

Rut hunting is also somewhat of a controversial topic. In many parts of the country, most notably where the whitetail is king, rut hunting is very acceptable and, in fact, considered a necessity if any deer are to be harvested. In other places, particularly in mule deer and Columbia blacktail areas, many old-timers think that hunting during the rut amounts to little more than an unsportsmanlike slaughter of a defenseless animal.

In deer herds that are being managed properly by state game departments, shooting deer during the rut has no more effect on herd dynamics than harvesting them a month or two earlier. In fact, just the opposite may be true, as states like Colorado have learned with early high country four-point-or-better hunts that see lots of hunters concentrating solely on trophy-class bucks. Some biologists believe that it is better to hold as many deer seasons during and after the rut as possible, to allow any bucks that will be harvested one last chance to breed before winding up in the freezer.

Dynamics of the Rut

What triggers the rut? Ask that question around the campfire and you're bound to get several different answers. Even the scientists really aren't 100 percent sure. Many hunters believe that a cold snap triggers the rut, and while this may seem to apply, most biologists believe that photoperiodism—the response to light—is the primary trigger. In layman's terms, that means that the proportion of daylight to darkness at a specific time of year is the signal for the rut to begin, as well as end. There are also other factors involved, however. For example, poor diet may cause a late or irregular breeding season. An overabundance of food may also delay the season; it has been shown that obesity will cause a doe to come into estrus later than normal. There are many other such examples of exceptions to the rule.

Photoperiodism will obviously create rutting seasons varying with latitudes. That's why in the extreme northern latitudes, peak rutting cycles occur in early to mid-November. Further south, the rut may not be going strong until December, though special circumstances may cause radical exceptions. A study conducted in New York state years ago showed that peak deer breeding takes place during a 60-day period, but the breeding season itself may extend for 120 days or more. This study of 894 deer found that the earliest breeding date was October 1 and the latest February 9, with the peak of the activity between November 10 and December 15. These time spans seem to be typical of North American species of deer. Although peak and start dates of the rutting cycle differ from area to area, somewhere in the middle will be up to 40 days of really intense activity. California's coastal mule deer, for example, which begin rutting in earnest mid-September and continue until near the end of October.

The length of the rut ensures at least partial fawn survival in case of some unusually harsh spring occurrence. And photoperiodism ensures that does breed at a specific time, and therefore drop their fawns at a time when spring weather is likely to be mild and food plentiful, conditions that favor fawn survival and growth.

A single buck may breed with only four or five does during the 60-day peak cycle, or with as many as 20 or 25. Because rutting activity leaves bucks little time to eat, they often lose 25 to 35 percent of their body weight. Does may conceive during their first estrus cycle but if they are not bred then, or for some reason do not conceive even if they are bred, they will come back into estrus in 26 to 28 days. It is very unusual for a doe not to be bred during her first or second estrus cycle, but if she doesnot, she will come into heat a third and perhaps even a fourth time before going barren for the spring.

Successfully hunting the rut is more than just hitting the woods willy-nilly, expecting some female-crazed monster buck to come blindly strolling past your stand. In fact, hunting the whitetail rut is very different from hunting the mule deer rut, and while blacktails tend to act more like muleys during this time, with them the game is a bit different yet.

There have been volumes and volumes written on how to hunt the rut

Western whitetails rub objects other than live flora, as this freshly-rubbed Colorado fencepost shows. The size of the rub often corresponds to the size of the buck that made it. (Photo by Todd Smith)

A special late-season hunt allowed Robb to hunt this near-record book blacktail during the rut. He took the deer from a small herd of does as it fed in an open meadow at mid-day.

successfully, and it's easy to see why. The more you get into it, the more complex—and fascinating—the subject becomes. Space in this book doesn't permit an in-depth treatment of the topic. Instead we have outlined the basics, hoping to offer some usable information and to stimulate enough curiosity to encourage you to explore the subject further.

The Whitetail Rut

Perhaps the most important thing a hunter must know about hunting rutting whitetails is that the bucks let the does come to them, not the other way around. Dominant bucks stake out breeding territories, marked by secretions from the glands located at the forward corners of the eye, and glands located on the forehead. These secretions are rubbed onto bushes and shrubs, many of which are thrashed with the antlers. These are the "breeding rubs," significantly different in appearance and freshness from velvet-removing rubs made a couple of months earlier.

In his breeding territory, the buck also makes one or more scrapes. Sizes of scrapes vary, but they are pawed-out spots in the ground perhaps two feet by a foot and a half, almost always located on a trail. A series of scrapes on a trail is called a scrape line. Bucks urinate in primary scrapes in such a posture that the urine runs down over the tarsal glands, carrying the tarsal secretion to the ground with it. The scrape is pawed and/or torn up with antlers until it is a muddy, smelly mess that the buck may even ejaculate in. This scrape is the buck's way of telling the world that he's here, and ready to breed.

When the urge to mate overcomes a doe, she comes looking for a buck. She can smell the scrape, and it draws her like chocolate draws a child. If the buck's not home when she arrives, she may urinate in or near the scrape and move off. The buck, who checks his scrape line at least once a day (or night), smells this female invitation and follows. He will put his nose to the ground and follow her every step, much like a hound trailing a raccoon. When he finds her, the mating is brief, and he returns to his breeding area to await another receptive female.

It is interesting to note that whitetail bucks that fight during the breeding season do not do so over specific does, but rather over territory. They guard their territory most jealously, and while small bucks may be permitted to enter it, no other breeding males can do so without a challenge.

For the antler rattler, this is an important point. If a dominant buck believes that one or more breeding bucks have entered his territory and may be fighting or rubbing their antlers on small trees or shrubs in mock battles, he will come to investigate with the intent of throwing the intruders out. Rattling, the banging together of a set of antlers to imitate such a battle, can be done successfully from a ground blind or tree stand, with many hunters preferring to rattle from the ground unless the cover is so thick that bucks can easily sneak up on you

they may lock horns and shove each other around for a bit to see who gets first dibs. If several does are in heat at one time, though, I've seen more than one buck in a herd breeding at a time. There are no hard and fast rules; it's every buck for himself.

As we've seen, mature mule deer bucks live a solitary life, often in habitat near does and fawns but far enough away that the two rarely meet—until the breeding urge overwhelms a buck's good sense. Then he leaves his sanctuary to find a ready doe, breeds her, and perhaps spends the following day resting with her. Then he's off in search of his next conquest.

One of the differences between mule deer and whitetails during the rut is the country in which they live. In most mule deer country the animals migrate from summer to winter range, the trek often covering several miles. Snows are the most common driving force in this migration. When the snow's deep enough to make finding food a problem, the deer head down the mountains looking for easier pickings. Trophy-class bucks will stay in the harsh, snow-covered country longer than does and fawns, except when the rut is on. When that happens, all bets are off, but it's a point one should remember, as we'll see later.

Often the best way to hunt rutting mule deer is to find a small herd of does, and stay with them. One or more will soon be in heat, and when that happens, the bucks are bound to be there. This was a favored technique—and well-kept secret—of the great Nevada outfitter Jerry Hughes. Jerry passed away in the fall of 1988—in his deer camp, after a hard day's hunting, the way he would have preferred. But in his last seasons, after he discovered this technique of watching a doe herd from afar, he took several Boone & Crockett candidates for his clients. According to Jerry, "The secret is to be patient. If you know the rut is on, just wait it out. It might take most of a week, but if you keep watching those does, sooner or later a really good buck will show up."

By November, when most mule deer rutting activity occurs, the deer are already on winter range where there are open sagebrush flats, meadows among the trees, and small parks to glass for does. It pays to get up to a high vantage point in good deer country well before first light and set up a comfortable glassing station. It may pay to sit and glass from a single spot all day during the rut, because the deer are very active day and night then, and can show up moving about at any time. It works well to glass from a single spot first thing, then hike along a ridgeline, poking in and out of small protected canyons and cuts to see what we can see.

Once a buck is spotted, a stalk is often in order. This may not be a real problem if you only have to move within rifle range, but stalking a rutting buck with bow or muzzleloader can be more difficult because the deer are usually moving. Stalking is much easier when the deer are bedded. Be constantly aware of the does during the stalk, because though the bucks may be crazed with the need to breed, the does are often as jumpy as a bagful of Mexican jumping beans. More often than not, a stalk is blown during a rut hunt by a nervous doe, not a wary buck.

If your goal is a truly large set of antlers, find your does and see what's with them. If there is nothing but small bucks around, don't think there are no good bucks in the area. Often there will be only one very good buck with any small herd of does, and he might have a hot doe off somewhere for the time being. Chances are he'll be back. But if you can't see any good bucks after a few days and if it's really late in the season, it is possible that what you're witnessing is in fact a "false rut."

The false rut is a term for the time when the main rutting activity has ceased, and the bigger bucks have already done their breeding. The smaller bucks may have been kept from breeding by more dominant animals, and they're still around hoping to get in on a little of the action, at least. The bigger bucks have really already gone back up the mountains as far as they can go, ready to resume the bachelor life they prefer. Hunt up higher than the does you're seeing, looking for large tracks in the snow and finding, if you're lucky, small bachelor groups of big bucks trying to eat as much as they can to recoup their strength and regain the weight the breeding season has cost them.

Some hunters have also begun using doe-in-heat-type scents during the rut, setting up stands and hoping these scents will draw an animal within shooting range. These scents have proven that they can be effective, though difficult to use. For example, I've tried leaving them overnight in hopes of sneaking in on a big buck at first light, only to find that the scent bottles have been dragged off by raccoons, coyotes, and other critters. They do have merit, but they are not a substitute for learning about deer behavior and the lay of the land.

The Blacktail Rut

Blacktail deer are closely related to mule deer, and act much the same. They prefer the bachelor life until the rutting urge hits them. Blacktail rutting occurs in November, with the Sitka blacktail starting a couple of weeks earlier than their Columbia cousins.

With Sitkas, spot-and-stalk hunting is by far the best method during the rut. Hunt the snow-line and look for deer, and you'll be in business. With Columbia blacktail, it's a bit different because the country they inhabit is often thick, nasty rainforest-type stuff. Also, states like Oregon offer a rut-season, blacktail hunt only for bowhunters, so the object is not only to find a buck but to get one into range for a good bow shot. In California, the private lands management program run by the state allows a few ranches to offer rifle hunts during the rut.

During the bow seasons, rattling has proven itself an excellent technique for getting a shot at a good buck. In very thick country, bowhunters often need to get up off the ground to be able to see down into little open pockets; otherwise, even if a buck moves in, the hunter may not be able to see him in time, or may not be able to get an arrow through the dense cover.

Charles Barnum operates the Redwood Creek Ranch near Eureka, California, property under the state's private lands-management program. Charles and I have experimented with deer decoys during the blacktail rut, placing a taxidermist's full-body-mount mannequin in an open meadow. The form is painted, medium-sized antlers attached, and buck deer tarsal glands attached for scent. We've seen does walk right to the form, and bucks come into the meadow, look the mannequin over, and assume a dominant strutting posture. More needs to be done with this technique to see just how valuable it might be. We began thinking that if it works for pronghorn hunters, why not deer hunters, too? It just might, but caution is advised when using this kind of set-up on public land where another hunter might mistake the mannequin for the real thing.

Other than that, the method Charles uses most is spot-and-stalk, looking for bucks in the open parks and meadows that checkerboard his heavily-timbered ranch. It's been very successful, with the 1988 season producing 9 bucks for 10 hunters, 3 of which grossed scores over the 130 points needed to make the Boone & Crockett record book.

The Coues Deer Rut

Coues deer are little whitetails, but the country in which they live dictates the way they are hunted—and that's by the spot-and-stalk method, pure and simple. Deer densities are such that any other method would be folly.

Coues deer generally rut in December, and in Arizona, where getting a tag is still awfully easy, the hunting can be very good and the general rifle season occurs at this time. All you have to do is climb into good country, set up a glassing station well before first light, and start looking. Buck/doe ratios are generally good in most areas, meaning that once you spot deer, you'll more than likely have a buck located, too. These little ghostlike deer are hard to see as they float in among the desert flora, so look hard, mark the deer you do find carefully, and make that first shot count.

Other than the occasional drive, we have used no method except spot-and-stalk to hunt Coues deer, rut or no rut. In the terrain they live in, this seems to be the most practical approach, given the big country and the low deer densities. However, knowledgeable hunters have told us that Coues deer will respond readily to calling, and can respond to skillful horn-rattling. Not the strident clashing a Texas hunter might use, but rather more subtle "social" sparring—the same kind of rattling that seems to work with blacktails in dense cover. Under most conditions, the deer densities make such methods very haphazard unless deer have already been spotted—but such techniques could, once in a while, be a

Commercially-prepared scents can aid deer hunters in several ways; estrus-based scents are used in making mock scrapes, and masking scents used to help conceal human odors. Modern packaging like this Scent Wafer from H.S. Scents make the smelly stuff easier to use than ever before.

When hunting rutting mule deer, look for a small herd of does. Even if no bucks are present, stay with the does. When one comes into heat, a buck will appear sooner or later.

useful part of a Coues deer hunter's repertoire.

In some parts of the country, regular deer seasons may coincide with the rut, especially in the eastern whitetail woods. In the West, it often is a matter of drawing a special tag for a late-season hunting opportunity. Whatever it takes, if you get a chance to hunt during the rut, do so. It's your best chance of all to be in the right place when that monster buck of a lifetime makes a mistake.

CHAPTER XXVI

GLASSING FOR DEER

When I first began deer hunting, I approached the game with as much enthusiasm—and about as much success—as I did chasing girls. I figured that the more ground I covered, the more deer I'd see, and therefore the better my chances at success. So I'd hit the slopes early and start hoofing it, up, down, and all around, hoping my legs would be the key to success.

I shot my share of deer, too, though none was of trophy quality. And every year I'd come back to camp dead tired with little to show for my efforts but sore feet, and the same overweight, plodding fellow would be there with stories of all the deer he'd seen. Of course I knew he was fibbing, but before the week was over he'd punctuate his stories with a pretty fair buck.

This made no sense to a vigorous young buck with a jockstrap mentality like me. But the third year in a row this happened in our camp in western Colorado, I swallowed my pride and asked for some advice.

"All you need to do is quit running around like a teenager in heat and start hunting," my friend told me. "Try letting your eyes do the walking for a change, and you'll be surprised how many deer you see."

I must have looked halfway between skeptical and pathetic, because he offered to take me to where he'd killed a pretty solid 27-incher the day before. "Just give it one morning, and if you don't believe me go back to the way you've been hunting," was all he said.

To say that my eyes were opened would be a gross understatement, because in reality that morning determined how I hunt big game almost all the time now. We climbed the highest point in our area that next morning, getting on top about half an hour before the first rays of sun graced the sky. By 10:00 a.m. I'd seen nearly 50 mule deer—more than I'd seen in five days of racing around—and 13 of them were bucks. A nice, solid 24-inch 4x4 came within range of my perch, and when I shot him with my dad's vintage 1930 Model 70 in .270, I was flabbergasted.

Instead of hunting deer haphazardly, I now had a plan. I'd spot them from long distance, then move in closer for a shot. Spot-and-stalk hunting was my new method, and with it I was going to shoot just about every deer in the world.

The key to spot-and-stalk hunting is glassing. In Chapter XXIV we talked about many different hunting methods, and spot-and-stalk hunting itself is well discussed there. As the years have crept by and I've hunted deer wherever they live, I've found that glassing is just about the most important skill a hunter needs to learn to be successful. This holds true for open-country western hunting, to be sure, but glassing can be an invaluable tool in the heavy whitetail woods, too.

Deer Hunting Coast to Coast

Optics for Glassing

Deer hunters spend lots of time fussing with their arms, whether they hunt with a rifle, bow, muzzleloader, or handgun. We all take pride in our marksmanship, and like to brag that we've worked up loads for ol' Betsy that have her shooting dime-sized groups at 100 yards. And that's all to the good. You can never practice too much on the range, or double-check your equipment often enough.

But the biggest mistake you can make in getting your hunting gear together is to spend four figures on a fancy rifle and scope combination, then buy a pair of binoculars for $29.99. In my opinion, there is no more important piece of equipment you can own as a deer hunter than your binoculars! If you hunt a lot, hunt slowly and look long and hard, you'll use your binoculars a million times more than your rifle.

Just like in everything else, you get what you pay for, and optics are no different. When the time comes to buy a pair of binoculars or a spotting scope, check your budget, decide how much you can afford to spend, then spend another hundred bucks. It may hurt at the time, but if you love to hunt deer, it won't take many trips afield before you'll be patting yourself on the back for making such a smart buy.

I own several pairs of binoculars and two spotting scopes. I look at it like a golfer. When I have a five iron to the green, I want my five iron, not the seven iron or the three iron or the wedge. When I'm hunting open western country, I want a higher-powered glass. When I'm sneaking around the thick woods, I want a lower-powered glass with more field of view. When I'm backpacking I'll sacrifice a little optical power for weight, but not much. My first rule of hunting is that if I have to carry weight, I want it to be glass. I'll leave something else out of my pack before I scrimp on my optics.

Hunting Optics

Before we get into the finer points of glassing, you need to know a bit about binoculars and what to look for when selecting a pair for hunting.

Magnification. In several different magnification powers, each designed to let you see distant objects as if they were closer. Magnification is represented in power (7X or 7 power, for example). The higher the magnification, the further away you can spot deer. There is a trade-off, however. The higher the magnification, the narrower your field of view.

Field of view. This is the width you can see at a given distance. The field of view in most binoculars is listed as so many feet at 1000 yards, so you can easily compare different types. When spotting game at long range, field of view isn't all that critical. However, in heavy cover a wide field of view can be a big advantage.

Exit Pupil. Magnification is important, but in deer hunting the exit pupil—the light-gathering capability—of your optics is a close second. Why? Because deer are neither a nocturnal (most active during the night) nor a diurnal (active by day) creature. Rather, they are crepuscular, which means they are usually abroad during those ghostly gray hours of dawn and dusk. Binoculars that have a large exit pupil help you see better in this half-light, making it much easier to spot deer when they're most active.

In order to use the maximum amount of this low light, the exit pupil must be as large as the pupil of your own eye. That's about five millimeters. To figure the exit pupil size of a binocular, simply divide the magnification into the size of the objective (front) lens. The first number listed for a binocular is the power, the second the objective lens. If you have a 10x50 binocular, divide 50 by 10 and you get 5. That's a glass with a large exit pupil. Conversely, an 8x20 binocular has an exit pupil of just 2.5, not nearly enough for low light conditions.

Depth of field. You can buy two types of binoculars today: center focus (those that are focused by a wheel or lever that moves both eyepieces simultaneously) and individual focus (where each barrel is focused individually). Once the barrels are individually focused properly, everything appears in focus from a certain distance, say 50 yards, to infinity. For deer hunting, those you must focus yourself (center focus) are the way to go.

Why? Because they have a large depth of field at long range, making looking over a mountain easy. But at short range they have a very shallow depth of field. This isolates detail, and is critical in stalking in heavy cover. You can focus right in on an antler tine, eyeball, or throat patch set in a tangle of branches; you might not have been able to distinguish it with the naked eye, but the shallow depth of field will fuzz out other nearby objects like branches, brush, and leaves, letting you see exactly what it was that caught your eye.

Lens coating. A microscopic film of anti-reflective coating, usually magnesium fluoride, is applied to every glass-to-air lens surface in a binocular or spotting scope. This reduces reflection and enables the maximum amount of available light pass through to your eye. Quality optics have coated lenses.

Roof vs. Porro prism. The two basic kinds of binoculars are the Porro prism kind, the traditional humpback design you see at football games, and roof prism glasses, which have straight barrels, or tubes. For the same magnification, roof prism glasses are much smaller and lighter than Porro prism glasses.

There's a cost factor involved here. For comparable optical quality, roof prisms are considerably more expensive than Porro prisms because to obtain that quality, a roof prism glass must be made much more precisely than a Porro prism.

That's the technical side of binoculars. However, there are other considerations. As mentioned before, buy quality. Cheap binoculars will fail in the long run, and in the short run their poor optical quality will give you a headache. In top-quality binoculars, lenses are polished to give a crystal-clear image; in cheap glasses, specifications aren't as precise. Quality binoculars are built to avoid fogging, but cheap glasses will fog up sooner or later. I wouldn't hunt without binoculars that aren't rubber armored, either. Not only are they quiet, but the armoring helps cushion the shock of banging against rocks or trees.

A top-quality pair of hunting binoculars will set you back at least $200, and some of the very best cost closer to $750 on today's market. Zeiss, Bausch & Lomb, Leupold, Leitz, Swarovski, Redfield, Nikon, Brunton, Pentax, and others familiar throughout the hunting business all make top-quality binoculars. The key point to remember in optics is, you get what you pay for. If you don't have a pair of first-rate binoculars, put off buying that new rifle and invest in glass. You'll be glad you did.

For most western hunting, I find binoculars in the 8x40 to 10x50 class the best all-around choice. A 7x35 is acceptable, but I prefer a bit more power. In the heavy timber, thick oak brush, and whitetail woods a 7x35 is excellent. Bowhunters and other heavy brush still hunters might want to look at Ranging's 5X binoculars. They're a very good glass for stalking and still-hunting through thick cover.

Spotting Scopes

It's the same with spotting scopes; you get what you pay for. Many hunters prefer lightweight spotting scopes, but even for backpacking I use a full-size, rubber-armored spotting scope with a variable eyepiece of 20-60X. A 15-45X eyepiece is also a good choice, and in many cases a 10-30X eyepiece will do the job. Many people like the fixed 20X or 25X eyepieces, and they're often fine. But I like to see what I'm looking at, and at extreme ranges that's just not enough power. The small, mirror lens spotting scopes are great to carry around, but they're difficult to center on a deer at long range, and their optical quality isn't good enough for my tired eyes. Also, the mirror lens optics need lots of light for maximum effectiveness, making them almost useless on dark, stormy days.

One thing many hunters overlook when shopping for spotting scopes is the tripod. A sturdy tripod is a must, to keep the scope steady in the wind. However, most really sturdy spotting scope tripods I've seen don't raise your glass high enough to let you peer over tall grass and weeds. You may have to do what I've done, and buy a tripod at a camera shop to get what you want. I've yet to see a spotting scope manufacturer offer a top-quality hunting tripod with their scopes.

Optics aren't only for seeing deer a long ways off, they're also most helpful for spotting bucks in thick cover. Careful glassing will separate the mule deer from his aspen home.

Deer Hunting Coast to Coast

Optical Systems

It should go without saying that you should always have your binoculars ready for use when hunting, not stowed away in the bottom of your day pack. Start the day by making sure the lenses are relatively clean.

My hunting buddies and I always carry an optics system when hunting the open western mountains and prairies. That system includes my binoculars, spotting scope, and tripod (the exception is noted below). The spotting scope is the constant. The binoculars change with the country. If I'm looking for deer at a mile or more away, the 8x40s or 10x40s come along. If I think I'll be glassing a shorter distance, or perhaps have to go into the timber or thick oak brush, I may use a 7x35.

Duwane Adams taught us a new system for spotting deer at long range. Duwane is a real trophy hunter and outfitter in Arizona, specializing in Coues deer, but his system also works on mule deer and elk. Duwane carries a low-powered pair of binoculars only for really close-in spotting, and doesn't bother with a spotting scope. Instead, he sets up a pair of 15x60 Zeiss binoculars on a tripod, gets comfortable, and sits on top of the hill and looks for deer. He lugs these big binoculars around the mountain on his pack frame.

"I like the big binoculars because I can use both eyes to spot deer a very long way off," Duwane says. "And I don't get the eyestrain that someone trying to squint with one eye through a spotting scope all day will get."

Watching Duwane at work convinced me. I now own a pair of the Zeiss 15x60s, and it's one heckuva good system for spotting deer at ranges of one to four miles. Setting up that tripod at eye level, getting comfortable, and meticulously glassing a mountainside is just like looking through a pair of eyeglasses, and I can spot the slightest movement through them. The catch is that they're heavy, and you need a solid tripod to mount them on. They also cost a bit more than $1,000 a pair.

Dwight Schuh is another hunter who learned Duwane's system, and Dwight uses it extensively when bowhunting. Dwight uses a pair of 20x80 Steiner binoculars and is happy with them.

Whatever system you choose for open country hunting, make sure that the components complement each other. When hunting with a friend, that's much easier to do. Dwight and I went bowhunting in the San Juan Mountains of Colorado in 1988, and our combined optics let us cover all the options. Dwight carried his 20X80 Steiners and a pair of 8x42 Elite binoculars from Bausch & Lomb. I packed along my 10x42 Brunton binoculars and a Redfield spotting scope with 20-60X variable eyepiece. We'd climb up a hill early and set up, glassing for hours. No matter what the conditions were, we were prepared.

Spotting scopes help hunters size up animals at the extreme distances they can be found in open Western terrain. A steady tripod is a must to keep a high-powered scope steady in the wind.

Ultra-high powered binoculars, like these 15x60 Zeiss mounted on a camera-quality tripod, are the ultimate way to glass large expanses of open Western country for all deer species.

How to Glass

There's really no deep, hidden secret to using your binoculars effectively to find deer. This is true in the open country of the West, the whitetail woods, or wherever you might be hunting. It is a little more difficult than throwing your glasses up to your eyes and seeing a deer magically appear in the lenses, however. You have to know how to glass.

First and foremost, you have to be comfortable. That holds true whether you're still hunting, sitting on top of a mountain peak, or in a stand. When I hike up to a good vantage point in the mountains and before I begin glassing, I make myself a nice comfortable place to sit. I don't want to be fidgeting around once I start looking for deer. When still hunting the whitetail woods or thick oak brush, before raising the glasses to my eyes, I make sure my feet are solidly planted, my hands are free, and I can lean against a tree trunk or other steadying object if at all possible. And always make sure you have enough clothes to keep you warm and dry, and block the wind.

When glassing with binoculars of between 7X and 10X, be sure you can rest the glasses on something. That may mean using your elbows on your knees as you sit, laying them over a log from the prone position—whatever it takes to keep the glasses steady and save your arms from fatigue. The exception is still-hunting heavy cover, when the binoculars might be used for just a quick glance.

Be patient! You can always tell an inexperienced optics user. He's the guy who gives the panorama one quick sweep, says "Well, there's nothing here!" and moves on. If you're in good deer country and have a good vantage point, be prepared to sit and glass for at least an hour before moving. There are lots of places for a deer to hide out there, and it may take some time for him to walk out from behind a bush or tree or boulder or contour line.

A good example of that is a hunt I took with Jack Atcheson, Jr. and Lloyd Harvey of Toby Creek Outfitters in British Columbia one September. Both the deer and elk were in the timber, and the three of us sat in one spot for hours, glassing hard right into the heavy timber until one of us found an animal we could all zoom in on. Cursory, half-hearted glassing would have had us leaving the country thinking there was no game at all, yet we saw lots of bull elk and shot three really dandy old mule deer bucks.

When glassing large expanses of open country, Duwane Adams likes to use the grid pattern method. He places an imaginary grid on the country in front of him, and glasses it square by square, beginning at the skyline. He looks at his first grid square for a bit, then moves his glasses slightly to the side and meticulously picks apart the next square. When he reaches the end of the panorama, he drops down and sweeps back, using the same meticulous method.

It's a little more complicated than that. For example, a good early-morning vantage point high atop a mountain will have you looking anywhere but directly

Binoculars should be worn so that the hunter can get to them immediately. They should not packed away so that they are not available when deer are spotted with the naked eye.

By using binoculars that must be focused, one can separate a deer from heavy-cover with the's depth of field feature. It turns a mess of thick sticks into a crisp picture of a deer's face.

into the sun. It will also have the wind in your face, or at least blowing at an angle and not sending your smell directly into the country you're expecting to find deer. You should keep hidden as much as possible, certainly off the skyline and preferably with trees, boulders, or other silhouette-breaking features behind you and on either side.

Time of day is also critical. As we've mentioned, crepuscular animals like deer move most in the half-light of morning and evening. That means you need to be in position and set up to begin glassing well before the first rays of light kiss the sky in the morning, and again at least two hours before sundown. This way you'll begin to become one with the country, and by the time the deer begin moving about, they won't even know you're in the neighborhood.

That doesn't mean deer don't move during the day, because they do, and in heavily-hunted country there seems to be more and more evidence of really good bucks being killed around noon. However, I feel that the best time to spot deer is in the morning, and often on cloudy or stormy days the deer will be out in the open until mid-morning. I also like to spot in the morning because, under the cover of darkness, if I'm careful and don't make lots of noise, I know the deer can't see or hear me. Moving to a glassing spot in mid-afternoon one must be more careful, and sooner or later you'll get caught.

Another big advantage of spotting deer from afar is the "no pollution" theory. By getting into position unseen, unheard, and unsmelled, you can look over all the wildlife in the country without even a single coyote or songbird bothered by your presence. Maybe that's carrying it a bit too far, but the more you hunt true trophy bucks of *any* species, the more you'll begin to believe that they have some sort of mystical sixth sense that alerts them to your presence. I believe that this happens far more than most of us care to think about, and the big bucks head for the heavy cover—or another county—without our even knowing they were there.

The Eye Catchers

It would be nice if every time we held up our binoculars a beautiful buck stood broadside in the lenses, just like the pictures we see in the sporting magazines. The truth of it is that rarely, if ever, happens. If you do glass large expanses of country, the deer standing right out in the open will jump out at you like a big neon sign; you really don't have to look for them at all. It's more important to look for the eye catchers.

The standard articles tell you to look for a horizontal backline in woods full of vertical trees: a black nose, a white rump patch, a twitching ear. And that is good advice. But what you really need to do is get a feeling for how the deer look in the country you're hunting. An extreme example of what I mean is that before taking my first African safari, I spent several days in a large national park, just watching the animals and tuning in to how they look in their natural habitat. If you have a chance to observe deer in parks, farm fields, or other such country before you begin hunting, do so. It will help you see exactly what colors, shapes, and sizes to watch for, and how the animals you are hunting look in the natural habitat.

When glassing for deer in the vast expanses of the West, often you'll see what appears to be a bush or a clump on a mountain. Watch it for several seconds. Does it move? There's your answer. In picking apart hillsides with high-powered optics, look for the pieces of deer mentioned above, as well as antler tines. In heavy cover, pieces are all you're ever likely to see. I remember hunting mule deer one year in Idaho, glassing them as they went into the timber to bed, then sneaking in to try to find them. For days I found nothing but empty tracks and empty beds, until I tried getting down on hands and knees. Then I began seeing the deer at their level, and spotting legs, noses, and antlers. I shot a very nice three-point buck in his bed after looking at a jungle of tree limbs for 30 minutes, only to discover that part of that jungle was a set of antlers.

When glassing for bucks, it's important to remember not to look at the mountain, or timber patch, or brush pile, or whatever, as a whole. Break it down and look at each individual part. Look in each shady patch, into each sagebrush pile, through each lodgepole thicket, hoping to see a piece of a deer. When that becomes second nature, you're well on your way to getting the most out of your optical system.

But nothing can replace experience in glassing for deer, or any other big game animal for that matter. As with becoming a skilled plumber or painter or mechanic, the more you work at the craft, the better you'll become. Every time we hunt together, Jack Atcheson, Jr. amazes me with his ability to find game with his binoculars. But then, he's been at it almost all of his life. If you spend lots of time learning to use your optics, spotting deer will become second nature to you, too.

And perhaps then you'll spend most of your time looking at deer, instead of for them.

CHAPTER XXVII

NOTES ON DEER RIFLES

The campfire arguments over suitable rifles and cartridges for deer are endless, and there's no way to solve them. Nor, except in unusually extreme cases, are there winners or losers. There is a lot of great deer rifles and a lot of great deer cartridges—and darn few that are really unsuited for hunting America's most popular big game.

In any discussion of deer rifles and the cartridges they fire, there are three elements that should be discussed: the cartridges, the rifles, and the sights those rifles are equipped with. There really isn't any proper order, but we'll start with the cartridges.

A full human lifetime ago the great gun writer, Colonel Townsend Whelen, theorized that a cartridge suitable for deer would deliver 1,000 foot-pounds of energy at the animal. At this late date, it is impossible to determine on what criteria this assumption was based. Colonel Whelen was an astute and thorough writer, and he experienced some virgin hunting in the Canadian Rockies that no writer of today can hope to duplicate.

However, Whelen's heyday came at the nadir of big-game populations in the United States. The generation of writers that followed him, with Jack O'Connor and Warren Page at the forefront, were able to gain much more extensive experience in deer hunting than Whelen ever dreamed of. Today's writers, your scribes included, are not only more mobile in our jet age, but are able to hunt in a time when deer are more plentiful and more available in more areas than ever before. And yet, in spite of—and possibly because of—more varied and more extensive field experience with deer, there seems no reason to dispute Whelen's 1,000 foot-pound theory. No, it isn't an absolute, nor was it ever. But it still seems to make sense.

There are many cartridges that meet this criterion, depending on the distances involved. The .30-30, America's classic deer cartridge, delivers 1,902 foot-pounds at the muzzle with the 150-grain bullet, and 1,827 foot-pounds with the slower 170-grain bullet. At 200 yards neither bullet weight makes the grade, but both are just barely there at 150 yards. No surprise. The .30-30 is a 150-yard deer cartridge, period. Both the .243 and the 6mm Remington, considered by most writers to be the minimum calibers for deer, retain enough energy to meet the 1,000 foot-pound minimum a bit beyond 300 yards with 100-grain bullets. Flat-shooting cartridges from the .25-06 on up provide that kind of energy out to 400 yards and beyond, provided they're loaded with aerodynamic bullets. And the brush cartridges, from .35 Remington up to .444 Marlin and .45-70, lose that edge just beyond 200 yards.

There are some holes in the theory, but not many. One hole is to be found in the fact that the hot .22 centerfires from .222 Remington on up all develop 1,000 foot-pounds and more at the muzzle, and the .22-250 and .220 Swift retain more than that at 100 yards. The truth is that these cartridges will indeed kill deer—just like lightning, given proper bullet placement. In expert hands that can deliver such bullet placement, they're deadly—but they aren't deer cartridges. The bullets they fire were not designed for penetration, but rather for rapid expansion on varmint-sized game.

So the first caveat to Whelen's rule is that the bullet must be designed for use on deer-sized game. This rules out not only the .22 centerfires, but also the very light-for-caliber varmint bullets available for the 6mms, the .25s, the 6.5s, and even the 7mms and .30 calibers.

The second qualifier comes from the simple fact that not all deer are created equal. A cartridge that is totally adequate for small whitetails, blacktails, and Coues deer that weigh under 130 pounds may not be sufficient for mule deer and northern whitetails weighing three times as much. For the largest deer, a 1,500 foot-pound energy threshold seems to make more sense. At that energy level, the .30-30 becomes slightly less than a 100-yard cartridge, and the .243 and 6mm not much more. To carry that a step farther, the .25-06 would be limited to 250 yards for the largest deer; the .270 and .280 to 300 yards; the .30-06 to about 350 yards; and the 7mm Remington Magnum to 400 yards. None of that seems to sound unreasonable.

Energy figures aside, there are generally two classes of deer cartridges: the so-called "brush cartridges," heavy of bullet and caliber, slow of velocity; and the faster, flat-shooting long-range cartridges that are actually general-purpose cartridges. The brush cartridges start with the great .30-30 and include the .32 Winchester Special; the .35 Remington; the .348, .358, and .356 Winchester; the .375 Winchester; the .444 Marlin; and the .45-70. All are relatively short-range cartridges, and all use relatively heavy, slow-moving projectiles that hit extremely hard.

Although the .30-30's paper ballistics are hardly impressive, its efficiency on deer-sized game is not only legendary but justified. Part of the reason, perhaps, is its flat-nosed projectiles that set up quickly in game and impart a full dose of that admittedly unimpressive energy. At short ranges, it remains America's standard—and all the other cartridges mentioned are even more devastating, perhaps more so than necessary. None of the big boys, by the way, will actually plow through more brush than lighter, faster bullets—nor is any bullet particularly stable in brush. But cartridges from the .35 Remington on up, with large frontal areas and big, bluff bullets, will indeed flatten deer-sized game and greatly simplify finding animals that have been hit.

The hunter who prowls very heavy cover and knows that shots will come at

It shouldn't be forgotten that a properly sighted or scoped shotgun like this Mossberg is a devastating deer gun—and millions of deer hunters are obligated to use shotguns. (Photo by Todd Smith)

The bolt action is the most common action type among today's deer hunters nationwide. Accurate, dependable, and chambered to flat-shooting cartridges, it's not the only action available—but there are plenty of good reasons to choose it.

very close range is indeed well-served by such "brush cartridges"—just as our grandfathers were. The problem with the cartridges is simply that they're limited in range, while the flat-shooters, with proper bullets, do just as well at bayonet range as they do way out there, which is why cartridges like .270 Winchester and .30-06 have become nearly universal in deer country everywhere.

Rather than flat-shooting cartridges, let's call this group the general purpose deer cartridges. They start with the .243 Winchester and the slightly hotter 6mm Remington—and they go up as far as you want to go, all the way to the .300 magnums and larger. Earlier on, in our discussion of energy requirements, it may have sounded as if we were slamming the 6mms. Indeed we were. On smaller deer at reasonable ranges, the 6mms are just fine—but they are not long-range deer cartridges, nor are they well-suited for our larger deer. For the careful marksman who picks his shots, they're deadly—but those little 6mm pills lack the penetration and power for surefire results on bad-angle shots, long-range shots, and any shots on the very largest of deer. For these very reasons, they are not sound beginners' rifles. Youngsters and women looking for light-recoiling cartridges are much better served by rounds like the 7mm-08 and 7x57, somewhat limited in range but totally reliable for penetration and power.

The above remarks regarding the 6mms could also be applied to the milder .25s, the .250 Savage and the .257 Roberts. Both offer a bit more than the 6mms, but not much—and thus are well-suited for smaller deer at medium ranges, in the hands of experienced hunters.

The real general purpose deer cartridges begin with the .25-06 using 117- or 120-grain bullets. From there, excluding belted magnums, excellent choices include the uncommon 6.5x55; the .270 Winchester; the 7mms—.284 Winchester, 7mm-08 Remington, 7x57, and .280 Remington; and the .30s—.300 Savage, .308 Winchester, and .30-06 Springfield. This short list, though not complete, is America's deer cartridges. The extreme ranging capabilities of a belted cartridge are rarely needed. But, in fairness, to this list could be added the .264 Winchester Magnum; 7mm Remington Magnum; .257, .270, and 7mm Weatherby Magnums; and all the .300 Magnums. All are clearly powerful enough for deer, and are actually quite suitable—especially in very open country.

There are times and places for larger rifles in the vast spectrum of American deer hunting. In the forests of western Montana, where the whitetails are huge and elk and grizzles roam, enough locals carry the .338 to make a case for its suitability. And when Remington introduced the .35 Whelen, some 13,000 slide actions so chambered were ordered almost immediately. Clearly a whole bunch of folks in the deep timber of the Northeast felt a need for such a hard-hitting deep-woods rifle that would reach out twice as far as the time-honored .35 Remington. Sitka blacktail hunting on Alaska's Kodiak Island is fraught with enough danger from the biggest of all bears that one has to question the sanity of anyone who hunts deer with a lesser cartridge than a .338 or, better, a .375 H & H.

Special circumstances aside, the truth is that most hunters could shoot a .270, .30-06, .280, or 7mm magnum interchangeably, year in and year out—and neither they nor the deer they hunt would notice an appreciable difference. Nor is bullet selection particularly critical. The best deer bullets, caliber for caliber, are neither the lightest nor the heaviest, but the medium-weight bullets.

Deer are relatively light-boned animals, and except on the very largest of deer, a good deer bullet will expand relatively quickly (although not blow up). On average-sized deer, few bullets will remain in the animal on a broadside shot—and that's just fine. A bullet that stays inside on a behind-the-shoulder shot on a mid-sized deer could be worrisome on a strongly quartering-away shot. On the other hand, bullets designed for deep, controlled penetration on larger game may not expand adequately on deer. A very hard bullet—and a heavy-for-caliber bullet well-suited for game such as elk—can lead to an unnecessary tracking job on deer, even with a fatal hit. They can also lead to disaster on a hit that's off the mark by just a bit.

Users of factory ammunition can rely on medium-weight bullets in any caliber; chances are good they were designed for deer. Handloaders might be best served by the "standard" component bullets—Sierras, Hornadys, regular Speers rather than Grand Slams, and Ballistic Tip or Solid Base rather than Partition Noslers.

Choice of caliber will, to some extent, dictate choice of action. And that's just fine. Any action type available, whether bolt, lever, slide, semiauto, or single shot, will make a fine deer rifle. Most lever guns are chambered to the more specialized short-range cartridges, but both the Browning BLR and Savage 99 are available in flat-shooting cartridges, as were excellent but long-gone rifles like the Winchester Model 88 and Sako Finnwolf. The fast slide action's great stronghold is the Northeast, and modern semiautos like the Remington Model Four and Browning BAR have their fans. Ruger's great Number One single shot has its following, as do the single shots from Browning and Thompson/Center. And then there's the bolt action, America's most popular action today.

Why? Well, why not? The bolt action is generally the most accurate, and is certainly available in more calibers. Choice of calibers is the lever action's biggest drawback; it can be had in .308-length cartridges, but no cartridges suited for the most open country. The slide action is available in cartridges such as .270, .280, and .30-06—but the only slide action is Remington's. The single shot, though limited in models and makes, is available in almost any imaginable chambering. And although the one-shot concept is appealing, it isn't appealing to everyone. The single shot also has the drawback of being either fully loaded or fully unloaded, which is a problem in a saddle scabbard or while negotiating tough terrain on foot. The semiautomatic has almost no drawbacks, except that it is slightly less accurate, gun for gun, than a bolt action. However, it is also limited in makes and models, and noisy for the foot hunter since the bolt must be slammed into battery to make sure the round is fully seated—and the foot hunter in tough country may load and unload his rifle often.

When you get right down to it, though, the best action type is whatever action an individual is most comfortable with—all are adequately suited for American deer hunting. But whatever action type is chosen, the rifle should fit the hunter, come up quickly and on target, and be a rifle he or she has confidence in. That, after all, is the most important consideration.

The last consideration is sighting equipment. This is a scope world, and there's good reason for that. We shoot better if we see better, and we can see better through a scope. The target image is magnified, even if only slightly. More importantly, though, a scope puts deer and hunter on the same plane, plus gathers in more light so he can see better at first and last light. A scope is also faster to use under any and all circumstances, so long as it isn't overly powerful. With open sights the eye must focus on the front sight, the rear sight, and the target. With a scope everything is on the same plane; all that is necessary is to superimpose the reticle over the target.

In very close cover—and in constant rain or heavy snow—a case could be made for iron sights. Those should not be open sights, however, but rather the aperture or peep sight. The peep sight is actually an optical sight, although it has no lens; the eye will naturally center the front sight in the aperture, and all the shooter must do is place the front sight on the aiming point. The peep sight is fast and accurate, and those who choose it and are happy and successful with it should use it—but the scope remains the ideal sighting equipment for deer hunting; in fading light there is simply no comparison.

What kind of scope? In open country, the scope could be 4X, 6X, 2-7X, 3-9X, 2-1/2-8X, 3-1/2-10X, 4-12X—you name it. The scope should be of the highest quality the user can afford, and it should be set in solid, properly-installed mounts of similar quality. And if a variable scope is chosen, it must be kept on a medium setting; all too much game is lost by a close encounter that finds the scope at the highest setting, and all that can be seen is a furry blur. For close cover hunting, the scope can be 1X (no magnification at all), 2X, 2-1/2X, 3X, 4X, or a low range variable such a 1-3/4-5X or 1-1/2-6X. For general use in all terrain, a fixed 4X is just fine—and a 2-7X or 3-9X equally good.

The reticle chosen is up to the shooter; whatever is comfortable. Extremely fine crosshairs, hard to see in poor light, are not a good choice. Bold crosshairs are fine, and the "plex" type reticles—thick at the edges and thin in the center—are superb. The dot-and-crosshair is very good, especially on moving game.

The complete deer rifle will generally be reasonably light, especially for the hunter who expects to carry it all day in tough terrain. In wet country or high

The traditional "brush cartridges" are well-represented by this selection of .35s: from left, .35 Remington, .356 Winchester, .358 Winchester, .350 Remington Magnum, and .35 Whelen.

Here are some good open country, long-range deer cartridges: from left, .257 Weatherby Magnum, .264 Winchester Magnum, .270 Winchester, .270 Weatherby Magnum, .280 Remington, and 7mm Remington Magnum.

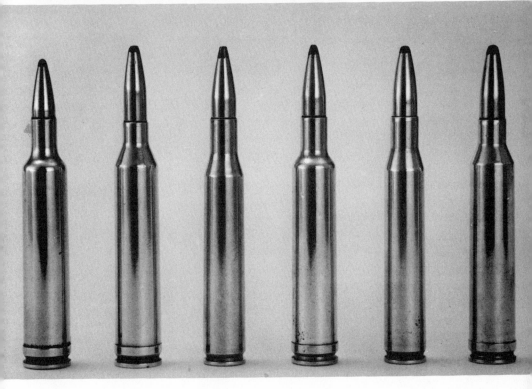

mountains, it could well have a synthetic stock or a laminate, but that's a personal preference. In open country it may have a long barrel, but for close cover hunting it should be reasonably compact. It should have sling swivels; even if you always carry your rifle in your hands while hunting (as you should if an encounter with a buck is possible), a sling will leave both hands free while you drag a buck out of the woods. It doesn't have to be a tack-driver—but it should possess adequate accuracy to handle any shot the hunter who owns it is likely to encounter.

And above all, it must be a rifle that you know will do its job each and every time you do yours!

Remington's long series of slide-action rifles have been traditional choices among close-cover hunters. Remington's new .35 Whelen chambering in their slide action is a superb, highly versatile rifle/cartridge combination.

Boddington used a semiautomatic Remington on this Texas hunt while his partner used a bolt gun. In practical field terms, all the action types offer more than adequate accuracy for deer hunting.

CHAPTER XXVIII

DEER GEAR

Deer hunters are gadget freaks. Always have been, always will be. Even back in the "good old days" before the turn of the century, hunters were always looking for a gimmick that would give them an extra edge, and make the harvesting of game simpler and easier.

It's much the same today. Modern deer hunters continue to search for those little extras that will help them succeed in their sport. And thanks to the inventive human mind and advances in technology, there are more gimmick items than you can shake a stick at on today's market, all touted as something to make you a better hunter.

These technological advances include everything we hunters need, and then some, from the clothing we wear to the camping gear we use to the food we eat to our arms and ammunition, and more. It's gotten so a fellow believes that he's not ready to head afield if he's not packing half a sporting goods store along on his person, with the other half back at camp "just in case."

Dwight Schuh and I were commenting on this on a recent backpack bowhunt for mule deer in Colorado's rugged San Juan Mountains. We had Dwight's llamas along to carry camp in for us, and therefore had a small scale to weigh packs before loading the animals up. After about the fifth day of brutal mountain assaults, we were getting a bit tired, and wondered what we could leave out of our hunting packs each day. We put them on the scales, and each weighed right in the neighborhood of 20 pounds!

"Good grief!" Dwight said. "Whatever happened to the days when a guy could put a book of matches in his pocket and head out hunting?"

He had a very valid point. Our packs were overloaded partially because of our profession. Included in mine were eight pounds of photographic equipment, and I had a full-size spotting scope and tripod that added almost seven more pounds. That's a lot of weight to carry for 12 or 15 miles a day at 11,000 straight up-and-down feet day in and day out, and illustrates something I see happening to the modern deer hunter.

In this fast-paced world we live in, people want instant answers to their problems. Many hunters believe that by purchasing gimmickry, they can substitute for field experience. If they use a rutting-type scent late in the season, for example, all they have to do is put some out there and watch a big buck come in to the bottle, nose high and defenses down, without bothering to learn about a buck's habits during the rut, or the lay of the land. An ultra magnum rifle, huge variable scope, and speed-of-light ammunition are all it takes to whack a big buck in open country; there's no need to learn about how to first find the deer, much less get close to them. Little time is spent on the range learning how to shoot such a rifle at reasonable ranges, much less the extreme distances for which such a rig is designed.

The point is this: There's absolutely no substitute for acquired field experience in deer hunting. Don't think you can go out and buy instant success at the local sport shop or through a catalog, because you can't.

That said, there are nevertheless lots of interesting items that will help us as deer hunters, if we use them not as replacements for basic hunting skills, but rather as tools to help us solve some of the problems we may encounter in the field. Here, then, are some things to look for when the urge to add equipment to your probably already-overloaded hunting closet strikes.

Clothing

There have been more advances in clothing for the outdoorsman in recent years than in any other category of items we deer hunters need. This is one area where modern "gimmicks" are really scientific breakthroughs that can make you a much more comfortable, and therefore efficient, hunter.

The trend is towards lightweight synthetic fabrics that replace or greatly enhance natural fibers. One example is the new polarfleece garments that retain their ability to keep you warm even when wet, just like pure wool, yet dry out in a fraction of the time wool takes. Polarfleece is just as quiet as wool, too. Synthetic undergarments, like long underwear, will wick perspiration away from the skin and prevent that old-time clammy feeling from developing, yet still keep you warm. Synthetic insulators found in jackets, coats, vests, and sweaters will keep you as warm as natural down even when wet. You can choose between bulky insulators like Holofill, Qualofill, and others, and ultra-thin insulators like Thinsulate. There are also gloves, booties, and facemasks made from neoprene, the same material that wetsuits are made from, for really bitter weather.

In the same vein, hot weather hunters will find shell-type garments made from Supplex nylon blends that are cool, dry extremely quickly, and are also relatively quiet in the woods. Cordura/Supplex blends offer toughness and quiet in both hot and cold-weather garments. The new "Quiet Cloth" — type garment shells are made from various blends of Supplex nylon. They are not only much quieter than standard nylon, but wear like iron.

Tremendous strides have been made by the W.L. Gore company in the laminating of Gore-Tex fabric to hunting garments to avoid leaking at seams and other potential trouble spots. Today's Gore-Tex garments are lightweight, waterproof, and breathable, too, from heavy parkas and coats to lightweight rain suits to hunting boots. They are definitely worth investigation by serious deer hunters. Garments that have a Gore-Tex liner are still a bit noisier than garments without one. However, this is a problem that is being corrected rapidly, and before

Portable tree stands are a very effective tool for deer hunters everywhere. These lightweight tools allow the hunter to quickly adjust his stand sight as hunting conditions change. (Photo by Nick Sisley)

A backpack camp must be simple yet contain as many conveniences as one can manage to carry in. Hunting with a buddy lets you split the load with a friend.

any hasty judgments are made, you should try the garments on in your local sporting goods shop.

An entire book could be written on modern clothing advances alone. If you haven't been down to the store in a while and seen what's currently available, you'll be very surprised. In five years' time we'll all be even more amazed, because the clothing revolution is just beginning.

At the same time, the old tried-and-true natural fiber garments are also evolving. Wool is still an excellent material for wet- and cold-weather hunting, just as 100 percent cotton is a superb material in hot weather. The key is to examine your needs closely, then carefully look over what's available and balance the whole equation against your check book. If you look hard enough, you'll probably find clothing that's exactly what you need and at a price that meets your budget.

Optics

The trend in optics today is towards quality, a trend reflected by the latest offerings from companies like Bausch & Lomb, Zeiss, Leitz, Leupold, and others. We're also seeing a trend away from the miniature pocket-sized binoculars back to full-sized binoculars, something I'm glad to see. Binocular companies are finally getting the message that hunters need full-sized glasses that gather lots of light at the critical dawn and dusk hours, can take wet and nasty weather, and stand up to the pounding serious deer hunters give them in the field.

Spotting scopes are undergoing the same transformation. The trend is toward variable eyepieces in the 15-45X and 20-60X sizes in a spotting scope that is fully waterproof, dustproof, and fogproof. There still isn't a decent hunting-sized spotting scope tripod available from the optics companies, but that should be rectified very soon. I buy mine at a camera store now.

Riflescopes haven't changed much, but again the trend is toward scopes that can take bad weather, field abuse, and gather lots of light. Compact scopes are showing up only on smaller rifles where they balance well.

Hunting Pack

Hunters almost always carry a pack of some kind. When hunting flat ground with lots of road access, like eastern and midwestern whitetail country, a day pack is sufficient. More and more western hunters are carry pack frames not only to tote their ancillary gear, but to help them get the meat back to camp.

Pack sacks are now being made from polarfleece-type material, something that allows the hunter to sneak through the heavy cover without fear of that nerve-wracking scraping noise nylon pack sacks make. I rarely hunt with a nylon pack anymore.

Pack frames are also now being designed specifically for the hunter, pioneered by the Dwight Schuh hunting pack. Dwight began putting a camouflage polarfleece sack on a nylon Coleman Junior pack frame a few years ago, and it's really a good idea. The frame doesn't stick up above your head, which means you can raise your head and see when hiking uphill, as well as sneak through brush with minimal hanging up. You can also pack 100 pounds of meat at a time with this set-up, more than most of us ever want to carry. His latest pack sacks feature outer pockets that permit carrying extra gear into base camp, then come off with the help of Velcro in camp while hunting.

Today, for the first time, we're starting to see a variety of day packs and frameless backpacks made especially for hunters. The Roosevelt hunting packs, in sturdy cotton duck and dark green in color, are designed for packing boned meat as well as all the extra gear we all carry, and they're excellent. Another new item is the Port-A-Pack, a polarfleece fanny pack that carries aluminum tubing that—in a flash—converts to a compact pack frame for carrying out game. Of course, in spite of some new developments, some of the old standbys are still hard to beat. For packing out really heavy loads, we don't know of anything that beats the good old Camp Trails Freighter pack frame.

You'll find an excellent selection of daypack and backpack sizes and designs at any backpacking or mountaineering store.

Cutlery

We all need a hunting knife, and there have been several innovations lately. Handles from many companies are now being offered in no-slip synthetic materials that are also lightweight. Blades are being offered in softer steels, making it much easier to touch up the edge during field-dressing. One of the better blade set-ups to come along was first offered by Western Cutlery and called the Rough Cut. This lock-back folding knife has two blades, one a standard drop-point hunting blade and the other a self-sharpening serrated edge. The "rough-cut" serrated edge will zip right through tendons, briskets, and other tough animal parts, as well as rope, small twigs, and other bothersome things around camp.

Another new knife type is the Game Skinner, made by Outdoor Edge. It's a pistol grip-type knife with a unique blade and handle design that allows you to skin a buck quickly with a downward stroke. The knife also has a gut hook, a feature that is becoming more and more popular today with both knife manufacturers and hunters.

Field-sharpening tools are changing, too. Diamond-impregnated crock sticks have been around a while, but now diamond-impregnated flat stones are also available. They're excellent for keeping a knife as sharp as it needs to be.

For deer hunting, keep in mind that you don't need a knife with a blade much over four inches in length. A drop-point blade of this length is all that's necessary to field dress an animal, and even bone him out if need be.

Deer Hunting Coast to Coast

This and That

There are a million and one little items available for hunters to haul to camp or stuff into their packs. They are too numerous by far to mention individually, so here are a few that we think are really useful.

If you drag your deer to camp instead of carry it, a wire drag is worth looking at. Marketed by Whitetail Strategies, among others, it's made from heavy cable and machined aluminum, and is a solid product that beats the heck out of just grabbing onto the antlers.

A synthetic firestarter should be in your pack during mountain hunts or whenever rain or snow might come along. Two kinds work well. One comes in a squeeze tube, the other in lightweight sticks. You may think this is ludicrous stuff, but it will get a fire going even with wood soaked by a rainstorm that would make Noah nervous. And forget the matches; carry a butane lighter that's foolproof in bad weather.

For carrying around binoculars, the wide neoprene binocular straps made by Butler Creek Corporation and Michaels of Oregon can't be beat. They give a little when walking, taking some of the strain off the neck and shoulders, and the inch-wide strap is much more comfortable than the tiny plastic straps that come with most binoculars. There are rifle slings made from the same material, and they do the same thing as well as being easy to wrap tightly into when shooting. They go especially well with the new synthetic rifle stocks.

For field-dressing, there are several items that will make the job easier. Folding aluminum gambrel hooks, like those offered by Black Timber Products, are great for hanging carcasses in camp. There's even one gambrel set-up that comes complete with rope, small block and tackle, and the whole thing folds neatly into a small zippered stuff bag. It's made by Sierra Game Products.

Game bags are something that should be included in every deer hunter's duffel. Lightweight cheesecloth bags are inexpensive, and they'll certainly keep the bugs out. Heavier cotton bags are a better choice for colder weather, and the best can be washed and used again.

If you hunt from a vehicle, a small fisherman's tackle box or two will enable you to compartmentalize small items in a no mess, easy-to-find manner. I keep field-dressing gear, including Swiss army knife, whetstone and oil, skinning knife, extra cheesecloth game bags, moist towelettes, plastic liver and heart bags, folding gambrel hook, and paper towels in one. Another is my "spares" box, containing extra rifle cartridges, knife and whetstone, compass, compact binoculars, nylon cord, bootlaces, butane lighter and firesticks, maps, state game regulations, gunsmithing Allen wrenches and screwdrivers, etc.

Just a few years ago deer scents were nearly unheard of—but today there's a bewildering array of scents, lures, scent masks, scentless soaps, you name it. It's confusing. The truth is that none of the scents is a panacea for success, nor will

When dragging a deer out of the woods, try and keep your back upright as much as possible. A piece of nylon cord, rope, or small-diameter wire will help accomplish this.

One should never head into the deer woods without basic survival items in his pack. When planning what to carry, assume the worst in terms of weather and what's needed to cope with it.

they make up for bad hunting tactics. But they can help.

The rules for their use are simple, although some of the ways they're employed, such as in mock scrapes, are far from simple. First, the scent must be natural for the area. Apple is a good cover scent, as well as a possible attractant, in areas where there are old orchards. But pine scent in an oak forest and apple scent in an evergreen jungle won't do you much good. As we said earlier, rutting activity covers an extended period—but sex lures are unlikely to have a positive affect if the rut is some time away or completely over. Bathing with scentless soap is certainly a good idea—but regardless of the scent used, the most successful method for fooling a deer's nose is to stay downwind.

Almost as bewildering as scents is the proliferation of deer calls—fawn bleats, grunt tubes, and more. They do work, and they aren't hard to use. On the other hand, no gadget will help if you haven't done your homework and found an area where there are deer to hear you! Most of the companies that make deer calls, such as Lohman, Jerry Peterson's Woods Wise, and Knight & Hale offer excellent instructional tapes and videos to demonstrate their use. Unless you know someone who has had success with these techniques, such training aids are extremely valuable. A couple of companies, including Woods Wise, even market excellent synthetic rattling horns—which, of course, are a deer call of a type—that are as good as or better than any you can make.

Every hunter needs a flashlight, and modern technology has given us several options. The various Mini Mag-type lights are excellent, compact and lightweight. There are also lights that clip onto your hat, or utilize a headband, thereby keeping hands free for field-dressing or pushing aside brush during an after-dark walk in the woods. Spare batteries and an extra bulb are a good idea.

Compasses are an item that hunters should not only carry but should also learn how to use correctly—and that's not all that difficult. There are several different sizes and styles available, and just as with optical gear, you get what you pay for. Companies like Johnson Camping (makers of the Silva compass line), as well as Brunton's excellent line of compasses, are good places to start looking.

There are lots of Cordura nylon carriers for all sorts of items made by Michaels of Oregon. These include everything from cartridge carriers to flashlight and compass holders to knife sheaths and more. The more you see and use this stuff, the more you'll want to have some — and wonder how you ever got by without it!

There are also several small, compact cleaning kits available that feature drop-through cleaning rods designed to be carried in your daypack. All are a good idea, and can solve simple away-from-camp problems as well as maintain a firearm in inclement weather conditions. It's always a smart idea to keep a standard aluminum cleaning rod in camp to solve major problems like snow or mud packed in the muzzle after a fall or tumble. And while on the subject of gun-related gear, there are several different scope covers on the market today as well. Most work, even in the worst of weather, but in reality a piece of old innertube will do the job just as well. One of the most useful items you can carry is a small roll of high-quality electrician's tape. This can be used for a thousand and one around-camp chores, from sealing a gun muzzle against rain and snow to taping together a boot sole that's come unglued to repairing cooking utensils to fixing minor tent and tack troubles.

Don't overlook items you can find at a backpacking store that don't appear in general sporting goods shops. Plastic water bottles beat the heck out of a conventional canteen, for example. Small nylon stuff sacks make organizing your pack much easier. Lightweight plastic holders for everything from toothbrushes to eggs keep weight down but protect fragile items. The old "space blanket" remains a heckuva tool for everything from a glassing pad in wet conditions to a wind break shelter to a survival blanket.

The point is, there are more potential inclusions in your deer hunting gear than you can shake a stick at. All of them have merit, and most all of them work the way they're supposed to. But as Dwight Schuh would say, "Good grief! Do we really need all this stuff?"

Yes, and no. You have to balance your wants against your real needs afield. In a base camp that you'll be visiting regularly, extra equipment can be a blessing, stored away carefully until the very moment it will be useful. On a backpack hunt, unless you're the Incredible Hulk, you can't afford to carry the whole sporting goods shop on your back for days on end. You have to pare your gear down to the bare essentials, carrying only the most basic survival items, hunting tools, and lightweight foods.

Hunting deer is rarely a comfortable stroll in the park; you have to expect to make do as best you can with the bare minimum most of the time. You begin a life of deer hunting, it seems, by carrying a rifle or bow and little more except that proverbial book of matches in the pocket. Then, as you get into it more and more, you keep adding more and more extra "essentials" until you have packs that weigh as much as Dwight's and mine. You then realize how crazy that is, and begin eliminating lots of this stuff until the pack is manageable once more. The secret is to choose your deer gear specifically for each hunt, carrying everything you definitely need, and nothing else.

That way you won't spend all day worrying about an overloaded pack, but can concentrate on the task at hand—finding a deer. After all, isn't that what it's all about?

JAGUAR HUNTING IN THE MATO GROSSO AND BOLIVIA

With notes on other game.

by Tony de Almeida

1989 CA, 319pp including 44 pages of illustrations. Foreword by Bert Klineburger. Not since Sacha Siemel has there been a book on jaguar hunting like this book. Tony de Almeida is the most successful guide for jaguars in the history of South American hunting. He has guided some of the most famous people in the world to the world's largest jaguars. This fascinating book chronicles Tony's career from the very beginning. In the pages of this book you will penetrate the remotest parts of the "green hell"—South Americas endless jungles. Here you will encounter the king of the jungle, the jaguar, in his domain. Along with stories about monster jaguars, you will read about deer, cougar, caiman, and more. A fascinating book. $35.00

INDIAN HUNTS AND INDIAN HUNTERS OF THE OLD WEST

by Frank C. Hibben

1989 CA, 228pp including 32 pages of authentic photographs from the author's files. Professor Hibben has written a fascinating account of the old West as told to him by Juan de Dios, a Navajo by birth who was captured by the Spanish in a slaving raid. Dios was twenty-one years old when Lincoln freed the slaves—Indian as well as Negro. He was ninety years old when he recounted his tales to Professor Hibben—these tales are all authentic. Prof. Hibben actually rode with Juan de Dios to the places where the events took place. A sampling of some of the chapters include: Massacre at Medio Dia, The Purgatoire Grizzly, Dead Man's Stampede, Big Medicine Lion, Big Bucks Sleep Lightly, The Bear That Walked Like a Man, and many more. A recommended work—a mixture of hunting and Southwestern Americana! $24.95

BELL OF AFRICA
by W. D. M. Bell

1989 CA 236pp, map, illus. In 1950 Walter Bell wrote his life-long friend, Col. Townsend Whelen, to ask help in publishing his memoirs. His autobiography was eventually published in the U.K. after Col. Townsend Whelen edited it. Adventures in the Yukon, South/East Africa and during W.W. I. Also Bell's drawings, his early days in Africa and lots hunting for big tuskers. $24.95

KARAMOJO SAFARI
by W.D.M. Bell

1989 CA, 288pp. Tale of the journey into Karamojo (now Uganda) some 70 years ago when it was still completely unknown to Western man. He brought back 18,762 lbs of ivory! $24.95

THE WANDERINGS OF AN ELEPHANT HUNTER
by W.D.M. Bell

1989 CA 187pp, illus. The greatest of all elephant books by the greatest of all elephant hunters, "Karamojo" Bell. Foremost an elephant title but also includes buffalo and lion. $24.95

NB: All three Walter Bell titles are available as a slipcased set for $65.00

CAMPFIRES AND GAME TRAILS
by Craig Boddington

1989 CA, 295pp, illus. Readers will learn a vast amount about how to hunt America's big-game species—about arms and equipment, scouting, specialized hunting techniques for various kinds of game in various kinds of habitat and terrain, getting the game home in good condition, getting along in the wilderness, and a host of other skills. You'll hunt with Boddington for all varieties of deer and for elk, antelope, wild sheep, mountain goats, bison, caribou, moose, black bear, grizzlies, wild boar, javelina, the great cats, Arctic game—and even the immigrant species, the so-called exotic game animals that can now be hunted in many parts of the country. Boddington reveals his deep love of game and the wilderness through his writing, and he evokes the joys to be experienced in the great outdoors. $23.95

WHERE THE GIANTS TROD
by Monty Brown

1989 CA, 431pp, illus in color and black & white, 2-color fold-out map in rear pocket, bibliography, index. WHERE THE GIANTS TROD is a narrative of pioneering men, their failures and their triumphs; it is also the chronicle of Kenya's northern desert region. The subjects are, each in their own individual right, varied and absorbing. They include prehistory, the background stories of the indigenous tribes living in the territory, a detailed account of the exploration of Lake Rudolf (now Turkana), and finally a narrative of the white man's efforts to administer the land up to the year 1920. The core to the book deals with the thirteen expeditions to explore Lake Rudolf. Organized by an enthusiastic cross-section of famous Europeans and Americans, each had his own tale to tell, each took a different route, and each made his own contribution to geographical knowledge. Described here are the expeditions by Von Hoenell/Count Teliki, Chanler, Neumann, Donaldson Smith, Delamere, Roosevelt, and Stigand, among others. The historical accuracy of the book is supported by a fascinating collection of photographs—some over 100 years old! Foreword by Sir Vivian Fuchs, the renowned Antarctic explorer and president of the Royal Geographic Society. We highly recommend this fascinating work! $54.95

ELEPHANTS OF AFRICA

by Hall-Martin A. & Bosman P. (illustrator)

1989 CA, 176pp, oblong folio, 120 color & 120 b/w illus. ELEPHANTS OF AFRICA contains reproductions of 24 outstanding pastel paintings of elephants in representative habitats throughout the continent. In addition, there are superb color cameos and eloquent pencil drawings of both elephants and the many other creatures—some of them rare or endangered—that share the elephant's varied environments: the Zaire peacock, the gorilla, the bongo, the zebra duiker, the Lord Derby eland, the lion, the leopard, and man. The text is both informative and scientifically accurate, yet written in a personal and anecdotal style. It is also realistic, squarely facing all the pertinent issues of elephant biology and conservation: the decline of the elephant in some areas because of poaching and the increase of human population; the ivory trade; the over-population of elephants in some sanctuaries; the conflict between elephant and man—all these issues are discussed by one of the leading authorities on African elephants. A magnificently illustrated work on the African elephant. $44.95

AFRICAN HUNTER

by James Mellon

1988 CA, 3rd edn, 522pp, 382 photos, large format, dust jacket. Nothing has been changed in this third edition. The same high-quality print and paper as before. Generally regarded as the most comprehensive title ever on African hunting. There are 380 first-class black and white pictures on the 522 pages. It has 52 chapters that focus on 20 African countries. The scope of this book is more exhaustive than ANY other book on African hunting. It sweeps the reader along with stories of the most dangerous and exotic animals of the dark continent that will keep you thrilled from the first to the last page. Covers absolutely ALL African game animals. $100.00

HUNTING ON THREE CONTINENTS WITH JACK O'CONNOR
by Jack O'Connor

1987 CA, 303pp, 32 pages of photos, hardcover, dust jacket. During the years 1973 to 1977 Jack O'Connor wrote for Petersen's HUNTING magazine. Safari Press obtained the rights to take the best material the old master wrote and make it into a book. This book contains entirely new material, never before published in book form. Containing sections on sheep & mountains, Africa and Asia, guns and ammo, North American hunting and much more, this is a book that the O'Connor fan will not want to miss (or anybody else for that matter). Many O'Connor affectionados feel that his best work was produced in his later years. What else is there to say? A new masterpiece by an old master. $35.00

HUNTING IN THE ROCKIES
by Jack O'Connor

1988 CA, 297pp, illus, dust jacket. This book is about Rocky Mountain game animals and how to hunt them throughout the entire R.M. region. Practical, helpful, and specific as to methods, it is also highly informative regarding animal habits and behavior and the conditions the hunter will encounter. Special chapters deal with equipment, binoculars and cameras, rifles, marksmanship, and planning the Rocky Mountain trip. The result is the best book on the region for the hunter, and one that offers excellent reading for the armchair traveler too. Includes bighorn and thinhorn sheep, elk, moose, caribou, goat, deer, antelope, the grizzly and the black bear. This edition has 48 pages of new photographs. $29.95

USE ENOUGH GUN
by Robert Ruark

1988 CA, 330pp, illus, dust jacket. This is more than the record of a lifetime's bag; it is the story of a man's education as a hunter. The lessons that Ruark learned from his grandfather still applied when he shot his first lion on safari in Africa, more than twenty years later. Then there were new lessons to be learned from Harry Selby, the Kenyan professional who became Ruark's close friend. Ruark hunted in India and Alaska, in Mozambique and Uganda, Kenya and Tanganyika. No matter where or how he traveled, in the end the thing that mattered was the nature of the hunt itself; the relationship of the hunter to the animal he killed; and the investment of skill and bravery in a grand endeavor. $32.50

HORN OF THE HUNTER
by Robert Ruark

The story of an African hunt. 1987 CA, 315pp, 50 photos, dust jacket. Another sought-after Ruark title is back in print. No other book will give you the "feel" of Africa like this book can. Ruark will take you to the land that every hunter longs to see...Africa! Here in the jungles and the plains, the reader will come to know the ferocity of the wounded buffalo and the acid sweat of fear. Virginia and Robert Ruark started their safari in Nairobi where they hired Harry Selby, one of the best known professional hunters in the business. With a group of native runners and bearers, a jeep and an old lorry, they ventured into the bush for a nine-week safari in Kenya and Tanzania. In this book Robert Ruark will share with you the excitement of his new love—big-game hunting. $35.00

PONDORO—LAST OF THE IVORY HUNTERS

by John Taylor

1989 CA, 354pp, illus. Pondoro means lion in Chinyungwe. It was the natives' name for John Taylor when he first began to hunt in Africa, on the lower Zambesi in the early part of the 20th century. For more than thirty years, Taylor—Pondoro was a professional hunter, often out of touch with civilization for as long as three and four years at a time: Pondoro Taylor said that he did not learn of WWII until some of his men brought back provisions wrapped in old newspapers! Find out what Taylor had to say about the most dangerous animal, how to get down-wind of your elephant, what makes a maneater and how to track it, how hippos navigate in water, when poisonous snakes attack, where to aim when an animal is charging you, and why the zebras are considered bad-mannered creatures. $29.95

THE EDUCATION OF NAGOMO

by Jacque & Ludo Wurfbain

Debra Weckbaugh, Illustrator

1990, CA, 64pp, profuse color & b/w illus. A beautifully illustrated children's book whose focus is on the "hot" environmental issues of today. Through the techniques of magic and imagery, this book teaches children about the thorny problems facing animals (and us) today. Its purpose is to give children insight into such ideas as conservation, habitat destruction, overpopulation, poaching, and extinction by looking with great sensitivity at certain endangered animals, including the rhino, elephant, addax, cheetah, and gorilla. Seen through the eyes of a little eight-year-old native boy from Zaire and his magical friend and mentor, the Patron Wizard of the animals of Africa, this book is sure to delight both young and old alike. Foreword by Michael Dee, curator of the LA Zoo. Recommended for ages seven through adult. $17.95

SAFARI PRESS LIMITED EDITIONS

In 1986 Safari Press started a series of limited edition books. Originally these books were reprints of scarce early hunting books. However, after three reprints it was decided to publish only original books in the limited edition series, and we will continue to do so.

The following books were published by Safari Press in strictly limited editions of 1000 or 500 copies. All are numbered and many of these books are signed by the authors. Please note that some of these books were also issued in regular editions for popular reading.

CLASSICS IN AFRICAN HUNTING SERIES

1- WHITE HUNTER ....John Hunter
   Limited to 1000 numbered and slipcased copies.
2- HORNED DEATH .... John Burger
   Limited to 1000 numbered and slipcased copies.
3- AFTER BIG GAME IN CENTRAL AFRICA .... Edouard Foa
   Limited to 1000 numbered and slipcased copies
4- FROM MT. KENYA TO THE CAPE.. Craig Boddington
   Limited to 500 numbered and slipcased copies signed by the author.
NB: numbers 1, 2 and 4 are sold out.

CLASSICS IN BIG-GAME HUNTING SERIES

1- HUNTING ON THREE CONTINENTS ....Jack O'Connor
   Limited to 500 numbered and slipcased copies signed by the author's son
2- INDIAN HUNTS AND INDIAN HUNTERS................................ Dr. Frank Hibben
   Limited to 500 numbered, leatherbound, slipcased, and signed copies by the author.
3- JAGUAR HUNTING IN THE MATO GROSSO.......................by Tony de Almeida
   Limited to 500 numbered, leatherbound, slipcased, and signed copies by the author.
4- DEER HUNTING COAST TO COAST................. Craig Boddington and Bob Robb
   Limited to 500 numbered, leatherbound, slipcased, and signed copies by the author.
NB: number 1 is sold out.

HUNTING AT HIGH ALTITUDES SERIES

1- WITH A RIFLE IN MONGOLIA...........................Count Ernst Hoyos-Sprinzenstein
   Limited to 500 numbered and slipcased copies.